The Presidency in the Twenty-first Century

THE PRESIDENCY
IN THE
TWENTY-FIRST
CENTURY

Edited by
CHARLES W. DUNN

THE UNIVERSITY PRESS OF KENTUCKY

Copyright © 2011 by The University Press of Kentucky

Scholarly publisher for the Commonwealth,
serving Bellarmine University, Berea College, Centre College of Kentucky,
Eastern Kentucky University, The Filson Historical Society, Georgetown
College, Kentucky Historical Society, Kentucky State University,
Morehead State University, Murray State University, Northern Kentucky
University, Transylvania University, University of Kentucky, University of
Louisville, and Western Kentucky University.
All rights reserved.

Editorial and Sales Offices: The University Press of Kentucky
663 South Limestone Street, Lexington, Kentucky 40508-4008
www.kentuckypress.com

15 14 13 12 11   5 4 3 2 1

Library of Congress Cataloging-in-Publication Data

The presidency in the twenty-first century / edited by Charles W. Dunn.
    p. cm.
  Includes bibliographical references and index.
  ISBN 978-0-8131-3402-4 (hardcover : alk. paper)
  ISBN 978-0-8131-3403-1 (ebk.)
  1. Presidents—United States—History—21st century. I. Dunn, Charles W.
II. Title: Presidency in the 21st century.
  JK511.P777 2011
  352.230973—dc23   2011019758

This book is printed on acid-free paper meeting the requirements of the
American National Standard for Permanence in Paper for Printed Library
Materials.

Manufactured in the United States of America.

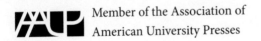 Member of the Association of
American University Presses

CONTENTS

INTRODUCTION

The Presidency in the Twenty-first Century: Continuity and Change

Charles W. Dunn

The tyranny of the legislature is really the danger most to be feared, and will continue to be for many years to come. The tyranny of the executive power will come in its turn, but at a more distant period.
—Thomas Jefferson to James Madison, March 15, 1789

Isaac Newton's first law, the law of inertia, states that an object once in motion will continue in motion unless acted upon by outside forces. In 1787 when the Founders of the United States set presidential power in motion, they created a force far more powerful than their intentions. Now for 225 years the momentum of presidential power has gradually accelerated. And as its power has increased so, too, have the public's expectations. The combination of increasing power and rising expectations has generated friction as outside forces have acted to limit presidential power and as presidential performance has failed to live up to expectations. Simply put, the history of the presidency reveals a disparity between the power and the promise of presidential leadership and presidential performance.

Thomas Jefferson understood that presidential power and presidential leadership were like an optical illusion. They are not what they seem, especially in the twenty-first century. So it was that in 1789 Jefferson forecast the fundamental problem of today's presidency. He foresaw that while the Constitution of 1787 appeared to create a presidency constrained by constitutional boundaries, it actually created opportunities for expanded power. Now, more than two centuries of expanded presidential power have placed the presidency and the president on a pedestal far above the Founders' intentions. A new set of laws, reflecting continuity and change, serve as the parameters or axioms of presidential power in the twenty-first century.[1]

LAW NUMBER 1: THE LAW OF HISTORY

The American presidency, a magnetically powerful attraction for presidents, presidential candidates, press corps, and the public, is simultaneously potent and impotent. Assured of their power, but frustrated by their weaknesses, presidents must perform a tightwire act in the center ring of American politics.

Although outside forces have acted to check presidential power, notably during the scandals of the Nixon and Clinton presidencies, presidents remain preeminent in American politics. Presidents more than anyone else determine the national agenda, setting priorities and proposing policies. Modern Americans, who can hardly imagine their president as anything less than the preeminent leader of their nation and the world, have lost sight of the presidency's constitutional origins.

The executive article illustrates flexibility, America's widely acclaimed constitutional virtue. Accommodating myriad demands and many interpretations, the executive article has allowed presidential power numerous opportunities for expansion. Aside from its unclear and imprecise limits, this article, along with the legislative and judicial articles, instituted a doctrine not so much of *separation of powers* as of *fusion of powers*. A doctrine of strict separation of powers would have clearly defined the limits of executive power. The fusion-of-powers doctrine has allowed the presidency to develop legislative, judicial, and executive responsibilities. Today's presidents are not passive participants, watching and checking the legislative and judicial branches, but active influences in shaping what those branches do. Flexibility, achieved through fusion of powers, has placed presidents at the apex of influence in American government. Stretched like elastic, presidential power has expanded to meet the needs of changing times and circumstances.

At the summit of power, presidents are vulnerable. Rising popular expectations make them susceptible to public distrust and dissatisfaction when their leadership fails to produce satisfactory results. Economic, political, and social conditions cause people to look to the president for leadership, but in leading the president divides, satisfying some and alienating others. As though playing a game of chess, presidents constantly face checkmate from Congress, the bureaucracy, the courts, the press corps, and interest groups. It is as though the power and promise of presidential leadership outstrip performance.

The American Founders in the Constitutional Convention of 1787 sowed the seeds of this irony of power and promise, which simultaneously escalate and circumscribe presidential power. So it was with President Obama, whose poll numbers suffered one of the largest drops in presidential history, plummeting in one year from a seemingly invincible peak to a seriously dangerous low, weakening his leadership and threatening his party's control of Congress. Presidents in the twenty-first century serve in a turbulent environment, tossed to and fro like a wave of the sea driven with the wind.

LAW NUMBER 2: THE LAW OF RHETORIC

Successful presidential leadership requires the merger of good campaigning with effective governing and the recognition that presidential rhetoric is much more than the spoken word. To effectively communicate their ideas and policies to the public, presidents must properly stage their rhetoric as in a campaign, recognizing that the substance of excellent ideas and policies requires an appropriate style of presentation. Thus, just as campaigning and governing must come together, so, too, must style and substance.

Proper rhetorical staging enables candidates and presidents to communicate their messages effectively to the American people, who can then judge whether they approve of those messages. Candidates and presidents, even the well-financed, who fail to stage their rhetoric properly, falter along the political wayside.

John McCain's 2008 campaign for the presidency received a shot in the arm from Sarah Palin's surprisingly successful acceptance speech at the Republican National Convention in St. Paul, Minnesota, but the McCain campaign failed to appropriately utilize her rhetorical skills during the campaign, thereby losing opportunities. Indeed, the McCain campaign insulated and isolated her from the media by carefully orchestrating her public appearances, a tactic that caused press and public to wonder about her abilities. A strong asset became a weak link in the

McCain campaign. In 2004 former Vermont governor Howard Dean had more than ample resources to win the Democratic nomination, but faulty rhetorical staging fatally wounded his candidacy, beginning with his feverishly frenetic, apparently uncontrollable response to defeat in the Iowa caucuses.

Thinking that presidents should govern, not campaign, people may react negatively to the idea of a seamless garment of campaigning and governing, which smacks of just more politics. On the positive side, however, the seamless garment benefits democracy through the effective communication of messages between leaders and followers. As the best simulation of the presidency itself, the presidential campaign tests whether candidates can organize and communicate their ideas to the people. In this light rhetorical staging in presidential campaigns benefits democracy.

Perhaps the primary reason for President Obama's political success rested in his communication skill. His keynote address at the 2004 Democratic National Convention unveiled his political potential on the national stage, and from there he continued to woo and wow audiences throughout America, culminating in his phenomenal acceptance speech at the 2008 Democratic National Convention in Denver, Colorado. That speech may stand out as the most successful in presidential campaign history, given its crowd size, media appeal, and crafting of themes for the campaign.

Spectacle is more important than speech. Speeches, even if worthy of the term *speech*, have become part of presidential image making. The value of presidential rhetoric now rests less in what a president says and more in how and where he says it, making form more important than substance. Presidents do not so much contribute to a substantive dialogue on major issues as they seek to control the dialogue through style. Speeches are like accent pieces on a table rather than the centerpiece. Or, put another way, they accent presidential presence more than they define the essence of a president's policies. They are the stagecraft of presidential leadership.

In the seamless garment of campaigning and governing, which separates successful candidates and presidents from the unsuccessful, proper rhetorical staging serves as a critical test of leadership. Presidents in the twenty-first century must master the art and science of weaving their campaigning and governing together as an undivided whole.

LAW NUMBER 3: THE LAW OF THEORY

Presidential leadership is not only bigger than the sum of its parts, but also bigger than any single theory. Presidents cannot rely upon any one theory of presidential leadership to ensure a successful presidency. Moreover, successful presidents may differ as to which theories benefit them more. Since individual theories of presidential leadership address only parts of the whole, they are like pieces of a puzzle.

Theories about presidential leadership have addressed many questions. Among them are these. From George Washington to Barack Obama, how many leadership styles have presidents had? How can we explain their different styles of leadership? What are the most effective leadership styles? Do common themes appear in the various leadership styles? Do some leadership styles work better than others? Should Americans prefer one leadership style to another? Should presidents try to emulate the successful leadership styles of their predecessors? Obviously no single theory can answer all of these and other questions.

Theories—like sex, drugs, and money—are good if in their proper place. But if not, dangerous results may occur. *Theory* comes from the Greek *theoria*, the "act of viewing, contemplation, consideration," and so a theory reflects an idea or a scheme, a philosophy or a model used to explain a subject, such as presidential leadership. A theory draws upon a limited body of evidence to explain the behavior of the whole. When stipulated as fact, however, theories may invite criticism, since they are at least in part indicative, suggestive, and speculative rather than inclusive, comprehensive, and definitive. Their primary value rests in partially explaining a subject.

Four themes typify theories about presidential leadership: (1) power, (2) the exceptional person, (3) history and culture, and (4) paradox. All theories focus in some way on presidential power to classify presidents, concentrating particularly on the sources of power and how presidents use their power. Explicitly or implicitly these theories point to an ideal use of power in the hands of an exceptional president. Paradoxes emerge, however, when human nature and other factors challenge a theory's discrete categories and conclusions.

Although theories enhance understanding of presidential leadership, they possess limitations. All theories of presidential leadership allude to, if they do not clearly state, the presence of paradoxes and their influence on presidential leadership. If Americans understood all of the contrary demands on presidents, they might exercise greater understanding in their judgment of them. If presidents always understood the paradoxes, they could more effectively lead the nation, distinguishing the possible from the unattainable and educating the public accordingly. In short, understanding the paradoxes of presidential leadership can help both the populace and presidents understand reality.

On the artist's canvas of effective presidential leadership, theories constitute parts of the picture, but not the whole picture. Taken individually, they help to explain the larger picture of presidential leadership, but they are not the picture itself. Theories selectively illuminate aspects of presidential leadership, but they do not explain the whole. In other words, theories point to the big picture by providing a better *understanding* of selective parts of presidential leadership. However, as noted, these theories do not make sense of reality as a whole. To the extent that theories instruct us about the paradoxes of presidential leadership, they help to unveil the big picture.

Thus, presidents in the twenty-first century must understand who they are, when they serve in history, what theory or theories of presidential leadership suit their needs, and how they can integrate the who, when, what, and how to achieve success.

LAW NUMBER 4: THE LAW OF CULTURE

In the words of Ronald Reagan, "politics is show business." If good leadership requires good acting, then to succeed, presidents must rely upon drama, especially in a culture greatly influenced by such institutions as the electronic media. Although the electronic media enable presidents to communicate more effectively with the public, they also produce unintended consequences, which may harm democracy.

The electronic media raise important questions for democracy. If style trumps substance, can the nation enjoy reasoned debate about serious ideas and issues? Have television and other electronic media unduly enlarged the importance of style over substance in presidential leadership? Do the electronic media cause presidential candidates and presidents to play to popular culture rather than to follow their conscience and conviction on issues? On one hand, the electronic media should enhance democracy by building better bridges of communication and understanding between leaders and followers. But on the other hand, they may subvert democracy by causing presidents and presidential candidates to emphasize their style of presentation over the substance of their ideas.

Public discourse in the national media, especially television, has shifted its emphasis from substance to style, making entertainment much more a part of American culture, so that entertainer-in-chief is now an important presidential role.

Americans once recognized their leaders through their writings, including copies of their speeches, but today's leaders find their images more important than their ideas. For example, in 1992 President Clinton captured the support of many young adults by appearing on MTV. What do we remember from that interview? His substantive answers to substantive questions? No. We remember his preference in underwear and his playing the saxophone with sunglasses on, which gave young people the impression that he was one of them. In 2000 Vice President Gore's poll numbers skyrocketed after "the kiss" of his wife at the Democratic National Convention. Obviously, this had nothing to do with the substance of his ideas or his vision for the United States, but it did portray him as a passionate family man, an appearance that boosted his image. Days later on the "Oprah Winfrey Show" when George W. Bush's poll numbers had declined, he gave her a "kiss" and then saw his poll numbers rise. Again, the "Bush kiss" had nothing to do with substance, but everything to do with image and entertainment. Barack Obama burnished his image on February 10, 2007, by announcing his candidacy on the steps of the Old State House in Springfield, Illinois, where Abraham Lincoln delivered his "House Divided" speech. And like all presidential candidates, he used content-free slogans: "Change We Can Believe In" and "Yes We Can."

In order to govern today, leaders must be able to use the electronic media, even though it may hamper their leadership in many ways. Leaders with good character will remember that the media are merely tools to help them serve the country, but these tools become dangerous in the hands of unscrupulous leaders who are willing to manipulate them and the country for their personal benefit.

The electronic media would appear to benefit presidential leadership by enabling presidents to communicate more effectively with the public and to learn what the public thinks. These two laudable democratic objectives suffer, however, from the unintended consequences. The electronic media strengthen the bridge of communication between presidents and the public through a democratic dialogue about issues and ideas, but they also weaken the bridge by emphasizing the images of presidents more than their ideas. As style has trumped substance, presidents have had to turn to more imaginative and entertaining ways of gaining public support.

Presidents in the twenty-first century face a daunting task, if they wish to be persons of sound character and conviction. They must sell their character and their ideas without stooping to sell their souls to an entertainment-crazed citizenry.

LAW NUMBER 5: THE LAW OF MORALITY

Successful presidential leadership requires that presidents function effectively in a culture of moral diversity and uncertainty. Not only do presidents bring their own personal morality to bear on their decisions, but they also confront division and dissent about what is morally acceptable in public policy. Both personal and public policy morality are now less clearly defined than in earlier generations.

Generally acknowledged as one of America's greatest presidents, Franklin D. Roosevelt placed morality on the center stage of presidential leadership when he said, "The Presidency is preeminently a place of moral leadership." Roosevelt understood that moral storm clouds hang over every major presidential decision. As people and groups fight to define what is moral and right for the family, art, education, law, domestic politics, economics, and foreign policy, presidents daily confront division and discontent about definitions of the morally acceptable.

Before the invention of computers, global positioning systems, or even accurate maps, sailors used the stars, particularly the North Star, to plot their course. With clear and certain guiding lights, they could find their way across stormy waters on dark nights. But presidents of the United States often navigate stormy political waters without clear and certain guiding lights, especially on moral matters. In short, they often find themselves without a moral North Star.

In their personal lives presidents also face differences about morality. Is a president's private morality a proper subject for public debate? Is there a relationship between a president's private morality and public policy? Should presidents lie if that would help them pursue a greater good for the American public? Some argue that a president's private morality should always remain private; others vehemently disagree. Some argue that the public interest always outweighs and overrides questions of personal morality; others believe the opposite.

On the canvas of presidential history, moral issues have painted a broad-brush stroke over presidents and presidential leadership. Inevitably all presidents, whether moral or immoral, face charges of moral corruption. Where their portraits hang in the museum of presidential greatness often depends on how well they handled moral issues.

American morality has become kaleidoscopic, reflecting an increasing variety of competing ideas about morals and religion, blurring the lines separating right and wrong. Although total agreement about American morality never existed, basic agreement was once more common. The directions of American morality have shifted from uniformity to diversity, from simplicity to complexity, and from singular to plural. America's moral kaleidoscope reflects an increasingly endless variety of competing ideas about morality. Never was there total agreement about American morality, but agreement was once much more common.

Kaleidoscopic morality makes presidential leadership more difficult. Presidents can no longer count on widely accepted moral standards to guide their actions. They must defuse moral land mines by trying to accommodate, appease, and appeal to differing moral interests.

Consider again the ship sailing at night. Whether the ship reaches its intended destination largely depends upon the captain's knowing and applying the laws of astronomy. Presidents are no different. Both their personal morality and their moral vision for America can significantly influence the destiny of their leadership and their place in history.

The presidency is a place of moral leadership, conditioned by personal moral character, the constraints and pressures that mold the nation's moral condition, and moral issues themselves. Together they shape the exercise of presidential leadership. History records how well a president's moral character intersects and interacts with the nation's moral condition and moral issues. On that may hinge the political life-span and legacy of presidents.

Morality, like beauty, is in the eyes of the beholder. Americans see morality through many lenses, including politics, religion, ideology, and language. Those entities determine the cut and shape of the moral kaleidoscope, the guiding lights of morality, because they define direction and purpose. American morality has become kaleidoscopic precisely because there is increasingly less agreement on the definition of morality, which makes presidential leadership more complex.

As the cut and shape of America's moral kaleidoscope have changed, voices have become more shrill and strident, speaking with greater assurance about the morality of their respective causes. Believing that their ideas occupy the moral high ground, people press their views on presidents, making more difficult their attempt to achieve compromise in the interest of national unity. To succeed in the twenty-first century, presidents face the daunting task of navigating the rocky shoals of morality.

Law Number 6: The Law of Politics

Long and sustained public careers together with stable political and public-policy strategies usually mark successful presidential candidates and presidents. Thus, presidents have customarily had their personal abilities, character, and policy inclinations tested along the way. The political system usually filters out candidates with policy ideas outside the mainstream of American politics, making "centrist" candidates and presidents the norm.

In the famous fable *The Tortoise and the Hare,* Tortoise personifies the law of presidential politics. Despite being slow, Tortoise won the race, defeating his faster and quicker opponent, Hare. Tortoise won with a simple strategy: remain steady and stay on course. Successful presidential candidates and presidents, like Tortoise, keep their eyes focused on the goal, winning election and reelection. They steadfastly avoid rabbit trails, which would slow them down and take them off course, and while bumps and potholes may slow them down, they continue their forward movement.

Before moving into the White House, the typical president has sustained a long public career, sometimes two decades or more, while serving in such positions as governor, U.S. senator or cabinet secretary, and also in the military. From Franklin D. Roosevelt through George W. Bush, that was true. Some critics contend that President Obama's leadership has suffered because his pre-presidential career included only a few years in the Illinois State Senate and one term in the U.S. Senate. Other than that, he served as a community organizer in Chicago.

This factor holds true for earlier presidents. Abraham Lincoln, for example, ran for office, winning and losing, over several decades, and Theodore Roosevelt served both as governor of New York and as vice president. But candidates who have not had a long public career, such as Wendell Willkie, the Republican Party's 1940 standard-bearer, usually come up short, failing to demonstrate to key leaders in politics, the media, and interest groups, as well as to the public at large, that they have the desire, dedication, intellect, organizational skill, and wisdom, among other things, to stay the course and go the distance. In 2004 U.S. Senator John Edwards (D-NC), who had served less than one term in the U.S. Senate, ran a credible campaign for the Democratic Party's nomination, but he lacked the nationwide breadth and depth of political and financial contacts to challenge the superior resources of U.S. Senator John Kerry (D-MA), which he had built over a much longer political career.

The complexities of America—political, economic, social, religious, geographic, and cultural—make the race for the White House a marathon run and not a hundred-yard dash. Presidential candidates and presidents must adjust to these complexities in order to survive, making appropriate compromises that will enable them to appeal to the American mainstream.

In *The Tortoise and the Hare*, the tortoise embodies the law of politics, steadiness and strategic thinking. While the hare slept, the tortoise walked on by. He won the race not because of speed or cunning, but because of his motivation and concentration on the goal of winning. Successful presidential candidates and presidents must exhibit the same quality: adhering to a strategy, despite difficulties along the road and temptations to go down rabbit trails. Most often their careers follow a pattern of serving in elective offices at the state and national levels, which in turn necessitates a long period of time to rise to the stature of a presidential candidate.

In the twenty-first century, both campaign and presidential challenges and responsibilities can overwhelm candidates and presidents unless they remain focused on a clear and coherent strategy that appeals to the mainstream of the American public.

LAW NUMBER 7: THE LAW OF MANAGEMENT

Successful presidents must master the complexities of management by indirection through political persuasion. The executive branch, al-

Charles W. Dunn

beit constitutionally accountable and responsible to the president, responds more favorably to indirect managerial methods than to those of command and control. And notwithstanding the lack of direct constitutional control in relationships with the legislative and judicial branches, presidents must still seek to influence those institutions, since the public holds presidents accountable for the implementation of their policies.

Constitutionally, presidents appear at the apex of authority in Article II, which would appear to give presidents the power to make command decisions and expect subordinates to carry out their orders. For example:

- "The executive power shall be vested in a President" (art. II, sec. 1);
- "The President shall be Commander in Chief of the Army and Navy of the United States" (art. II, sec. 2);
- The president "may require the Opinion, in writing, of the principal officer in each of the executive Departments, upon any Subject relating to the Duties of their respective offices" (art. II, sec. 2);
- "He shall from time to time give to the Congress Information of the State of the Union, and recommend to their Consideration such Measures as he shall deem necessary and expedient" (art. II, sec. 3); and
- The president "shall take Care that the Laws be faithfully executed, and shall Commission all the Officers of the United States" (art. II, sec. 3).

And also constitutionally, the president appears to have substantial authority or at least influence over the Congress. For example, among other things, presidents possess the power

- To veto acts of Congress (art. I, sec. 7);
- To nominate cabinet officers, ambassadors, and judges (art. II, sec. 2);
- To advise the Congress on the state of the Union (art. II, sec. 3); and
- To submit recommendations to Congress (art. II, sec. 3).

But appearances are deceiving. Mastering the complexities of managing by indirection through political leadership is the hallmark of successful presidents. Political persuasion to achieve goals usually works better than command decisions, which may create a defensive and hostile reaction from other parts of the government. Put another way, successful presidents lead primarily by indirection, exercising influence more than power, because an authoritarian manner makes them more vulnerable politically. Although theoretically presidents have the ability to direct, demand, and decree the carrying out of their decisions by subordinates in the executive branch, practically they do not.

Indirect methods, which require more nuance and subtlety, usually present the president as a more cooperative person. So persuasion is the hallmark of indirect leadership, while command is the hallmark of direct leadership. Thus, the nation needs political presidents more than managerial presidents. But circumstances sometimes dictate direct leadership when no other options exist or when presidents need to demonstrate overt strength. Those are usually decisions of last resort. When President Truman could not get General Douglas MacArthur to agree to his views about the Korean War, he had no choice but to dismiss him, a decision of last resort, which hurt the president's standing. MacArthur returned to America as a hero, addressing a Joint Session of Congress and enjoying a ticker-tape parade down New York City's Fifth Avenue.

Since the public holds presidents accountable for the implementation of their policies, presidents must exert influence not only over the Executive Branch, but also over the Congress and the courts, even though they lack the same measure of Constitutional authority over those institutions. Whether with the Executive Branch, the Congress, or the courts, however, successful presidents must master the complexities of management by indirection through political persuasion.

For presidents in the twenty-first century, the vast size and complexity of the government alone preclude managing effectively. Rather presidents must lead politically through articulating a convincing vision of their direction for the country.

Conclusion

These seven laws, parameters, and axioms of presidential leadership in the twenty-first century amplify the views of presidents Ronald Reagan and Harry Truman. Reagan said: "If I were really lucky, I wouldn't have this job." And Truman declared: "The Presidency is a killing job—a six-man job. . . . It requires young men—young in physical and mental ability, if not necessarily young in age." The first two presidents in the twenty-first century, George W. Bush and Barack Obama, have served under the same, but magnified, conditions, as presidents Reagan and Truman. And so it is that the presidency in the twenty-first century represents continuity and change.

NOTE

1. For an amplification of these ideas developed over more than thirty years of teaching, research, and writing about the presidency, please see *The Enduring Reagan* (Lexington: Univ. Press of Kentucky, 2009); *The Seven Laws of Presidential Leadership* (Saddle River, NJ: Prentice Hall, 2007); *The Scarlet Thread of Scandal: Morality and the American Presidency* (Lanham, MD: Rowman and Littlefield, 2000); *American Democracy Debated* (Glenview, IL: Scott Foresman, 1978, 1982); *American Government: A Comparative Approach* (New York: HarperCollins, 1994, 2000); *American Political Theology* (New York: Praeger, 1984); and *The Future of the American Presidency* (Morristown, NJ: General Learning Press, 1975), all authored, coauthored, or edited by Charles W. Dunn.

The Once and Future Chief Executive

Prophecy versus Prediction

Hugh Heclo

Thirty-six years ago, with the ashes of the Nixon and Johnson presidencies still glowing, a book on the same subject as this one, *The Future of the American Presidency*, presented the views of fourteen leading scholars, journalists, and politicians. Edited by Charles W. Dunn, it was a daring project.

Writing in 1975, how could anyone have predicted the future that was to come? Those subsequent years witnessed a seemingly hapless, unmanageable presidency under Jimmy Carter and a revitalized, emboldened presidential office under Ronald Reagan. Then there was the hugely popular Iraq war leadership but also electoral failure of George Bush senior. It was followed by the scandal-plagued, impeached, but politically successful William Clinton. And what shall we say of the second Bush presidency? Amid another Iraq War, this one a lingering disaster, and amid Nixonian assertions of unilateral executive power, George W. is the Bush whom the people rewarded with a second term.

Who could have predicted these and many other improbable presidential happenings over the past thirty-six years?

And now, in a moment suffused with even more uncertainty than 1975, Professor Dunn has launched the same daring—some would say reckless—project: asking eight mild-mannered and otherwise harmless scribblers to embarrass themselves by peering into the future of the American presidency.

At least two things might be learned from the past few decades. First, if you want to study America's presidency, you should have a keen eye for irony, a hearty appetite for paradox, and a strong stomach for tragedy.

Second, if nothing else, recent experience shows that the presidency is an extremely capacious office. It is capacious in the sense that, both theoretically and practically, over time it can accommodate a wide variety of leadership styles and interpretations of executive power.

So how can one predict what lies ahead as the parade of presidents continues? Who can foresee the singular personalities, events, and decisions that will swirl around this office in the future? My answer is that no one can reasonably make such predictions. And so I am not going to try.

This ends my presentation.

That is probably what a wise man would say. But of course, I have more to say.

PREDICTION VERSUS PROPHECY

Let me suggest a distinction, crude as it is, between the terms *prediction* and *prophecy*.[1] By prediction I mean trying to forecast things that will happen in the future. It is about foretelling what will occur. Prediction easily merges into clairvoyance, soothsaying, divination, and other kinds of "magical" news reporting about what lies beyond the historical time horizon.

Prophecy is more about forth-telling rather than foretelling. Prophecy claims to offer an authoritative, value-laden commentary about the truth of existence. Prophecy's communication is not a vision predicting the future, but a word seeking for attention. To ask what will happen is one thing. I am calling that prediction. To ask what will be happening when things happen is to search out deeper issues. That is prophecy.

The distinction is nicely illustrated by two small, juxtaposed verses in the biblical book of James. James 4:13 identifies the predictive vision: "Today or tomorrow we will go to such and such a city, spend a year there, buy and sell, and make a profit." The next verse answers prediction with a prophetic word: "You do not know what will happen tomorrow. For what is your life? It is even a vapor that appears for a little time and then vanishes away" (New King James Version).

I think this distinction is important because predictions suggest a closed quality to the future. Predictions offer us fixed pictures of what lies ahead, even when those pictures are tagged with different degrees of probability. The prophetic future is in this sense open, depending on choices people make in light of the prophetic word. Prophecy leaves room for freedom; it does not imply that the future is random or arbitrary. As one writer put it, a prophecy is "judged by its moral acuity—not by its predictive accuracy."[2]

In what follows I will not try to predict particular things about the future of American chief executives. My aim is to speak about what follows from the structure of the presidency's situation as it arcs into the future.

In trying to turn horizon into foreground, there will be two prophetic words. One is positive, the fulfillment of tendency inherent in republican constitutionalism. As prophecy, it tells forth a new and better realization of the possibilities of self-government—a transcending of our current dysfunctional way of doing politics. The other prophetic word is negative, the fulfillment of tendency in mass democracy. It tells forth the wreck of the republic. If you take them together, as I mean them to be, they are words of blessing and of woe, and thus of hope, depending on the choices citizens make.

THE FORM OF REPUBLICAN CONSTITUTIONALISM

Without claiming divine inspiration, I think it is possible to offer prophetic words about the future of the presidency. This is because there really is something called "form" in our political institutions.

By "form" I mean the essential qualities innate to something's nature. Form has to do with the controlling principles that make a thing what it is, rather than something else. The presidency is a certain kind of executive, the form of which is created by the Constitution. The presidency may be capacious. But as a constitutional office it is not formless. And its form derives from more than the bare words of Article II. The grounding idea of republican constitutionalism itself imputes a form—a calling to appropriate behavior—that is inherent within the structure of every president's situation in this constitutional order.

Respect for form does not mean hostility to change. Rather, it calls attention to the appropriateness of responses to changing circumstances. Appropriateness amounts to a developmental working out of what has heretofore lain hidden within the form of a constitutional chief executive. For example, as America emerged as a world power, it was wholly in keeping with the idea of a constitutional chief executive that the president should acquire new advisory and coordinating staffs such as the National Security Council. Without that, given changing circumstances, the form could not be realistically fulfilled.

By contrast, inappropriate responses consist in trying to build new things into the presidency—constructing, as it were, a new kind of office by adding materials from outside the form of a constitutional executive. Such additions "against form" make something less of what it is, not more. For example, puffing up presidential power through "signing statements" is a corruption rather than a fulfillment of constitutional form. Such statements allow presidents to rewrite rather than either approve or veto congressional legislation.

More than just the presidency is at issue. America's political identity is grounded in this historic achievement called republican constitutionalism. The drafters of the American Constitution understood that the purpose of the American Revolution was not to create a government based on the will of the majority. Willful government, whether based on the will of the one, the few, or the many, was simply a variation on the old theme of perverted, self-serving rule.

So they designed a constitution that would, among other things, suppress the immediate "will" of the majority and instead, hopefully, elicit the "judgment" of majorities. Representation would be the republican device for turning their goal of popular sovereignty into a practical possibility for governing. They understood, as G. K. Chesterton said, that while you can conceive of a democratic crowd "shouting a central and simple sentiment, good or bad, it is impossible to think of it shouting a necessary distinction in terms."[3]

To elicit judgments through law, rather than acts of majority will, the constitutional order had to be a complex system of representation. The people are represented in no one piece of the government. In a sense they are in the background of all the different moving parts and processes of the republican constitutional order. The Founders knew that leadership in republican government would be a problematic and fateful transaction between the people and their representatives. Republican self-government would be not just a top-down eliciting of consent or a bottom-up instructing of leaders, but a bottom-up and top-down transaction of reciprocal influence spread over time. Both elected "leaders" and electing "followers" would be citizens engaged in a deliberative transaction of mutual consent, guiding and being guided by each other over the long term. It was a reciprocating engine whose work would transcend the impossible choice between virtual and actual representation.

With the benefit of this properly complex institutional structure, one could, as James Madison put it, rest confident "on this great republican principle, that the people will have virtue and intelligence to select men of virtue and wisdom."[4] I think it is fair to say that the Founders' ultimate faith—and the underpinning of our entire political order—is not in leaders or in the common people, but in their interaction under the Constitution's design for ordered liberty.

On Presidential Form

What about the presidency? As presented in America's Constitution, the executive office is singular but the executive branch is not unitary. The power of the executive office is vested in a single person, not some plural head or collegial body. At the same time, the departments and agencies of the executive branch are created by the legislature. For their sustenance, they depend on the continuing flow of funds and authorizations from Congress. The substance of their work consists in laws and other types of guidance from Congress, often vague and inconsistent in nature.

This is, of course, the invitation to endless mutual struggle, bargaining, and compromise between separate institutions sharing powers. But it also imparts a form to appropriate behavior inherent within the structure of every president's situation under the Constitution. And that is not a calling to a "great man" theory of history or to executive unilateralism in governing. Rather the essential appropriateness inhering in the nature of this Constitution calls for presidential leadership to be a heavily collaborative form of government-by-discussion.

This is not meant to say that presidents should be expected to operate through committees or as chair of the board. Under the Constitution, the president has no equal colleague, no single or comparable bargaining partner. Collaborative leadership requires laboring together with other parties responsible for governing, sometimes leading from the front but also sometimes leading from the middle or the rear of the procession. A president who insists that other people bang their heads together to figure out some possible answers may be exercising a more subtle and productive form of leadership than the hyped-up kind of "follow me" leadership beloved by American pop-culture. It was basically in this collaborative form that the most "ideological" of modern American presidents, Ronald Reagan, achieved relative success in reforming Social Security and the federal tax code.

The Presidency: A Teaching Office

Understood in its constitutional context, there is also in the presidency an inherently didactic quality. It is a teaching office. As a national position representing citizens everywhere, there is nothing else like it in our constitutional order. That is not because Article II spells out vast executive powers. It is because the Constitution as a whole—as a way of ordering popular sovereignty through accountable representation—ensures that any president can command citizens' attention, thoughts, and emotions as no other official in the nation can, a least for as long as he or she retains their trust.

Teaching is not a "leadership style," to be picked up or set aside at will. Further, teaching is something much deeper than the smart use of public-relations techniques to "sell" the president's agenda. In the constitutional structure of the situation, there is no choice: presidents are always teaching, in ways intended and unintended, with words and with deeds.

But if form demands that presidents teach, does form suggest what they must teach? In a general way it does. Under the obligation to faithfully execute the office and to preserve, protect, and defend the Constitution, what presidents must teach amounts to one word: realism. That is the presupposition behind the entire effort to design and keep a republican constitution. The Founders were practical politicians. They realized that failure to sustain a realistic, trustworthy transaction between the people and their representatives would mean both sides would hear only what they wanted—rather than needed—to hear. It would mean people would fail to learn about and act on their true interests through their representatives. It would mean a self-governing people would literally lose touch with reality. Such a people would systematically misjudge both their internal problems and their foreign threats. And at that point, Americans would not be able to escape the ruin that has overtaken every other historical experiment in republican self-government. This, at its root, was our Founding Fathers' nightmare.

Often the political smart set seems to think that constitutionalism is an empty formality, or even a lie, because its reality often falls far short of its ideals. They are wrong. To paraphrase my late colleague Sam Huntington, republican constitutionalism is not a lie. It is an invitation to disappointment. But it can be a disappointment only because it is also a hope.[5]

The Modern Political System

And what about today? As boomers like to say, we've come a long way, baby. The Founders' plan was to promote deliberation among the people's representatives by insulating them from the shortsighted moods and easy courting of popular opinion. By now, virtually all such arrangements for an arms-length relationship have been dismantled or superseded.

But there is more to the story than these historical negations. At an accelerating pace during the twentieth century, a whole new way of doing politics insinuated itself into the constitutional design. There are at least six interlocking components of this self-serving and dysfunctional system:

- professional political management of the citizen-representative relationship;
- nonstop campaigning and media strategies to sell politicians and policies;
- dense networks of policy activists seeking to dominate the creation and execution of laws;
- nonstop fund-raising to finance this whole system of political and policy management;
- privileged access to decision makers based on this massive fund-raising;
- and, not least, sporadic convulsions of media attention for this and that hot topic—coverage devoted to stimulating eyeballs, not minds.

This political regime has been spurred on by new communication technologies and mounting policy expectations of the national government. It has grown over many decades, culminating with the idea of defining citizens as consumers. *The result of this new, unplanned system is a quietly spreading disintegration of the republican leadership transaction that undergirds our experiment in self-government.*

I wrote that last sentence two years ago. I went on to say that we should recognize that what is at work is something systemic. I wrote that it would take a crisis to break through and somehow transcend such a deeply embedded system.

If it takes a crisis to raze a system, is that where our nation is today?

I began by observing that we are considering the future of the presidency at a moment imbued with even greater uncertainty than in 1975. In summary form, I'd like to suggest for your consideration five differences between then and now.

First, two years ago we ended what many people—including many conservatives—regard as yet another failed presidency. President Bush's 66 percent disapproval rating in January 2009 matches that of President Richard Nixon when he resigned in August 1974. But that is merely a surface resemblance. George W. Bush put in place strong precedents for executive unilateralism. Bush left an executive office strengthened, not weakened. Ironically enough, an interpretation of unitary executive power that some conservatives hoped to use for cutting back the welfare state is now a tool sharpened and at hand for activist government in all spheres.

Second, unlike the case in the Watergate era, there is a general public indifference to issues of constitutionalism and executive power. When President Bush and officials in his administration repeatedly claimed broad, inherent executive powers, Americans seemed to yawn and await the results. This entire subject was hardly discussed during the longest presidential campaign in history—a sure sign that it had not registered among citizens in focus groups. President Bush's low approval ratings were a function of his failure to produce popular results, not his sweeping claims of executive power.

Third, in terms of political culture, American politics is at last moving past the 1960s. Not completely, of course, but the momentum is clear and it is generational. From the president on down, an emerging cast of political actors finds it quite irrelevant to argue about who was right or wrong on civil rights, Vietnam, the sexual revolution, and all the rest. Sixties-style civics teaches confrontation, mutual distrust, and ideological purity—an odd combination of aspiration and alienation in approaching public affairs. But there is an ever-increasing proportion of

Americans who simply were not there. The sixties' civics lesson has gotten old. And even worse, it has become uncool. Many younger citizens now think that the point of American political life is not to see through each other; it is to see each other through our common problems.

Fourth, we have entered a time when all the old inhibitions about the "appropriate role" of federal government have fallen away. President Reagan provided the rhetoric against big government but cut no major federal programs. President George W. Bush dropped the rhetoric and oversaw a vast expansion in federal intervention in the public school system and the prescription drug market. And now, amid a haunting sense of insecurity produced first by foreign terrorists and then by domestic mismanagement of our financial system, Americans seem to have no principled objection to any federal intervention. This includes semisocialist measures expanding powers of the central government to guide, manage, or own so-called private companies and economic institutions. Today the operative principle for federal power seems to be "Do whatever is necessary."

A final contrast with thirty-six years ago concerns the tools of democracy. Time will tell whether or not 2008 was a *realigning* election. But as for the organization of politics, 2008 was clearly a *redesigning* election. Through strategic use of modern technology, Barack Obama's twenty-month campaign organized supporters on a scale and depth never seen, or even imagined, before. More than 13 million people ended up on the Obama e-mail list, a million signed up for text messaging, and 3 million individual donors contributed a half billion dollars online. Beyond campaigning, there were new means to mobilize and sustain a popular movement. Networks of volunteers organized massive outreach efforts in a continuous two-way communication process between and among field-workers and campaign leaders. Obama's innovations made the vaunted Clinton machine and every other candidate look like characters from O'Connor's 1956 novel *The Last Hurrah*.

More than that, the interactive, Web-rooted process allowed individual citizens to connect—to experience politics as a personal, active presence in their lives. The new entryways to participation were laptops in the coffee shop, cell phones, forwarded e-mails, blog links, spontaneous discussion groups, house parties, and much more. And this is just the beginning. Thousands of political operators on all sides are now going to school on Barack Obama's campaign.

PRESIDENTIAL PROPHECY

So far I have distinguished between prophecy and prediction, emphasized the importance of constitutional form for prophesying, identified the modern system of politics, which has helped undermine adherence to such form, and summarized the unique elements of uncertainty in our current situation. It is time to conclude with words of prophecy.

At their best, prophecies seem to be rather brief. So first, briefly, the prophetic word of blessing.

The Positive Word: Empowering the Political Center

Precisely because of today's uncertainties, the stage is now set for a new and more positive era of presidential performance. It is new because for the first time in our history, interactive communication technology spread throughout the population makes such performance possible. And it is positive because, once matured, the new tools can offer a logical and much-needed development of form in republican constitutionalism.

This development consists of new opportunities to represent America's political center. The center, although longstanding in terms of general opinion, is now capable of being operationally mobilized as a political presence. Such a presence means human beings participating in public affairs with their resources of time and money. But above all, it means connected citizens sharing their personal experiences through mutual interaction, without any necessary top-down guidance. Governing from the center—filling that center with new currents of political participation—has become possible.

Politically empowering such centeredness is a deeply appropriate thing to do under our republican constitution. It moves beyond mere political salesmanship and professional management of representation. The connected, interactive nature of politics foreshadowed by Obama's campaign promises something more. It offers citizens multiple entryways into the public square. It makes it easy for people with common concerns to find each other, to organize, and to cooperate on- and off-line. It allows thousands of ongoing public conversations among citizens who are never gathered in one place.

Here then is the omen of turning to a more healthy political system, a postsixties era that teaches constructive rather than dysfunctional things about civil life. It teaches that trying to work with people who disagree with you is not selling out to the enemy. It's buying in to the democratic process. It teaches that compromise is not a sign of weakness but of common sense. It teaches that the point isn't to win an ideological battle. It's to find what works. It teaches that the leader's real task isn't to sell people with clever PR. It's to explain as clearly as possible why the leader is doing what she or he is doing.

Down this path lie positive innovations in governing. There can be more hard-working bipartisan groups, on the model of the 9/11 Commission. There can be not just the window-dressing of transparency but genuine public visibility into where citizens' money is going, into how and why decisions are getting made. There can be a more genuine petitioning of government—online for everyone rather than for those privileged with insider access. There can be Web-based political action groups far larger than the membership of any political party, coalitions spanning the inside-outside government divide. Such a better realization of republican constitutionalism can teach that politics, properly understood, is not something done to citizens, the *lumpen proletariat* of mass democracy. It is something done by citizens organized for a more representative and deliberative government. That is something different from government of the party base, by the base, and for the base.

For the future chief executive, all this offers new opportunities for collaboration and realistic teaching that correspond to the inherent form of republican leadership anticipated by the Constitution. It is a presidency mobilizing others to realize their collective strength, helping them learn about their situation, finding resources to work out the ongoing balance between their aspirations and their fears, understanding the ways of their opponents, and empowering the voiceless rather than the privileged. With its reciprocal top-down and bottom-up leadership mentality, community organizing may be excellent preparation for a constitutional chief executive. The president as community-organizer-in-chief? It's not a bad way of thinking about a positive future for the presidency.

The Negative Word: CREEPing toward Presidential Cults and Factionalism

But now too comes the prophetic word of woe. For the stage is also set for something much darker. If we end up interpreting our whole constitutional system as an extension of election-time horse-race thinking, supplemented by mass plebiscites, then something will have gone wrong. The effect will be to turn the constitutional rules for governance into so much fodder to be manipulated by interactively connected partisans trying to win at all costs.

The resources and incentives are now in place to produce something more dangerous than partisan mischief. A connected, Internet-driven politics invites presidential party–building. It is in fact an invitation to an anticonstitutional doppelganger presidency. This means the operating of one supposedly official presidency within the White House and another outside through the president's political communication and support system. This would have the effect of embedding a high-tech equivalent of Nixon's 1972 Committee to Reelect the President (the aptly named CREEP) into the heart of the political system. And the omens are already here. The Obama administration began life by legally dodging the intent of the Smith-Mundt Act and slipped its campaign e-mail list and potential propaganda machinery of "Organizing for America" into a wing of the Democratic National Committee.

This may be only the beginning. As more Americans abandon traditional broadcast news and information sources in favor of narrowcast media enclaves of groupthink, it becomes harder for any president to collaboratively lead and teach amid the din of voices. In fact there will be a powerful temptation for presidents to use all the advantages of our media-driven world, thereby distorting the office into another trinket in our celebrity culture. Consider Obama's 2009 inaugural parade. Were the models of the Oval Office and chunks of Air Force One just a wretched excess of constitutional bad taste? Or were they a harbinger of cultish fantasies to come? If the latter, we will make our system of government ever more insecure. We will be making the spirit and vitality of the whole republic dependent on one inevitably flawed mortal—as James put it, "a vapor that appears for a little time and then vanishes away" (James 4:14, NKJV).

It does not help that future generations will see an unending line of presidential libraries keep marching across the landscape from sea to shining sea. This ever-growing menagerie of ego monuments and repositories teaches citizens to denominate public affairs, the res publica of their republic, into presidencies—an unfortunate mimicking of the historical periodization found in monarchical nations.

A seemingly opposite danger but in fact one compatible with the "celebrification" of presidents is a denigration of the office. Why shouldn't citizens see organized presidential support as just another special interest group? It may have the imprimatur of the presidency, but that only makes the office itself part of an intensifying scramble of self-serving interests. It is what the Founding Fathers feared, and what they called factionalism.

Situational Constitutionalism and the Wreck of the Republic

There are some ugly truths about America's political condition. For more than fifty years, politicians of both parties have been teaching citizens what Richard Pious has called "situational constitutionalism."[6] Democrats and Republicans, liberals and conservatives, have supported and then pivoted 180 degrees to oppose expansive executive powers, all depending on whether or not it was their man in the White House. The yearning for partisan advantage has usually overwhelmed any principled commitment to constitutional values. And ordinary Americans appear to have been absorbing the lessons of situational constitutionalism that the political class has been teaching.

The implication should be sobering. The record of the last Bush administration suggests we may be reaching a point in this country where a president who (unlike Bush) *does* deliver the popularly desired results, despite disregarding the constitutional rules of the game, can expect to be publicly applauded rather than condemned. This is dangerous territory for a nation aspiring to be not only democratic but also constitutional. Down this path Americans will, in fact, be watching the wreck of the republic.

But American citizens probably will not see it, because most people do not understand how real wrecks occur in history. Most expect them to be the kind of dramatic events portrayed on evening news and in video games. But in real life, the corruption of institutions is as banal and dull as evil itself. How national wrecking occurs is captured in a little poem by Emily Dickinson:

Crumbling is not an instant's Act,
A fundamental pause.
Dilapidation's processes
Are organized decays.

And the last stanza:

> Ruin is formal—Devil's work
> Consecutive and slow—
> Fail in an instant, no man did.
> Slipping—is Crash's law.[7]

NOTES

1. I am setting aside the more technical notion of prediction in the scientific sense of the term, namely, a conditional statement taking the form of "if this is done, then such and such will follow." Instead my distinction follows along lines laid down by the Jesuit theologian Karl Rahner, although it is far cruder than anything he has to say. See Karl Rahner, *Visions and Prophecies* (1958; London: Burns and Oates, 1963 [English trans.]).

2. Lisa Schwebel, *Apparitions, Healings, and Weeping Madonnas: Christianity and the Paranormal* (New York: Paulist Press, 2004), 102.

3. G. K. Chesterton, "The Position of Sir Walter Scott," in *Twelve Types: A Collection of Biographies,* originally published in 1902 by Arthur L. Humphrey's of London.

4. James Madison, speech before the Virginia Ratifying Convention, June 20, 1788, www.constitution.org/rc/rat_va_17.txt.

5. Samuel Huntington (1927–2008). A passage in the conclusion of his *American Politics* states: "Critics say that America is a lie because its reality falls so far short of its ideals. They are wrong. America is not a lie; it is a disappointment. But it can be a disappointment only because it is also a hope." *American Politics: The Promise of Disharmony* (Cambridge, MA: Belknap Press of Harvard Univ. Press, 1983).

6. Richard M. Pious, *Why Presidents Fail: White House Decision Making from Eisenhower to Bush II* (Lanham, MD: Rowman and Littlefield, 2008), 275.

7. *The Complete Poems of Emily Dickinson* (Boston: Little, Brown, 1960), poem 997, written circa 1865.

Shall We Cast Our Lot with the Constitution?

Thinking about Presidential Power in the Twenty-first Century

Stephen Skowronek

As the reach and responsibilities of the federal government expand, so too do the stakes of any debate over the scope and limits of presidential power. In other words, the implications of our thinking about these matters have never been as weighty as they are today. All the more striking, then, is the determination in recent years to drive the debate over presidential power back to first principles. It is not just that the improvisations of prior generations have been called into question; that is to be expected. What is curious is that the way forward is no longer being charted by reformers candidly committed to political and institutional innovation. For all appearances, the prescription of the day is to consult the Framers and cast our lot with the Constitution.

The drive back to constitutional formalism and originalism has been led by advocates of a more *expansive* reading of the prerogatives of the presidency in modern American government. These advocates have staked their ground on the hallowed principle of the separation of powers and have decried latter-day institutional innovations that have allegedly compromised Article II's clear and deliberate vesting of "the executive power" in the president alone. These advocates have constructed a legal brief on behalf of the Constitution's "unitary executive" and have argued that contemporary incumbents need look no further than the Framers' design to justify sweeping claims to unilateral action and hierarchical control.[1] Skeptics have, quite naturally, responded in kind, and when it comes to touting hallowed constitutional principles, they are not easily outdone. Reminding us of a Revolution fought against overweening executive power, skeptics point to fresh signs of an "imperial presidency" and prescribe a reinvigorated system of constitutional checks and balances to arrest the drift toward unilateralism and unbridled discretion.[2]

There is, of course, much that might be said for a debate over first principles. What greater tribute could there be to the eighteenth-century experiment that launched American government than to hear advocates and critics of presidential power still, at this late date, invoking the Constitution as their ultimate authority? The determination on both sides to consult the Framers on controversial matters of power and prerogative is reassuring, if only because it is so quintessentially American. Great debates over the meaning of the Constitution serve the cause of keeping all of its various interpretations vital and available.

But there are troubling aspects to this resurgence of constitutional formalism as well. To the extent that the Constitution's meaning remains eminently contestable and fiercely contested, its capacity to clear common ground for a satisfactory resolution of the weighty controversies of the moment would appear quite limited. An extended debate over first principles is more likely to exacerbate constitutional confrontations and political crises than to ease them. There is no gainsaying the seriousness with which advocates of the unitary theory have embraced the intellectual challenge at hand. Advocates have delved deeply into the founding period to illuminate their case, and they have stipulated their claims meticulously with reference to the Constitution's text, structure, and ratification history. But in doing so, advocates have prompted the skeptics to do the same.[3] In effect, the history of the founding period has become just one more battleground in a political contest over the powers now in dispute. One suspects that contemporary advocacy of presidential power has taken the form of a legal brief precisely because prospects for garnering political consensus behind any one interpretation of the Constitution are today so severely limited and because judicial intervention has become the best hope for a favorable resolution of the issues in dispute. If this is indeed the case, the phalanx of legal scholars currently debating the claims of "the unitary executive" is indicative both of the high stakes at issue in the moment at hand and of the high premium to be paid for a coherent and consistent theory of American government in the twenty-first century.

Less obvious, but more troubling, is what gets sidelined in a debate of this sort. The old arguments from text and structure are familiar, but they are hardly exhaustive of prior thinking about the presidential power. Nor are they an especially accurate guide to the premises that transformed the resources and governing role of the presidency in modern America. Indeed, when attention turns to what the constitutional debate leaves out, any reassurance we might have found in its familiarity quickly dissipates.

The fact is that this is the first time since the founding generation when advocates and critics have been so singularly fixated on the formalities of constitutional design in trying to resolve the riddle of presidential empowerment and control. No sooner had Madison weighed in against Hamilton in the debates of the Washington administration than the search began in earnest to develop extraconstitutional devices that might bridge what the Constitution had separated. Reformers have persistently sought to ease the straitjacket of checks and balances with an eye to the greater attractions of institutional collaboration, elite cooperation, and collective control. I would go so far as to venture that no one has ever come up with a formal constitutional solution to the conundrum of presidential power in America; prior generations have all looked to auxiliary instruments and arrangements external to the Constitution itself to resolve the problem. Moreover, the various instruments and arrangements they conjured up proved attractive in their time precisely because they avoided any stark choice between releasing and restraining that power. They facilitated both goals at once and, in so doing, gradually altered the political foundations of presidential power.

In this essay, I would like to revisit the long history of these efforts at extraconstitutional improvisation. I want to pay particular attention to the improvisations of twentieth-century progressives, for they were especially self-conscious and aggressive in pushing against formal constitutional reasoning in the development of the American executive. For better or worse, progressive reformers built "the modern presidency," the office as we know it today, in an open "revolt against formalism."[4] Second thoughts about their handiwork notwithstanding, the premises and conditions upon which they expanded presidential power cannot but affect rather profoundly the practical significance of latter-day proposals to put the genie back in the bottle.

My more specific concerns in drawing out the extraconstitutional foundations of this office as we know it today are twofold. I want to say something about why the long tradition of extraconstitutional improvisation suddenly seemed to have failed us in recent years, and why advocates of presidential power have reverted to a more formal constitutional discourse to press the case forward. I also want to consider the implications of reverting to strict constitutional argumentation in light of what has gone before. I will suggest that the more seriously we consider the political development of the office—the sequence, premises, and prior impact of change—the less willing we will be to cast our lot with the Constitution in trying to resolve the problems now in view.

EARLY CONSTRUCTIONS OF PRESIDENTIAL POWER

For the better part of two centuries, the development of the American presidency tracked the democratization of the polity. The first half of this story, the nineteenth-century half, is familiar and fairly straightforward. Presidents were empowered through the primary instruments of democratization, the political parties. Parties eased checks and balances in exchange for new forms of collective control.

Ever since Henry Adams wrote about the presidents of the founding generation, we have known that Jefferson's conception of presidential power proved to be every bit as expansive as Hamilton's.[5] But contemporary scholars are quick to point out that there was a crucial difference between them. Whereas Hamilton sought to lodge presidential prerogatives in Article II of the Constitution, Jefferson sought to extricate presidential strength from the constitutional text and anchor it instead in externalized expressions of public opinion.[6] By claiming ground beyond the Constitution, Jefferson's construction was in some ways even less constrained than Hamilton's, and yet, its scope was kept circumstantial and subject in principle to the judgments of others. For Jefferson, extraordinary assertions of presidential power could be justified as a collective act of popular will, a mandate from the people, a populist intervention.[7] By implication, these interventions would extend no further than the people's collective action and political indulgence would take it. Checks and balances would be left intact as security against the impositions of individuals and factions who had less than overwhelming popular support.

Jefferson's construction of presidential power was reflected institutionally in innovations that played to the advantages of the political movement behind him. The formation of the Republican Party, the ratification of the Twelfth Amendment, the designation of the congressional caucus as a presidential nominating body, the selection of state electors in accordance with the party ticket—all served the cause of popular mobilization, political cooperation, and institutional cooperation. With them, Jefferson swept the field of his political opponents, secured his party's control over all the elected branches, reconstructed national political priorities, and exercised prerogatives that dwarfed those of his Federalist predecessors. But innovations such as these cut two ways, and they left Jefferson's successors to labor under their constraints. Once the insurgent Republicans were safely ensconced in power, the auxiliary institutions they instituted to express the public will strengthened the position of Congress and saddled presidents with norms that were deeply suspicious of the formal trappings of executive power.[8]

The Jacksonian construction of the presidency extended the Jeffersonian ideal of an office empowered through popular mobilization and institutional coordination, but the mechanisms deployed were very different. The Jacksonians rejected political control of the executive by Congress, and they found the ideal of a single party of national consensus unwieldy. Pressing his political priorities upon a nation more sprawling and varied in its interests, Jackson encountered stiff resistance to his priorities from the other branches of government, and his claims to a popular mandate for independent action grew correspondingly sharper.[9] When push came to shove, Jackson embraced the political divisions his policies were creating, proclaimed the presidency superior to Congress as an agency of democratic expression, and set about mobilizing majorities on the electoral battlefield sufficient to gain control of the Congress and secure deference to his will. These assertions fueled the organization and integration of rival mass-based parties designed to compete for power at all levels.[10]

Jackson created a presidency more fully extricated from congressional domination and more fully supported in its popular connection, but his followers saw to it that it was also more fully integrated into state and local politics. The characteristic institutional forms to emerge from the Jackson period—the party convention for nominating candidates and the spoils system of political rotation and partisan appointment in administration—paced the greater strength of the Jacksonian presidency with more disciplined instruments of collective control. As the party convention took candidate selection and programmatic commitments out of the hands of the Congress, it lodged them more firmly in a national coalition of local party machines. The spoils system, in turn, bolstered congressional support for the president by transforming the executive bureaucracy into a jobs program for the local party work-force. Whereas the party of Jefferson had articulated an accord among elites at the center of power and delivered it to the periphery, these new parties generated power from the bottom up; their candidates were, like Jackson, to deliver to the center an accord hammered out by political interests at the periphery.[11]

The new construction was tied conceptually to perceived inadequacies of the Constitution: the charge was that the Madisonian system had failed to resolve the presidential election of 1824 on sound democratic principles and that auxiliary mechanisms were needed to redress the problem.[12] The alternative put in place went far toward upending the original scheme of checks and balances, but it did not endorse separation as an alternative.[13] Rather, the instrumentality of party joined the presidency more tightly to other power centers. Together, the party convention and the spoils system created a near perfect community of interests for the release, control, and direction of presidential power. Fortifying the president with an organized base of popular support outside the constitutional apparatus made it easier for him to forge a concert of action with fellow partisans in the other branches and raised the political risks of his acting alone.

The party-based presidency reached its zenith during the Civil War under the insurgent Republicans. Eyeing the enormous war machine mobilized under Lincoln to contest the meaning of the Constitution, a Republican county convention in upstate New York neatly captured the prevailing arrangement: "He [the President] has no army, he has no navy, no resources of any kind except what the people give him. . . . He is powerless unless the people stand at his side and uphold his hands. . . . The Republican organization, in all its principles and all its members, is committed to the preservation of the Union and the overthrow of the Rebellion. It is the power of the State and the power of the Nation."[14]

THE PROGRESSIVE CONSTRUCTION OF PRESIDENTIAL POWER

Well before the Jackson insurgency began, the congressional nominating caucus that had empowered Jefferson had become "King Caucus," an authorizing agency reviled for compromising the independence of national and state officers alike. By the time the Progressive insurgency began, the party convention that had empowered the mid-nineteenth-century presidents had become the plaything of state and local "bosses" who held the executive branch hostage to the patronage demands of their local organizations. Both developments attest to the fact that the new forms of collective supervision devised by those early movements were more than merely cosmetic. Indeed, a pattern may be discerned: democratic reformers would ease checks and balances in exchange for newly improvised forms of control, and when those controls came to be perceived as too constraining, reform advocates would seek to renegotiate the bargain.

The third iteration of this pattern proved to be more sustained, more broad-ranging, and more systemic in its effects than either of the previous two. In successive waves of reform extending over the first two-thirds of the twentieth century, progressive reformers proceeded to expand the domain of national action, to construct an extensive administrative apparatus for intervention at home and abroad, and to concentrate power in the presidency on a scale that dwarfed all nineteenth-century precedents. This concerted shift toward national, executive, and presidential power has long marked a pivotal turning point in American political development, so much so that analysts often write of "the modern presidency" as an office categorically different in its operations and responsibilities from its nineteenth-century predecessor.[15] Moreover, ever since James McGregor Burns dubbed the new system "Presidential Government," the assumption has been that the deal the progressives struck weighed far more heavily on the side of presidential empowerment than on the side of control.[16] But we now find ourselves in a postprogressive world, a world in which arguments on behalf of presidential power are changing and progressive premises are very much at issue, and a world that affords a somewhat different perspective on what those twentieth-century reformers had in mind.

Three aspects of the progressive departure have marked it as especially radical. First, the progressives broke with the nineteenth-century reliance on party mechanisms for easing constitutional constraints and balancing presidential empowerment with collective control. As the centerpiece of the received solution, party power stood out to early-twentieth-century reformers as the central problem to be overcome.

Progressives saw the party machines as increasingly indifferent to the interdependencies of industrial society; party competition appeared to them to perpetuate outmoded conflicts and to submerge the common interests upon which a new national government might foster greater social cohesion. More pointedly, the progressives wanted to recast the institutional bond between president and Congress around an expandable bureaucracy capable of reconciling national economic interests and tying them to coherent national purposes; and that ambition placed them at odds with mechanisms of government previously developed to hold the president more directly accountable to state and local concerns.[17] Mounting a sharp critique of the principal instruments of Jacksonian democracy, the reformers worked to displace the selection of candidates by party conventions with a primary system, and they sought to displace the disembodied bureaucracies created by spoils appointment with more contained and capable administrative units. Their primary system was to tap the entrepreneurial skills of individual leaders and render political coalitions more responsive to timely policy innovations; their meritocracy was to advance the values of policy expertise, professional competence, and "enlightened administration."[18]

Second, the progressives unleashed a critique of the Constitution that was more direct and sweeping than anything the Jeffersonians or the Jacksonians had contemplated.[19] There was much for these critics to admire in the Framers—realism, nationalism, reconstructive instincts, leadership of public opinion.[20] Rather than defer, however, progressives proposed to emulate their forefathers with a "new nationalism," one that would overthrow what they now regarded as "the monarchy of the Constitution."[21] Their legal realism turned all theories of the state, including the Framers' theories, into so many "justifications or rationalizations of groups in power or seeking power—the special pleadings of races, religions, or classes on behalf of their special situations."[22] Progressive political realism described all institutional arrangements, including the Framers' arrangements, as contingent expressions of the power of interests.[23] Realism in both forms served progressive purposes by upending unreflected premises about government carried over from an earlier day and by legitimating experimentation with alternative arrangements addressed to "the facts" of current circumstance.

The progressives wanted to strip discussions of power of their constitutional pretenses so as to force the defenders of established arrangements to engage in a pragmatic, open-ended, and explicitly political debate over what the largest interest, "the public interest," demanded in the moment at hand. They located the public interest itself in the evolving concerns of an "organic" society. A government continuously attentive to the current interests of the public required a "living" Constitution, one that would operate as the protean instrument of an ever-evolving democracy.[24]

Finally, the progressives seized upon the possibility of constructing a *presidential* democracy. Parties were too decentralized; courts were too tied to precedent; Congress was too cumbersome and beholden to special interests. Only the presidency seemed to have the national vision to articulate the public's evolving interests, the political incentive to represent those interests in action, and the wherewithal to act upon them with dispatch. Key to the progressive design, presidential power was advocated as the means to a more effective fusion of public opinion with "enlightened administration," and the reformers put the president to work accordingly. They constructed an office in which incumbents would be duty-bound to assume political leadership of the nation on an ongoing basis. Rather than enclose the office in the Constitution, the progressives sought to break down the boundaries around it, to render presidential authority less self-contained and more radically externalized. Each incumbent was individually charged to consult with policy experts on the pressing issues of the day, to manage the interests of the industrial economy, to keep national opinion mobilized behind great public purposes, and to engage the Congress for concerted national action.

To speak of this as a "broad construction" of presidential power is to misconstrue the progressives' ambition. As Charles Beard saw it, the objective was to break American politics free of debates between "finely spun theories about strict and liberal interpretations of the Constitution." Theodore Roosevelt's declaration of a presidential stewardship was not, for Beard, a new constitutional doctrine; it was the liberation of national statesmanship from tired doctrinal disputes. In this same spirit, Henry Jones Ford declared the work of the presidency "the work of the people *breaking through* the Constitutional form." Similarly, Herbert Croly touted the rise of Roosevelt as a release from the narrow-mindedness of "government by lawyers" and an acknowledgment "that the national principle involve[d] a continual process of internal reformation."[25]

It is easy to understand why commentators have tended to mark progressive reform as a great divide; the new vision was sweeping in its ambition and thoroughgoing in its practical impact on American government and politics. But though the progressives pushed harder and farther away from original conceptions of American government, there was also much that they drew forward from nineteenth-century precedents. Like the Jeffersonians and the Jacksonians, they perceived themselves as democratizers promoting institutional innovations that would make American government more responsive, more responsible, and more collective. They were willing to empower the presidency, but only on the condition that the office was opened up to more broad-ranging influences; enveloping the executive in a new community of interests was an essential part of the deal. Moreover, the progressives, like the Jeffersonians and the Jacksonians, built institutions that expressed their faith in a discernible public interest outside of government, and they never flagged in their efforts to bring those institutions to bear more directly on their new presidency-centered system.

In forming the progressive "administration state," the progressives sought, first and foremost, to deliver on the promise of "enlightened administration." This meant building administrative agencies that would instill confidence in a more powerful national government. Progressive administrators were to be insulated as much as possible from "politics"; they were to develop an independent voice based on their own professional expertise and gain authority from their capacity to distill the facts objectively from the situation at hand.[26] Second, while weakening the role of party organizations in presidential selection and ejecting the local parties from their pivotal coordinating role in national administration, the progressives also built up an extensive "para-state" apparatus—universities, graduate schools, think tanks, professional associations, information clearinghouses, journals of national opinion—all with an eye to surrounding and infusing new concentrations of national power with what they thought would be truer and more reliable distillations of the interests of the whole.[27] All in all, the progressives felt safe in finessing constitutional divisions and subverting institutional competition because they, like the Jeffersonians and the Jacksonians, were confident in the new mechanisms they were devising to discover the public interest, promote political cooperation, and induce elite collaboration.

And over the years, they kept refining these instruments. Progressives emerged from World War I with a more sober view of the capacity of the people to express the public interest directly, and in response, they began to put greater stock in group representation and pluralist bargaining. Charles Merriam, a champion of academic political science who later served Franklin Roosevelt on his Committee on Administrative Management and on his National Resources Planning Board, proposed an ongoing mobilization of "the political prudence of the community" into the policymaking process. The assembled wisdom of the nation was to circumscribe governmental power and infuse it with "the facts essential to intelligent national government." In part this was just another brief for experts, for deploying in government the resources of the nation's new universities and graduate schools, and for consummating a marriage of positivism with power. But, on inspection, Merriam's offensive on behalf of the prudential authority of the public was remarkably multifaceted. Merriam insisted on representation for "all phases of opinion," for he saw that confidence in progressive government would come to hinge on the public's perceptions of "the impartiality of the prudentes who were brought together." He envisioned integrating and coordinating mechanisms that would tap "the wisdom of the few more skilled and experienced" while remaining sensitive to the "general level of judgment and insight reached by the mass of the community itself."[28] Merriam's efforts to surround formal power with extraconstitutional agents fill out an expanded potpourri of progressive prescriptions—civic education for the common man, data-gathering by specialists, clearinghouses to collect and make public information from all sources, objective analysis and expert advice from top administrators, outreach to diverse communities, national economic interests, and professional associations.

Important aspects of this new conception of the balance between presidential empowerment and collective control were incorporated into the institutional capstone of the progressive presidency, the Executive Office of the President (EOP). Though it tagged the president with new responsibilities for planning and forecasting and bolstered the institution of the presidency with new resources for policy development and administrative oversight, the EOP was less an instrument of unitary command and control than an instrument designed for institutional coordination and collective action. Its offices served interbranch and interagency relations, not just the president. They anticipated a new governmental partnership, a partnership built on assurances to Congress that executive actions and recommendations were grounded in the best managerial practices, the latest forecasting instruments, and the most reliable data. President Truman was initially wary of the formation of the National Security Council and the Council of Economic Advisors within the EOP because he perceived the elevation of professional managers and expert advisers to positions of authority within the executive branch as a constraint on his constitutional prerogatives.[29] But it was precisely by means of this technocratic interposition that the progressive presidency was to meet other centers of power on common ground and solicit their collaboration.

The progressive construction of American government tilted radically in the direction of "presidential government," but as Richard Neustadt so astutely observed in 1960, its presidents were well-advised not to depend on the Constitution. Whatever the original meaning of the separation of powers, American government had developed in practice into a system of "separated institutions sharing powers." The last of the great progressive tracts, *Presidential Power,* described an office engrossed in interactions with others outside its own sphere and charged to orchestrate the far-flung interests of the whole.[30]

DOUBLING BACK TO THE FRAMERS

The reformers who built the presidency as we know it today did not proceed unchallenged. Efforts to expand presidential power by shifting its ground and developing new instruments of control outside the Constitution proper were resisted at every turn by conservatives who insisted that presidential power rests on the Constitution alone. This was Henry Clay's case against the pretensions of Andrew Jackson and William Howard Taft's appeal against the pretensions of Theodore Roosevelt.[31] Both Clay and Taft rejected populist trumps to constitutional strictures, both refuted the notion of an "undefined residuum" of presidential power, both sought to hold the powers and duties of the chief executive to a stringent textual standard, and both were swamped by the democratic movements they challenged. Late into the period of progressive dominance, conservative intellectuals like Willmore Kendall, Alfred De Grazia, James Burnham, and James Buchanan were still juxtaposing the Constitution against the progressives' presidency-centered system. Voices in the wind, they invoked formalities of text and structure to defend the local and congressional prerogatives.[32]

But political developments during the 1970s and 1980s scrambled the terms of this debate, and today the old progressive-conservative divide over the question of presidential power has evaporated. On the one side, progressives began to abandon their own handiwork. As progressives came to see things, the controls that twentieth-century reformers had relied upon to ease checks and balances and regulate the release of presidential power had proven themselves woefully inadequate. True to their vision of the modern presidency as a collective instrument of democratic rule, progressives recoiled at what they belatedly perceived as incumbents' overwrought pretensions to imperial rule and as new forms of privilege operating behind the facade of a public interest in the administrative state.[33] "Power invested, promise unfulfilled" was their summary judgment of the twentieth century's great experiment in presidency-centered government.[34]

No doubt, the progressives had a lot to account for. Latter-day charges that the progressives had eviscerated constitutional restraints, exacerbated political agitation, and sanctioned demagoguery all had a ring of truth. By the 1980s, the once-confident invocation of public opinion, enlightened administration, and group representation as effective balance wheels for executive power in the modern state appeared reckless, naive, and half-baked. And given the energy and candor with which the progressives had assaulted the formalities of the Constitution, a revisionist recasting of the Framers as the more hard-headed and enlightened realists became nearly irresistible. In one way or another—either by redirecting the argument for control back to the original system of checks and balances or merely by exposing the hopeless confusion and derangement of modern practices—the Constitution came to leverage a new generation of criticism of the modern presidency.[35]

THE BIRTH OF THE UNITARY THEORY OF THE EXECUTIVE

What distinguishes the most recent period, however, is not just that the progressives' premises for presidential empowerment collapsed; it is that conservatives armed with an alternative set of premises for empowerment thrust themselves into the vanguard of advocacy. As the progressives were recoiling and the intellectual foundations of their modern presidency were crumbling, these new advocates dispensed with the standard progressive nostrums in favor of a formal, constitutional case for presidential power in modern American government. The conservatives criticized the modern presidency not because progressives' experimentation with new forms of control had proven inadequate, but because such controls presented an illegitimate intrusion on the president's constitutional prerogatives.

Given past episodes in the development of the presidency, it is certainly no surprise that advocates of presidential power have proved impatient with checks and balances. Nor is it surprising that conservatives would prefer to rest the case for presidential power on the Constitution alone. But the combination of impatient advocacy with formal constitutional reasoning has not been so prominently displayed since the days of Alexander Hamilton. Instead of proposing new machinery to surround presidential power and hold it to account; instead of justifying a relaxation of checks and balances in the name of superior forms of institutional coordination and collective control; instead of pushing the foundations of presidential power further out into polity at large; the arguments of the new conservatives cut radically the other way. The new conservatives claimed that everything needed to justify an expansive indulgence of presidential prerogatives today is to be found in the "text, structure, and ratification history of the Constitution."[36]

With both critics and advocates of modern presidential power returning to first principles and defending formal constitutional arrangements, the historical insight of all prior generations—that executive empowerment entails the invention of auxiliary mechanisms of control outside the constitutional frame—has gone into remission. But what appears at first to be a sudden failure of political imagination turns out on reflection to be an intellectual adaption to new political circumstances. It is certainly no coincidence that the 1970s and 1980s witnessed the rise of a national political coalition hostile to progressive political priorities and capable of dominating presidential contests. Suspicion of the sprawling bureaucratic state spawned by the progressives, anger at the progressives' repudiation of the Vietnam War, resistance to the progressives' penchant for market regulations, and rejection of their social and cultural permissiveness all came together in these decades in a formidable political tide.

The plight of the conservative insurgency in American national politics tells us a lot about why advocates and critics of presidential power hunkered down in the Constitution. The election landslide of 1972 amply demonstrated the potential of this new coalition in presidential contests, and yet in the short run at least, any hope of its gaining control of the Congress appeared a pipe dream. American politics entered into a long period in which conservative insurgents were on the offensive ideologically but unable to consolidate their hold on national power. Shorn of an interbranch consensus on foreign and economic policy and faced with the stubborn persistence of divided government, they could anticipate little but frustration for their new national majorities.

The alterations conservative intellectuals made in the ideational foundations of the presidency-centered system follow directly. The quest for unity in government, which had hitherto prompted political solutions to the problem of *constitutional* division, now prompted a constitutional solution to the problem of *political* division. Like all previous reform movements, this one was playing to its political strengths. It recognized that the progressives' main stipulation for the release of presidential power—a clear public voice—had become problematic, and it seized upon the instrument in hand, the expanded potential for presidential government, for a solution. The new construction sought unity in the executive because there was little prospect of bridging the interbranch divide. The new construction demanded strict administrative subordination to the will of the president because the ideal of administration in service to government as a whole had become vacuous. The new construction emphasized the separation of powers and the president's capacity for unilateral action because so much power had already been concentrated in the expanded executive establishment. All told, a return to formalism in defense of expansive presidential prerogatives promised to facilitate programmatic action in the absence of an overarching political consensus; the "unitary executive" was a theory designed to promote the political reconstruction of a divided polity.[37]

Political context also offered something of a democratic defense for the conservatives' assault on collective control, and it was on this count perhaps that the legacy of progressivism has been most deeply implicated. It is not just that the presidency-centered government built by the progressives had made it easier to imagine incumbents resourceful enough to go it alone as agents of a conservative reconstruction. At least as important was the fact that progressives had pushed presidents upon the public and raised their political profile as spearheads of a "continual process of internal transformation," for this lent common-sense plausibility to presidency-centered efforts on behalf of the new governmental vision. And most important of all was the fact that progressive governance had fallen short by its own professed standards of democracy. With the exposure of interest-group control of the bureaucratic networks of modern government and with the idea of "enlightened administration" in disrepute even among progressives, the stage was set for another great reversal, another redirection of presidential power against the instruments that had previously justified it. A populist attack on the power of overbearing and irresponsible bureaucrats was now of a piece with the traditional demand of all democratic insurgents to subordinate power to clear public expressions of national purpose; it justified the release of presidential power within the executive branch as a restoration of responsibility and accountability in government.

All the conservatives needed to do to tap this sense of democracy was to constitutionalize the public voice; to tie the fact that the president is the only officer in American government who represents the nation as a whole more closely to the notion that the selection of the president had become, in effect, the only credible expression of the public's will. Originalists in their legal theory, the unitarians rely for this point on a degree of political realism that would make their progressive predecessors blush. Once the public voice is fused more tightly to the will of the incumbent, extraconstitutional controls can be rejected as inconsistent with democratic accountability, and the vast repository of discretionary authority over policy accumulated in the executive branch can be made the exclusive province of the incumbent.

The Nixon administration anticipated at a practical level what the new theory would soon seek to elevate as a standard of rule. While he was quick to remind his critics of precedents among his progressive predecessors for everything he sought to do, Nixon was also acutely aware of the very different circumstances in which he was invoking them: he was acting in a government otherwise controlled by his political enemies; there was no cohesive national sentiment on which to base expansive claims to power; his was a "silent" majority. Faced with these circumstances and emboldened by his great victory in 1972, Nixon tapped the historical development of presidency-centered government to sharpen the argument for presidential independence and to press forward on his own with a transformation of American government and politics. Using many of the tools already available, Nixon worked to undercut institutions put in place to foster interbranch collaboration and collective control. The statutory offices of the EOP were downgraded by compromising their neutrality and negating their promise of cooperative action. At the same time, Nixon worked to bolster institutions put in place to enhance his own governing capacities. Nixon concentrated resources in the White House office itself and extended the political supervision of the White House deeper into the permanent bureaucracy. When asked what was to prevent a president so empowered from overreaching, Nixon invoked the retroactive sanction of voters: "A president has to come before the electorate."[38] Here then was a clear road map showing how to move away from the idea of governing more collectively *through* the presidency toward the idea of governing more exclusively *within* the presidency.[39]

The key assertions in what would become the unitary theory of the executive circulated through the conservative movement in the tumultuous years between the precipitous collapse of the Nixon presidency at the hands of the political enemies he so feared and the capitulation of George H. W. Bush to a Democratic Congress on the signal conservative issue of taxes in the budget agreement of 1990. Persistent political division and stiff institutional resistance to the conservative turn sharpened arguments in and around the White House for the subordination of all executive power to the presidential will. The unelected Ford presidency inspired administration insiders to new thinking about the constitutional foundations of presidential authority and how it might be sustained in the face of a hostile and resurgent Congress.[40] The basic ideas were already in place by the time Dick Cheney instigated the minority report of the congressional investigation into the Iran Contra affair.[41] Terry Eastland's *Energy in the Executive: The Case for a Strong Presidency* (1992) expanded the case with reference to battles of the G. H. W. Bush administration.[42] The subsequent extension of the conservative movement into a national legal establishment, a development skillfully traced by Steven Teles, disseminated these arguments and linked them to potent political and intellectual networks.[43]

PROSPECTS FOR THE NEW FORMALISM

The same political logic that has driven contemporary conservatives to expound upon the constitutional separation of powers and the hierarchical design of the executive branch has driven their critics to mount a stronger defense of constitutional checks and balances. In the 1970s in particular, a resurgent Congress responded to new assertions of presidential power and independence by attempting to strengthen its own position in the exercise of war powers, budget powers, investigatory powers, prosecutorial powers, appointment powers, and the like.[44] But with the wisdom of the Framers fueling constitutional arguments on both sides, things have grown increasingly unsettled. If anything, recent history has found the presidency engulfed in one constitutional crisis after another.

To the extent that this constitutional standoff has been the artifact of historically curious political circumstances, there is always a chance that it will be eased by new developments on the political front. Still, there are reasons for concern. Present-day critics of presidential power may lament what they now perceive as a misguided course of development, but the challenges to American government are mounting apace, and such challenges have always put skeptics at a decided disadvantage in debates over presidential power. By the same token, the strong constitutional claims now at the forefront of advocacy are likely to have a lasting appeal. The unitary theorists offer a principled foundation for practices that have become commonplace but difficult to justify by the received standards. Rather than demand that we reverse course, advocates of presidential power today are offering to capitalize on what the long history of advocacy on behalf of the presidency has actually produced by giving it newfound rigor and fixity as a sacred constitutional ideal.

Either way citizens look at it, a constitutional response to the collapse of the progressive paradigm is problematic. The presidency has accumulated a variety of different premises for its power over the course of its development, but familiar though they may be, historical premises are not readily interchangeable.[45] It is one thing to champion first principles but quite another to apply them to power arrangements that have developed over time on other grounds. American citizens may well wish to overturn the terms and conditions upon which presidential power expanded its reach and American government as a whole reoriented its operations, but citizens are unlikely to reclaim the wisdom of the Framers in the process.[46] At issue in the new formalism are the significance of political development itself, the impact of change on the range of future options, and the practical implications of older values.

While those who bemoan the power of the modern presidency have little difficulty mounting a constitutional critique of current practices, the practical problems of acting today on the basis of that critique are imposing. The building of the modern presidency affected institutions and procedures throughout the American polity. It transformed the operations of the Congress and the incentives of congressmen every bit as much as it changed the role of the president and the parties. That is why latter-day efforts to rein in the presidency have proved so disappointing. Convoluted in their design, halting in their application, doubtful in their effects, these efforts reflect nothing so much as the difficulty of dislodging the presidential office from the pivotal role it has assumed in modern American government and politics.[47] The course of political and institutional development is not so easily ignored. The perennial dream that Congress will reclaim its rightful role in a vigorous system of checks and balances runs up against a history that has moved steadily in another direction. Ever since the rise of political parties in the early nineteenth century, Americans have been looking for ways to ease checks and balances and build institutions that will release the powers of the government more efficiently.

The problems presented by doubling back to fundamentals in order to *expand* the power and prerogatives of presidents in modern America are a bit different. At issue is less the practicality of the move than the conceptual sleight of hand that it entails. The unitary theory of the executive advances the historical trend toward a more presidency-centered system of government and provides a principled defense of the modern presidency's expansive claims to power and prerogative, but the principles put forward reverse the ground on which that system has developed. Indeed, the current reversion to the Constitution in advocacy of presidency power appears to turn the whole sequence of institutional expansion into a brazen scheme of bait and switch. When powers that swelled on the promise of superseding constitutional divisions with more broadly based and democratic forms of control are recaptured, contained, and defended by the Constitution alone, collective claims on those powers are abruptly curtailed. Or to put it another way, when all extraconstitutional interventions are rendered superfluous and the powers of the office become wholly internalized, the accumulated resources of the modern presidency are redeployed on behalf of the personal form of rule that the institutional innovations of all previous reformers were at pains to qualify.

It will be observed that in reworking the case for presidential power, each of America's great reform movements has pulled forward prior advances while discarding those legitimating qualifications that no longer served its purposes. In effect, the idea of concentrating more power in the presidency has moved historically by leapfrogging constraints on the back of newly established baselines. The arguments of contemporary conservatives are no different in this regard. Much as the Jacksonians scooped the Jeffersonian model of the presidency from its Congress-based constraints, and the progressives scooped the Jacksonian model from its party-based constraints, today's conservatives have scooped the progressive model. Their return to the Constitution expands the domain of unilateral action by exploiting the progressive legacy of national power, administrative power, and presidential management.

But there is no mistaking the cutting edge of their new formulation. The arguments of the unitarians do not just scoop up the progressives' legacy of national and executive power; they also marginalize and stigmatize the extraconstitutional mechanisms on which the progressives had relied to surround and regulate their presidency-centered system. Public opinion, publicity, pluralism, empiricism, science, openness, technical expertise, professional judgment, administrative independence, freedom of information—all the operating norms on which the progressives pegged their faith in building the "modern" presidency—are sidelined by this appeal back to the Constitution. When Theodore Roosevelt addressed the question of how to limit his heady notion of a presidential "stewardship," he endorsed the idea of a popular recall of presidents who had lost the confidence of the public.[48] When an interviewer pressed Vice President Cheney on the decisive turn of public opinion against Bush-administration war policies, the quick retort—"So?"—offered a pointed lesson on the distance that has been traveled between these two constructions.[49] Democracy's claims on presidential power now end with the administration of the oath of office.

Had the ambitions of the conservative insurgency not met such stubborn resistance for so long, it might be harder to credit its heavy investment in the exclusivity of presidential control. As it stands, the unitary theory is a high-stakes gamble that leaves movement priorities no more secure than the next election cycle. More striking still is the theory's pretension to upholding constitutional intent, for a more personalized and internalized form of modern executive power threatens to render the whole of modern American government more volatile.[50] When the notion of a presidential stewardship is stripped of progressive provisions for collective oversight by the nation's "prudentes"; when the notion of a politicized bureaucracy is stripped of Jacksonian provisions for collective oversight by the party; when the notion of a concert of power is stripped of Jeffersonian provisions for collective oversight by the Congress—when the extraconstitutional ballast for presidential government is all stripped away and the idea is formalized as fundamental law, the original value of stability in government is all but lost from view.

FINAL THOUGHTS

At this juncture, the one thing that seems clear is that new ideas about how to assert presidential power are fast outpacing new ideas about how to hold that power to account. If it seems odd in such a circumstance to caution *against* constitutionalizing the problem of control, that is because we are not accustomed to reckoning with the practical effects that our political development has had upon the Constitution. On the one side, a developmental analysis suggests that the efforts of contemporary critics of the modern presidency to get Congress to reclaim its original role and to reinvigorate checks and balances are unlikely to get very far. On the other side, it suggests that advocates of presidential power who now want to claim the Constitution as a safe, familiar, and wholly adequate ground on which to venture an expansion of executive prerogatives are, in fact, pushing down a road that is unprecedented and likely to prove dangerous.

The sober option for twenty-first-century governance is one that reckons with political development directly and follows the example of the institution builders who transformed the American presidency in the nineteenth and twentieth centuries. They did not resist new claims of presidential power, but neither did they accept them at face value. Instead, they made fresh claims of their own on that power, claims that altered the premises and operations of American government as a whole. Their solution was to ease checks and balances in exchange for new forms of collective control. The best bet for a safe and effective resolution of the issue of presidential power today is not to cast our lot with the Framer's handiwork but to alter it by our own lights and reconstruct governmental operations candidly with mechanisms of our own.

NOTES

1. See, for example, Steven Calabresi, "The Vesting Clauses as Power Grants," *Northwestern University Law Review* 88 (1994): 1377–1405; Steven Calabresi and Kevin Rhodes, "The Structural Constitution: Unitary Executive," *Harvard Law Review* 105 (1992); Steven Calabresi and Christopher Yoo, *The Unitary Executive: Presidential Powers from Washington to Bush* (New Haven, CT: Yale Univ. Press, 2008); John Yoo, *The Powers of War and Peace: The Constitution and Foreign Affairs after 9/11* (Chicago: Univ. of Chicago Press, 2005); John Yoo, *War by Other Means* (New York: Atlantic Monthly Press, 2006).

2. See, for example, Louis Fisher, *Presidential War Power* (Lawrence: Univ. Press of Kansas, 2006); John MacKensie, *Absolute Power: How the Unitary Executive Is Undermining the Constitution* (New York: Century Foundation, 2008); A. Michael Froomkin, "The Imperial Presidencies: New Vestments," *Northwestern University Law Review* 88 (1994): 1346; Lawrence Lessig and Cass Sunstein, "The President and Administration," *Columbia Law Review* 94 (1994); Kevin Stack, "The President's Statutory Powers to Administer the Laws," *Columbia Law Review* 106 (2006).

3. Louis Fisher, Jack Rakove, and John Yoo, "The Imperial Presidency and the Founding," paper presented at "The American Presidency at War: War and Presidential Politics," Institute of Governmental Studies / UC–Berkeley School of Law Conference, Berkeley, CA, Sept. 19, 2008. For an online video clip, see University of California Television (UCTV), www.uctv.tv/search-details .asp?showID=15408, accessed Dec. 16, 2008; David Barron and Martin Lederman, "The Commander in Chief at Lowest Ebb—A Constitutional History," *Harvard Law Review* 121 (2008): 3–4.

4. Morton White, *Social Thought in America: The Revolt against Formalism* (Boston: Beacon, 1947).

5. Henry Adams, *History of the United States during the Administrations of Jefferson and Madison* (Upper Saddle River, NJ: Prentice Hall, 1963), originally published in 1889–91.

6. Jeremy Bailey, *Thomas Jefferson and Executive Power* (New York: Cambridge Univ. Press, 2007).

7. Bruce Ackerman, *The Failure of the Founding Fathers* (Cambridge, MA: Harvard Univ. Press, 2005).

8. Wilfred Binkley, *President and Congress* (New York: Vintage, 1962), 67; Richard McCormick, *The Presidential Game: The Origins of American Presidential Politics* (New York: Oxford Univ. Press, 1982), 76–163.

9. Stephen Skowronek, *The Politics Presidents Make* (Cambridge, MA: Harvard Univ. Press, 1997), 130–54.

10. Robert Remini, *Andrew Jackson and the Bank War* (New York: Norton, 1967).

11. McCormick, *The Presidential Game*, 164–206; Martin Shefter, "Party, Bureaucracy, and Political Change in the United States," in *Political Parties: Development and Decay*, ed. Louis Maisel and Joseph Cooper (Beverly Hills, CA: Sage, 1978), 218–25.

12. Gerald Leonard, "Martin Van Buren and the Constitutional Theory of Party Politics," *Rutgers Law Review* 54 (Fall 2001): 221.

13. Leonard White, *The Jacksonians: A Study in Administrative History* (New York: Macmillan, 1954), 558.

14. Oneida County Proceedings of the Republican Party Convention held in Rome, New York, Sept. 26, 1862, published in the *Utica (NY) Morning Herald*.

15. Fred Greenstein, "Continuity and Change in the Modern Presidency," in *The New American Political System*, ed. Anthony King (Washington, DC: American Enterprise Institute, 1979), 45–86.

16. James McGregor Burns, *Presidential Government: The Crucible of Leadership* (Boston: Houghton Mifflin, 1965).

17. Eldon Eisenach, *The Lost Promise of Progressivism* (Lawrence: Univ. Press of Kansas, 1994); Marc Stears, *Progressives, Pluralists, and the Problems of the State: Ideologies of Reform in the United States and Britain, 1909–1926* (Oxford: Oxford Univ. Press, 2002).

18. Stephen Skowronek, *Building a New American State: The Expansion of National Administrative Capacities, 1877–1920* (New York: Cambridge Univ. Press, 1982); Sidney Milkis, *The President and the Parties* (New York: Oxford Univ. Press, 1993), 21–146.

19. J. Allen Smith, *The Spirit of American Government* (Cambridge, MA: Harvard Univ. Press, 1965, 1907).

20. Charles Beard, *An Economic Interpretation of the Constitution of the United States* (New York: Macmillan, 1913), 151; Charles Beard, *The Supreme Court and the Constitution* (New York: Macmillan, 1912), 76; Herbert Croly, *The Promise of American Life* (New York: Macmillan, 1909), 35–38.

21. Croly, *The Promise*, 131–37; Eisenach, *The Lost Promise*, 73.

22. Charles Merriam, *New Aspects of Politics*, preface to 1st ed. (Chicago: Univ. of Chicago Press, 1925, 1970), 58.

23. Beard, *An Economic Interpretation*.

24. Howard Gilman, "The Collapse of Constitutional Originalism and the Rise of the Notion of the 'Living Constitution' in the Course of American State Building," *Studies in American Political Development* 11 (Fall 1997): 191–247.

25. Charles Beard, *American Government and Politics* (New York: Macmillan, 1928), 101; Eisenach, *The Lost Promise*, 216; Henry Jones Ford, *The Rise and Growth of American Politics* (New York: Macmillan, 1898), 293; Croly, *The Promise*, 136, 168.

26. The ideals of expertise and independence in administration were per-

haps best expressed by James Landis, in *The Administrative Process* (New Haven, CT: Yale Univ. Press, 1938). The ideal in practice is exemplified in Richard Kirkendall, *Social Scientists and Farm Politics in the Age of Roosevelt* (Ames: Univ. of Iowa Press, 1966); and Samuel Hayes, *Conservation and the Gospel of Efficiency* (New York: Atheneum, 1959). On the capacities of progressive administrators to combine these resources and fashion new centers of power, see Daniel Carpenter, *The Forging of Bureaucratic Autonomy* (Princeton, NJ: Princeton Univ. Press, 2001).

27. Eisenach, *The Lost Promise*; Michael Lacey and Mary Furner, eds., *The State and Social Investigation in Britain and the United States* (New York: Cambridge Univ. Press, 1993).

28. Charles Merriam, "Political Prudence," in his *New Aspects of Politics*, 246–63.

29. John Hart, *The Presidential Branch* (Chatham, NJ: Chatham House, 1995), 52–53, 68–69; Stephen Hess, *Organizing the Presidency* (Washington, DC: Brookings Institution Press, 1976), 53–54.

30. Richard Neustadt, *Presidential Power: The Politics of Leadership* (New York: Wiley, 1960), 42.

31. Henry Clay in *Register of Debates*, 23rd Cong., 1st sess., Dec. 26, 1833, 174; Richard Ellis and Stephen Kirk, "Presidential Mandates in the Nineteenth Century: Conceptual Change and Institutional Development," *Studies in American Political Development* 9, no. 1 (Spring 1995): 117–85; William Howard Taft, *The President and His Powers* (New York: Columbia Univ. Press, 1916).

32. James Burnham, *Congress and the American Tradition* (Chicago: H. Regnery, 1959); Alfred De Grazia, *Republic in Crisis: Congress against the Executive Force* (New York: Federal Legal Publications, 1965); Wilmore Kendall, "The Two Majorities," *Midwest Journal of Political Science* 4, no. 4 (1960): 317–45; G. Patrick Lynch, "Protecting Individual Rights through a Federal System: James Buchanan's View of Federalism," *Publius* 153 (2004).

33. Arthur Schlesinger Jr., *The Imperial Presidency* (Boston: Houghton Mifflin, 1973); Theodore Lowi, *The End of Liberalism: Ideology, Policy, and the Crisis of Public Authority* (New York: Norton, 1969).

34. Theodore Lowi, *The Personal President: Power Invested, Promise Unfulfilled* (Ithaca, NY: Cornell Univ. Press, 1985); Arthur Schlesinger Jr., *Journals, 1952–2000* (New York: Penguin Press, 2007), 260.

35. Fisher, *Presidential War Power*; Lowi, *The Personal President*; James Ceasar, Glen Thurow, Jeffrey Tulis, and Joseph Bessette, "The Rise of the Rhetorical Presidency," in *Rethinking the Presidency*, ed. Thomas Cronin (Boston: Little, Brown, 1982); Jeffrey Tulis, *The Rhetorical Presidency* (Princeton, NJ: Princeton Univ. Press, 1987); Milkis, *The President*.

36. Yoo, *War by Other Means*, 5.

37. Instructive on this point is Daryl Levinson and Richard Pildes, "Separation of Parties, Not Powers," *Harvard Law Review* 119 (June 2006).

38. Nixon-Frost interview, May 19, 1977, cited in Christopher Pyle and Richard Pious, *The President, Congress, and the Constitution: Power and Legitimacy in American Politics* (New York: Free Press, 1984), 74–75.

39. Richard Nathan, *The Plot That Failed: Nixon and the Administrative Presidency* (New York: Wiley, 1975).

40. Jim Mann, *The Rise of the Vulcans: A History of Bush's War Cabinet* (New York: Viking, 2004).

41. *Report of the Congressional Committees Investigating the Iran Contra Affair, with Supplemental, Minority, and Additional Views,* Senate Report No. 100-216, 100th Cong., 1st sess., Nov. 13, 1987.

42. Terry Eastland, *Energy in the Executive: The Case for a Strong Presidency* (New York: Free Press, 1992); also, L. Gordon Crovitz and Jeremy Rabkin, eds., *The Fettered Presidency: Legal Constraints on the Executive Branch* (Washington, DC: American Enterprise Institute, 1989).

43. Steven Teles, *The Rise of the Conservative Legal Movement: The Battle for Control of the Law* (Princeton, NJ: Princeton Univ. Press, 2008).

44. James Sundquist, *The Decline and Resurgence of Congress* (Washington, DC: Brookings Institution Press, 1981); Martin Shefter and Benjamin Ginsberg, *Politics by Other Means: Politicians, Prosecutors, and the Press from Watergate to Whitewater* (New York: Norton, 1999).

45. This is one of the main themes of Jeffrey Tulis's *The Rhetorical Presidency.*

46. An interesting response to this challenge is offered by Abner Greene, "Checks and Balances in an Era of Presidential Lawmaking," *Univ. of Chicago Law Review* 61 (1994): 123–96.

47. Andrew Rudalevige, *The New Imperial Presidency* (Ann Arbor: Univ. of Michigan Press, 2006).

48. Sidney Milkis, *Theodore Roosevelt, the Progressive Party, and the Transformation of American Democracy* (Lawrence: Univ. Press of Kansas, 2009).

49. Interview of the vice president by Martha Raddatz, ABC News, March 19, 2008, www.whitehouse.gov.

50. Jeremy Bailey, "The New Unitary Executive and Democratic Theory," *American Political Science Review* 102, no. 4 (Nov. 2008): 453–65.

Is the Constitutional Presidency Obsolete?

Robert J. Spitzer

The second Bush presidency made at least two major contributions to the study of the American presidency: first, it put the tenets of the separation-of-powers/checks-and-balances system front and center in contemporary political analysis; second, it reinforced the centrality of constitutional powers and institutional relations to any complete understanding of the contemporary presidency. After all, the George W. Bush presidency's overarching goal and master plan, spanning the gamut of routine day-to-day activities, on the one hand, to the administration's most important policy goals, on the other, was to redefine and enlarge the president's constitutional powers consonant with its singularly expansive view of the office. In this respect alone, the second Bush presidency prompts students of the presidency to examine the roots of this institution, the constitutional structure in which it is embedded, and the nature of executive power.

As Bush's successor, Barack Obama, has demonstrated, these questions are no less vital for the post-Bush presidency. Even though Obama campaigned against the ideological and policy directions of the Bush presidency, Obama found himself, in at least some instances, endorsing controversial Bush-era policies that raise important constitutional and legal questions. For example, the Obama administration continued some Bush administration counterterrorism tactics; it also defended in court the Bush-era policy of warrantless surveillance conducted by the National Security Agency, a policy the defense of which was based on the controversial doctrine called the "state-secrets privilege."

This essay examines the future of the American presidency by considering the impact of the second Bush presidency. My examination begins by explicating the legislative-dominant separation-of-powers system established by the Constitution's founders, the evolution of that

system toward the modern strong presidency established in the twentieth century, and the interrelationship of presidential constitutional
powers with political powers acquired by presidents, the latter issue
viewed from the perspective of the most influential presidency schol-
ar of the last several decades, Richard Neustadt. These developments
are then considered in the light of the Bush administration's executive
governance theory, known as the unitary executive theory. I argue here
that while most past presidents have attempted to grab more power, the
unitary theory sets up a game-changing paradigm in presidential power that may spell the beginning of the end of the separation-of-powers
system as it has functioned in the nation's first two centuries. As some
actions of the Obama administration suggest, the appeal of the unitary
theory may well span ideology and party.

THE FOUNDERS' CONSTITUTION AND
THE CHANGING SEPARATION OF POWERS

As political scientist Louis Fisher once noted, "To study one branch
of government in isolation from the others is usually an exercise in
make-believe."[1] In a governing system composed of "separated institutions *sharing* powers,"[2] the essence of governance is found in the friction points between governing institutions. So any understanding of the
future of the American presidency must incorporate both its historic
arc and its interrelations with the other branches, but most importantly
with Congress. These Constitution-based institutional interrelations become even more important with the contemporary juridical and political mania for constitutional "originalism."

These features converge at a fundamental asymmetry underlying the separation of powers: that the legislative branch was designed
to be the first, most important, and most powerful branch among the
three. If this comes as a revelation to twenty-first-century Americans,
it was not to those of the eighteenth century. John Locke noted then:
"In all cases whilst the government subsists, the legislative power is the
supreme power. . . . the legislative must needs be the supreme, and all
other powers in any members or parts of the society [are] derived from
and subordinate to it."[3] The American three-branch federal system was
emphatically not one of three coequal branches; it was to be legislative-
centered.[4] James Madison's dictum on this was clear enough when he

proclaimed, "In republican government, the legislative authority necessarily predominates."[5] What the political scientist Clinton Rossiter referred to decades ago as the "fact of legislative primacy" arises from the
constitutional document itself,[6] where "Congress is granted a breathtaking array of powers . . . the bulk of governmental authority as the Founders understood it."[7] This principle applies to foreign as well as domestic
powers.[8] Yet legislative dominance rests not only with the lengthy laun-
dry list of powers granted to it in Article I, but in its power relationship
with the other two branches of government.

Formal Powers of Congress

The legislature's power to make laws is, first, government's most important function. "Without prior legislation," historian Garry Wills notes,
"there is nothing to be executed or adjudicated. The other two functions [executive and judicial] necessarily serve the first."[9] Beyond this,
congressional preeminence is reflected in the trump cards that institution is granted in the Constitution. Congress can remove from office
members of the other two branches through impeachment; neither the
executive nor the judicial has any reciprocal removal power over members of Congress. Congress establishes and provides pay for the members of the other branches; determines the structures of the other two
branches, encompassing the cabinet departments and other agencies of
the executive branch, as well as all "inferior Courts as the Congress may
from time to time ordain and establish" below the Supreme Court; and
sets the number of judges that serve on all federal courts, including the
nation's highest court. As the Constitution says in Article I, section 8,
Congress not only has an express grant of power to "make all laws which
shall be necessary and proper for carrying into Execution the foregoing
powers," but also is granted "all other Powers vested by this Constitution
in the Government of the United States, or in any Department or Officer
thereof." Congress also has final say in the veto process, as well as in the
approval of treaties and executive appointments by the Senate. Congress
amends the Constitution with approval of the states, a process in which
the president has no legal role. In the checks-and-balances system, each
branch could indeed claim checks on the others, but those of Congress
were final trumps. As Wills concludes: "No matter what the sequence of
action . . . Congress always gets the last say (if it wants it)."[10]

None of this is to suggest, however, that Congress's Constitution-based preeminence was untrammeled—far from it. Aside from the checks of the other two branches, Congress was checked by its division into two houses, making it the only branch of the three divided against itself; the extensive list of powers granted Congress in Article I, section 8, was immediately followed by a specific list of limitations described in Article I, section 9; and the First Amendment of the Bill of Rights, completed two years after the Constitutional Convention, begins with "Congress shall make no law . . ." followed by the specific prohibition that Congress is not to infringe on individual liberties enumerated in the First Amendment. Beyond this, considerable evidence supports the related proposition that the framers, and especially James Madison, cultivated and favored a closer relationship between the executive and judiciary as a counterbalance to the aforementioned legislative supremacy.

Madison stated at the Constitutional Convention: "There was an analogy between the Executive & Judiciary departments in several respects. The latter executed the laws in certain cases as the former did in others. The former expounded & applied them for certain purposes, as the latter did for others."[11] A further evidence of Madison's predilections was seen in his vigorous, if unsuccessful, advocacy for creation of a council of revision—a body consisting of the president and the members of the Supreme Court that would come together to collectively exercise the veto power (such a power was exercised by the governor and state judges in New York until 1821).[12] While the proposal was not accepted, it reflected the idea that these two branches had an affinity, founded both in similar functions and in the need to effectively counterbalance the legislative branch, not shared by either with Congress.[13]

Further evidence of legislative dominance arising from the Constitution was the functional relationship between the branches in the nation's ensuing century. Those founders who participated in governance operated and behaved in a manner consistent with legislative supremacy.[14] By the middle of the nineteenth century, the imperatives of the American "patronage state," so delineated by political scientist Theodore J. Lowi, further favored "congressional dominance," such that Lowi dubbed this period one typified by near-parliamentary governance.[15] Writing in 1884, Woodrow Wilson identified "Congress as the central and predominant power of the system," adding that "unquestionably, the predominant and controlling force, the centre and source of all motive and of all regulative power, is Congress."[16]

Yet it is not only true, but a truism, of the three-branch relationship that it has been dynamic, not static, in American political development. The modern three-branch relationship would appear to little resemble anything like a legislative-dominant system (and one might certainly argue that such a development was not only necessary but desirable), but that is a consequence of more than two hundred years of institutional evolution. No further evidence need be marshaled than to cite the reality of contemporary executive-branch dominance in national governance. The proposition that presidential power has significantly increased in the past two centuries, yielding a "modern strong presidency" in the twentieth century, is one of the most well-established and widely accepted tenets of the institutional presidency and American governance.[17] Many contemporary analysts argue that presidents of recent decades have found that the demands and expectations placed on the office outstrip its powers, placing modern presidents in an often untenable political situation, but this assertion does not contradict the truism of the long-term rise of presidential powers and the relative eclipse of Congress. Among his many writings, Louis Fisher provides careful case analysis of how this shift has taken place in such key areas as war powers and spending.[18]

Congress's Ineffectual Final Checks

Many factors account for the legislative-executive reversal of fortunes, beginning, but not ending, with the limiting specificity of Congress's Article I powers as compared with the delimiting vagueness of presidential Article II powers. A second, if seldom noticed, factor related to these powers is that Congress's just-described final checks have proved in practice to be less than utilitarian. Yes, Congress could check the executive and judicial branches by reducing their size—surely an effective method to rein in excessive power of the other branches. Yet the founders could not have reckoned with the feature of modern (post-Weberian) bureaucracy that says once a job, agency, office, or department is established, it is very much more difficult to abolish the same. Thus, the reduction in size, scope, or personnel of another branch of government has scarcely functioned as a viable check.[19]

The same can be said of the power of impeachment. Drawn directly from British law, by the seventeenth century "impeachment by the British House of Commons and trial by the House of Lords had evolved into the standard means of enforcing responsibility of the King's ministers to Parliament."[20] Yet Congress's impeachment power has functioned nothing like a "standard means of enforcing responsibility" in American governance. Since 1789, the power has been used rarely. The House of Representatives has approved impeachment charges in only seventeen instances: thirteen times against federal judges, twice against presidents, once against a senator (the Senate later decided that expulsion was the proper means to remove senators), and once against a cabinet member. Of the fourteen who went to trial in the Senate, seven were convicted and seven acquitted. In the case of the two presidents brought to trial in the Senate, Andrew Johnson and Bill Clinton, neither episode provides confidence that impeachment was or is an effective check on the presidency, or that it was properly used.[21] A check so rarely used can scarcely be considered an effective check, even if our founders contemplated otherwise.

A similar, if less drastic, argument can be made regarding Congress's veto override power. Yes, congressional override gives it the final word, but its successful application is rare. Of the approximately 2,500 bills vetoed by presidents from Washington to the second Bush, Congress's rate of successful override is only about 7 percent (although it rises to about 19 percent for major legislation). When the power of presidential veto threats and veto-related bargaining is added into the calculus, actual practice supports the conclusion that the veto is a potent and important presidential tool but that the prospect of successful override, for the most part, is not.[22] In law, it's Congress that gets the final say in the veto process; in fact, it's generally the president.

The historical record regarding treaties and presidential appointment confirmations makes a similar point. From 1789 to 2007, less than 1 percent of all treaties have been rejected by the Senate, and presidents have turned ever more to executive agreements (not subject to Senate vote, although Congress may act to alter such agreements) rather than treaties to conclude agreements with other countries. At the start of the country's history, the number of treaties and executive agreements was roughly equal; in recent decades, executive agreements outnumbered treaties by a ratio of at least fifteen to one.[23] Congress has been a willing partner in this shift toward greater executive control over relations with other nations; nevertheless, the practical effect of Congress's final checks has been negligible. As for presidential appointments, those nominated to executive-branch positions are confirmed by the Senate about 99 percent of the time. In all of American history, only twenty-three cabinet-level nominations have been rejected by Senate vote. The highest rejection rate for presidential nominations is in the area of Supreme Court appointees, where the Senate has confirmed about 80 percent of those nominated by the president—still a very respectable presidential batting average.[24]

The realities of constitutional checks and balances lend credence to Thomas Jefferson's prescient prediction, penned in a letter to James Madison in 1789: "The tyranny of the legislatures is the most formidable dread at present, and will be for many years. That of the executive will come in its turn; but it will be at a remote period."[25]

THE EXECUTIVE QUEST FOR POWER

Power is the presidential narcotic, and the rise of the modern strong presidency is, as noted, one of the best-established axioms of American politics. There is much to examine and argue about regarding the particulars of this axiom (including the normative question of whether this trend is a good or bad thing), but its fundamental truth is beyond doubt. The rise of presidential power was made possible both by constitutional ambiguity and by the limited efficacy of Congress's final checks, but it was effectuated primarily by the acquisition and exercise of political powers and power resources. Writing in the 1950s, Clinton Rossiter, in his paean to the modern strong presidency, listed ten presidential roles. Five of them were constitutionally based (chief of state, chief executive, commander in chief, chief diplomat, and chief legislator), whereas the other five (chief of party, voice of the people, protector of the peace, manager of prosperity, and world leader) were the political add-ons acquired in two centuries of institutional evolution. No clearer statement of the limitations of the president's constitutional powers, and the importance of political resources, has been advanced than that of political scientist Richard Neustadt.

The Rise and Demise of the Neustadt Presidency

The prolific writing on the shifting balance of powers away from legislative and toward executive power encompasses both political and struc-

Robert J. Spitzer

tural change. Yet that change has, to some degree, outrun or outstripped the analysis of it. In political science, the dominant paradigm of the past four decades for understanding the presidency has been that of Richard Neustadt's classic *Presidential Power*.[26] In this work, first published in 1960, Neustadt sought to turn the focus of presidential power away from formal and institutional powers and toward informal political powers and resources. In his view, the president's formal, constitutional powers were spare. Neustadt thought formal, constitutional powers by themselves an insufficient basis for the vigorous presidency demanded by the country in modern times. The spare grant of power to the presidency is compounded by the inherent limitations imposed by the separation-of-powers system. Add in America's fragmented political parties, the massive bureaucracy, the American media, and the fickle public, and the net result is a president whose chief political task, according to Neustadt, is to rely on *persuasion* as the primary means for getting everyone else to do what the president would like.

The reality of presidential governance, in Neustadt's analysis, is neither command nor gallant heroic leadership but "the power to bargain"[27]—to plead, cajole, jawbone, entreat, negotiate. As this implies, presidents in Neustadt's view operate from a position of relative political weakness, not strength. He argues that presidents who rely on constitutional/command authority will fail, even if they succeed. To make his point, he examines in his second chapter, "Three Cases of Command," three instances when presidents exercised command power: President Harry Truman's decision to relieve Douglas MacArthur as military commander during the Korean War, Truman's order to take over steel factories in the steel seizure case, and President Dwight Eisenhower's decision to send National Guard troops to Little Rock, Arkansas, to enforce public school racial desegregation. In each instance, the president achieved a short-term goal (although the Supreme Court overruled Truman's decision in the steel seizure case, more properly known as *Youngstown Sheet and Tube v. Sawyer*). But in Neustadt's view, these accomplishments turned out to be "transitory" and in actuality revealed presidential weakness, not strength.[28]

Neustadt concludes: "Command is but a method of persuasion, not a substitute, and not a method suitable for everyday employment." Successful presidents, he argues, must master the persuasive arts; command powers are incompatible with an effective presidency in the modern era.

In essence, effective presidents use carrots, not sticks; honey, not vinegar. Why? Writing in a new preface to his book in 1989, Neustadt stated his argument this way: "Even a 'strong' President is weak. . . . *Weak* remains the word with which to start."[29] As Neustadt summarizes, the key to presidential effectiveness arises from three sources: the president's bargaining advantages, the expectations of those with whom he deals, and the estimates of others regarding how the public views the president.[30] Notably absent from this list is any mention of constitutional or other formal powers.

Neustadt's analysis of presidential power has been subject to substantial criticism and debate,[31] in part precisely because of the extent to which it underestimates the importance of formal and constitutional powers. Yet the Neustadt paradigm has dominated the study of the presidency in the past four decades, although it has met a rising challenge from the movement in political science toward new institutionalism. As political scientist William Howell asserted in 2003, "Neustadt sets the terms by which every student of American politics has come to understand presidential power in the modern era."[32]

I have always thought of Neustadt as the presidential Machiavelli,[33] whispering in the ears of chief executives about how to maximize their power. In that respect, Neustadt's advice is always timely, and timeless. But the Neustadt paradigm is nowhere more clearly inadequate than in explaining and understanding the second Bush presidency. Neustadt's analysis was necessary because the president's formal powers, by themselves, are indeed inadequate to explain modern presidential power. Yet his analysis seems utterly irrelevant to explaining the presidency of George W. Bush. This irrelevancy arises from the central tenet of Bush's approach to executive power: its reliance on a full-blown constitutional theory, the unitary theory of executive power. By its nature, this theory is all about executive command, not persuasion; formal powers, not informal political resources.

To pose the matter somewhat differently, if modern presidents typically seek more power for themselves and the office, is the Bush presidency really any different in its quest for executive powers from its predecessors? I believe the answer to be yes. Activist presidents from recent decades, such as Franklin D. Roosevelt and Lyndon Johnson, clearly expanded executive power. Yet they did so in a primarily Neustadtian manner, both in employing traditional persuasion, bargaining, and other political tools (as opposed to the "command" power disdained by Neustadt) to advance their substantial and ambitious policy agendas, and in avoiding grandiose claims to Constitution-based powers as the basis for their actions. Neither Roosevelt nor Johnson pretended that the New Deal or the Great Society was the just-discovered fulfillment of the Constitution's founders' conception of their office. Yet the essence of President Bush's unitary power claims are just of this sort—namely, the fulfillment or realization of some long-lost or misunderstood vision of the Constitution's framers regarding executive power. This claim is of the greatest importance for the future of the American presidency be-cause it is predicated on a broad assertion of how executive power in the original governing document was framed. But in order to understand its import, the theory itself requires explication.

The Unitary Theory: Article II on Steroids?

The unitary theory of executive power emerged in the 1980s in the Justice Department's Office of Legal Counsel under President Ronald Reagan. Under office heads Theodore Olson and Charles Cooper and Attorney General Edwin Meese, staff lawyers (including future Supreme Court Justice Samuel Alito) formulated the unitary executive theory. With coordinate support from the Federalist Society, the newly formed organization of conservative lawyers,[34] these young legal thinkers were looking for a way to limit federal power and curb, if not dismantle, the modern regulatory state, especially independent commissions. In the words of the Federalist Society, it is "a group of conservatives and liber-tarians dedicated to reforming the current order."[35]

The phrase "unitary executive" was derived from references in the *Federalist Papers* to "unity" in the executive.[36] The phrase appears most famously in Alexander Hamilton's Federalist Paper 70, in which he wrote that the "unity" of the executive was one of the important advantages of the executive office proposed in the new Constitution. But Hamilton's reference was far more straightforward than what is ascribed to it by the unitary theorists: Hamilton was simply comparing the presidency as an office occupied by a single individual with competing proposals of the day for a "plural executive," whereby the office would be composed of two or more people who would function as a kind of executive com-mittee.[37] Departing from the traditional conservative view that sought limited executive power,[38] the unitary view argued for even greater presidential power as a means of attacking, and routing, power in the rest of the government.

As applied during the George W. Bush presidency, the theory deigned to empower the president to exercise sole control over the removal of executive branch officials, to direct the actions of such officials, and to nullify the decisions or actions of others believed to impede the president's full control over the executive branch. In practice, this has meant that Bush felt at liberty to ignore provisions of laws with which he disagreed (most prominently by relying on signing statements),[39] reinterpret or set aside treaties unilaterally, determine the fate of enemy combatants, use tactics generally considered to be torture against enemy combatants despite strictures against such actions in federal and international law, allow warrantless surveillance of domestic phone calls contrary to existing law, and curtail judicial oversight, among other actions. Further, the unitary view questions the very constitutionality of government agencies (and the rules they issue) created to be independent of the president by law—that is, independent regulatory agencies, commissions, and other similar entities (the first of which, the Interstate Commerce Commission, was created in 1887),[40] notwithstanding the undisputed fact that presidents are empowered to appoint the heads of these agencies and that these agencies' constitutionality has been upheld since their creation.[41] In fact, the legal basis for the modern bureaucracy, including independent agencies, is one of the best-established features of modern governance.[42]

In addition, Bush's unitary approach asserted that the other branches of government could not interfere with presidential actions arising from these executive powers. It is on that basis that Bush argued that he could ignore laws, or provisions of laws, that, in his view, impinged on his so-called unitary power as chief executive. From 2001 to 2008, Bush used signing statements to void, or refuse to enforce, laws or provisions of laws in more than 1,100 instances (roughly twice the number of times they were used by all of his predecessors combined), asserting that these provisions infringed on his unitary executive power.[43] In addition, Bush administration lawyers argued that the courts may not adjudicate in areas the president deems within his executive power. Administration lawyers made these arguments in such court cases as *Hamdi v. Rumsfeld* (2004), *Rasul v. Bush* (2004), and *Hamdan v. Rumsfeld* (2006).[44] To date, courts have largely rejected the argument that they do not have a right to adjudicate.

Key to the unitary theory is the contrarian and counterfactual assumption that presidential power has declined, not increased, since the enactment of the Constitution in 1789.[45] In an essay published in 1989, Theodore Olson (who also served as assistant attorney general in the Reagan administration and as solicitor general in the second Bush administration) asserted that the presidency had endured "two centuries of unrelenting encroachments by Congress," during which time Congress had "adeptly and persistently eroded and disassembled executive power." The capstones of the congressional erosion of presidential power, by this view, were the War Powers Act of 1973 and congressional actions related to the Iran-Contra scandal of the Reagan administration.[46] In order to rectify this alleged imbalance and recapture presumably latent or dormant constitutional presidential powers, the unitary theory stakes out two sets of aggressive power claims.

The first is that presidents have sole and complete control over the executive branch. As then federal judge Samuel J. Alito said in a 2000 speech to the Federalist Society, "The president has not just some executive powers, but *the* executive power—the whole thing."[47] This power claim might seem unexceptionable on its face, but it presumes to extend presidential powers beyond the well-established understanding of the president's role as chief executive.

The first claim rests on a very specific reading of key phrases in Article II.[48] It cites the "vesting" clause—the first sentence of Article II—noting its slightly different wording, as compared with the first "vesting" sentences of Articles I and III, as a gateway to vastly greater executive power. Article I grants to Congress "all legislative Powers herein granted"; Article III says, "The judicial Power of the United States, shall be vested in one supreme Court" and in "inferior Courts." Article II says, "The executive Power shall be vested in a President of the United States of America." The unitary argument insists that the absence of strictly parallel wording (no "herein granted" in the Article II phrase) means that the founders gave the executive far greater power than the other two branches. Unitarians further reference the oath clause in Article II, section 1, where the president swears to "preserve, protect and defend the Constitution," and also the provision in Article II, section 3, requiring the president to "take Care that the Laws be faithfully executed," to argue that the president somehow has a special, independent responsibility to determine what is and is not constitutional, especially as related to the internal workings of the executive branch.

The unitary interpretation of these phrases rests, as it must, on an arcane and formerly unknown (that is, before the 1980s) interpretation. The more straightforward interpretation of the differences in the wording just quoted is that the "herein granted" in Article I was meant both to recognize Congress's vast enumerated powers (a list unmatched in Article II) and to limit this dominant branch in the manner described earlier. The vesting of executive power in the first sentence of Article II reflected both the relative vagueness of Article II's construction in comparison to that of Article I, owing to difficulties faced by the founders in deciding how the office was to be constructed, and the desire of a few to at least open the door to a stronger executive in the years to come. As Charles Thach concluded decades ago, this wording at the start of Article II reflected the embrace of "the characteristically American doctrine of coordinate departments. The unrestrained legislature and the subordinate executive had had its day, and, so far as the United States were concerned, had 'ceased to be.'" That is, the wording was an instrumental part of the birth of an independent executive within the separation-of-powers and checks-and-balances framework. It is also generally understood to reference some residuum of executive-type powers beyond those listed, as might be exercised by a president in times of emergency, although this matter continues to be hotly debated. The main dispute over the wording from Article III was another matter left unresolved: whether there should or should not be federal inferior courts below the Supreme Court. The constitutional convention punted by letting Congress decide at a later date, if it so chose.[49]

The unitary view insists on "an *absolute* separation of powers between the three branches of government."[50] This appears to be the root meaning of Alito's claim, quoted earlier, that the president possesses "*the* executive power—the whole thing." The claim rejects the very idea that powers are somehow shared or overlap between the branches.[51] The fact that this view flies in the face of the bedrock understanding of how the American three-branch system of governance works little deters unitary advocates. But note that the unitary view is predicated on an "originalist" or "original intent" reading of the Constitution. It is, after all, central to modern conservatism that contemporary governmental actions should conform to an originalist view of the Constitution; that is, that the modern exercise of powers should hew closely to a narrow or strict interpretation of the Constitution and the founders' intent behind it, as it was contemplated in 1787. The opposing "living Constitution" perspective, expressing the view that constitutional intent should be married to other considerations, including historical evolution and contemporary needs, is anathema. On its face, the unitary view reads more like the product of a living-Constitution than an originalist orientation, given its radical departure from constitutional text and received understanding, as well as its recent formulation. As mentioned, the provenance of the unitary theory dates to Justice Department lawyers and the Federalist Society, in the 1980s. Yet the theory's legitimacy hinges on the claim that its roots were founded in 1787, not the 1980s. As one architect of the unitary view admitted, "What the idea had lacked was an intellectual justification and defense."[52]

To frame the unitary theorists' claim to having discovered an entirely new theory two hundred years after the writing of the Constitution, imagine a scene from the first Indiana Jones movie, *Raiders of the Lost Ark,* when the hero (played by Harrison Ford) finds himself in an ancient Egyptian map room and uses a soft long-bristled brush to remove a fine sand and reveal the critical row of hieroglyphics that will tell him where to find the biblical Ark of the Covenant. Bush administration lawyers would have us believe this to be the essence of the unitary executive—that in the 1980s, lawyers working in the Reagan Justice Department and the Federalist Society similarly uncovered this originalist, unitary theory of executive power after removing the dust of history. But, one might ask, how could modern constitutional analysis uncover such a vast realm of heretofore misunderstood or unknown executive powers more than two hundred years after the document's writing, especially considering the mammoth degree of study, scrutiny, and writing to which the Constitution had been subject during that entire time?

The establishment of such a constitutional pedigree is not a task to be completed solely by political figures, as its credibility would rest squarely on its historical, academic, and intellectual integrity. That this enterprise began as a political rather than scholarly enterprise is clear enough. As one study noted, the Meese Justice Department under Reagan "became a giant think tank where these passionate young conservative legal activists developed new legal theories to advance the Reagan agenda." Another account of this period characterized the Justice Department during the Reagan administration as one that "saw increased presidential power across the board as one of the core missions of the Department of Justice."[53] Critical to this new theory's credibility and intellectual pedigree was the establishment of its academic integrity, and it was here that legal academic writings in law reviews played an indispensable role.

The Law Review Breeding Ground

Elsewhere I argue that legal training and law reviews are a breeding ground for wayward constitutional theorizing;[54] in the case of the presidency, legal academic analysis has provided critical scholarly legitimacy for at least some of the ideas that flowered in the second Bush administration (although this phenomenon is limited neither to the presidency nor to the Bush administration).[55] Legal training, including the adversarial process, advocacy, and client loyalty, are well suited to the American system of justice, where opposing, one-sided arguments collide to produce a just outcome. By its nature, the adversary process often has the effect of giving the presentation of truth a lower priority, as winning the argument becomes the most important goal. When these principles are applied to scholarly analysis of constitutional matters, the all-too-frequent result is selective analysis, overheated rhetoric, overstated conclusions, and distortion of facts and concepts. Such wayward theorizing too easily finds its way into print in the nation's more than six hundred law journals, where, unlike the case for literally every other academic discipline, the professional publications are run by law students, not faculty or other trained professionals, and peer review is almost never used to determine publication worthiness. The result is that publication decisions are not, and cannot be, made based on the substantive merit of the articles submitted. Admittedly, one can find much excellent writing in law journals. The problem is not that excellence does not exist, for it does; the problem is that there is no floor to errant writing.

The analysis that today fills law journals purportedly establishing the unitary theory's originalist provenance is an example of what some forty years ago was labeled "law office history."[56] This derisive term describes a long-simmering dispute between historians and legal writers, based on historians' claims that legal writers distort and cherry-pick history in the way that a lawyer in a courtroom presents only one side of a story, in hopes of persuading a jury to rule on behalf of the client. It's good legal practice but terrible history or social science. This is the essence of the problem with the research buttressing the unitary executive theory. It's law office advocacy and brief writing, not scholarship.

Articles referencing the unitary executive began to appear in law journals in the mid-1980s,[57] but the first full-blown and sustained explication and defense of the idea was published in 1992.[58] Thereafter, a lengthy series of articles appeared debating the merits of the unitary theory.[59] Capping the unitary argument was a series of four law review articles, amounting to nearly five hundred published pages, all authored by Steven Calabresi, Christopher S. Yoo, and other associates, that provide a chronological account of what they claim shows the infusion of the unitary executive throughout American history under the modern Constitution.[60] The sweep and ambition of this unitary-view writing is concisely encapsulated by legal writer Gary Lawson, whose breathtaking argument in his article on the subject is that, as per the unitary theory, "the post-New Deal administrative state is unconstitutional."[61]

The unitary-executive-theory literature found in law reviews suffers from four overarching problems endemic to the law journal writing referenced here:[62] it cherry-picks its evidence, often misrepresents the historical record, and ignores pertinent literature in other disciplines; it attempts to manufacture a constitutional pedigree for a purely contemporary political construct; it seeks to configure a constitutional basis for overturning existing case law that has long accepted the constitutionality of (in this case) the modern regulatory state; and it is a paradigmatic example of the lawyerly advocacy scholarship just described—which is to say, it is not scholarship at all. Perhaps the best example of this latter criticism is the fact that the unitary theory turns the related principles of separation of powers and checks and balances on their head. Any power identified as belonging to the president or the executive branch is, by unitary theory definition, beyond the reach of the other two branches,[63] despite the fact that the essence of the three-branch relationship is one of overlapping and interconnected powers (which does not deny that each branch does retain exclusive control over some aspects of its functions). One need go no further than James Madison, who wrote in Federalist Paper number 51, "Ambition must be made to counteract ambition." In order to effectuate the American governing system, said

Madison, "the constant aim is to divide and arrange the several offices in such a manner as that each may be a check on the other." As Louis Fisher concludes, "the model of the Unitary Executive was never adopted or intended, nor does it have any wholesale application today either in theory or practice."[64]

The Second Bush Presidency's Legacy

The George W. Bush administration's unceasing effort to rewrite Article II, including such activities as the prolific use of signing statements to rewrite legislation, expansive claims of executive privilege, unbounded declarations of secrecy spanning every manner of presidential (and vice presidential) action and document, warrantless wiretapping, war powers claims, detaining of suspects related to external threats, invocation of his commander-in-chief power as a basis for claims to unfettered power over military decisions,[65] and other actions, all ride on square *constitutional* claims made by the administration. While the substance of these claims is, at the least, open to dispute, George W. Bush was no Neustadtian president seeking to buttress puny formal powers by marshaling his persuasion skills to strike bargains with Congress or the bureaucracy— nor was his activist vice president, Dick Cheney. It was something entirely different, not because the second Bush presidency was the first to expand the powers of the office, but because it was the first to attempt to do so by implementing a wholesale rewriting of the office's constitutional and legal powers under the banner of the unitary executive.

In regard to the second Bush era, the Neustadt power-to-persuade line of analysis seems not only obsolete but positively quaint. It is no surprise that Neustadt's formative thinking about presidential power began in the Truman presidency. One might hypothesize that, had Neustadt come of political age during this Bush presidency, he would have written a book entirely different from, perhaps even contrary to, *Presidential Power*. As a "how-to" guide for presidents, Neustadt's paradigm may have been verified by Truman, Eisenhower, Kennedy, and Johnson, but it is falsified by the Bush presidency. The idea of Bush and his administration's seeking gamely to persuade Congress, or jawbone obstreperous bureaucratic officials into adoption of some policy or other, is positively laughable. For the Bush presidency was all about command, not persuasion, and constitutional command at that.

One may be tempted to dismiss these criticisms as the mere consequence of ideological politics—Bush political opponents seeking to mask partisan criticism in the guise of charges of an excessive executive branch power grab. This objection fails in the first instance because it fails to address the gaping problems associated with the unitary arguments and provenance, extending to law office history, advocacy as scholarship, and law journals controlled by students. Second, this objection fails to note that criticism of the Bush unitary view spans the ideological spectrum; many on the political right have expressed grave reservations about this new turn in hyperexecutive politics.

American conservatism came under no little stress during the Bush presidency, especially as those who hew both to originalism and to a more traditional view of conservatism that remains skeptical of too much power concentrated in too few hands (although the two do not necessarily coincide) viewed the Bush administration's unitary view with no little alarm. Columnist and unitary-theory critic George Will, for example, noted with originalist skepticism that "only one delegate [at the Constitutional Convention] . . . favored vesting presidents with an unfettered power to make war." Former Reagan administration lawyer Bruce Fein has been a harsh critic of Bush administration unitary power claims, including abuse of executive privilege (which Fein dubbed "executive nonsense"), violation of the Foreign Intelligence Surveillance Act (FISA), and Bush's suspension of habeas corpus for detainees. Former Bush federal attorney David Iglesias referred to Bush's power claims related to executive privilege as "executive privilege on steroids" and "executive carte blanche." Joseph Baldacchino, president of the National Humanities Institute, referred to the "failures" of the Bush administration, singling out the administration's "warrantless searches and spying [and] the concentration of power in the executive branch at the expense of Congress, the courts and the states." Writing in *The American Conservative,* Claes Ryn wrote with disdain about "the so-called 'unitary' executive—the notion of the pre-eminence of the president, who is to be as little constrained as possible by checks and balances and the rule of law. Their goal is wholly at odds with the constitutionalism of the framers." The Cato Institute's Gene Healy is the author of a book that warns of "America's Dangerous Devotion to Executive Power" on its front cover. Healy dubs the Bush unitary view "Unitarian Heresies" and offers a lengthy analysis that undercuts the tenets of the unitary view and is especially critical of Bush lawyer and University of California at Berkeley law professor John Yoo, primary author of the administration's torture memos and arch proponent of a nearly unlimited war power for the president.[66]

Conclusion: The Post-Bush Presidency

George W. Bush was no Neustadtian president seeking to buttress puny formal powers by marshaling his persuasion skills to strike bargains with Congress or the bureaucracy. Throughout his presidency, Bush showed little patience for, or interest in, the kind of constructive political engagement and bargaining commonly found among his predecessors. Bush's effort to portray nearly every significant decision and policy as somehow consonant with an originalist reading of the Constitution and to then justify these actions in the "command"-like terms Neustadt denigrated separates him from previous activist presidents. What's more, even if the Bush unitary view is rejected by his immediate successors, one important lesson of the presidency is that, if the past is any guide, some future administration will surely be tempted to resurrect and embrace this theory, like the fabled ring, "the one ring to rule them all," in J. R. R. Tolkien's trilogy *The Lord of the Rings*. When executive power is in play, any president may be prone to Gollum-like behavior. Even Barack Obama, who ran in part on a platform of rejecting Bush's expansive views of presidential power, has been subject to escalating criticism from some of his political allies for embracing some of Bush's expansive power claims, including Obama-administration efforts in court to protect the secrecy surrounding the National Security Agency's warrantless wiretapping program conducted under Bush, continued support for extraordinary rendition, and qualified continuation of the use of signing statements to interpret legislation signed into law.

Bearing this in mind, the lessons for the future are reducible to a series of propositions:

Proposition 1: The Constitution simply does not have all the answers to the riddle of executive power. This fact alone points to the flaws of certitude and generality that typify originalism as constitutional doctrine.

Proposition 2: The arc of presidential power from past to present is rooted in, but cannot be adequately explained by, Article II powers alone.

Proposition 3: Like the Constitution itself, Article II is not a Rorschach ink blot, the meaning of which is to be interpreted in any manner by whoever happens to be viewing it. All theories are not equally tenable; not every constitutional debate consists of two equally valid and legitimate opposing points of view. Text and historical evidence provide some answers. On the other hand, some questions simply cannot be answered.

Proposition 4: An originalist reading of the Constitution leads to legislative supremacy, not to the unitary executive.

Proposition 5: The unitary theory fails on the merits in its attempt to bridge its grandiose power claims with an originalist reading of the Constitution. It is faux originalism. Despite its pretensions to seriousness, it is the product of a pseudoscholarly enterprise that, at bottom, suffers from a fatal flaw: it rejects the essence of the separation-of-powers/ checks-and-balances system (while falsely claiming obedience to it) precisely because it deems to vest in the president a constitutional power to reject or ignore statutory law if the president decides solely for him- or herself that such law trammels executive prerogatives. The unitary theory further denies to the courts the right to adjudicate matters that the executive deems, by any self-made standard, beyond the court's reach. The unitary theory is not just against the Constitution; it's bad law, bad governance, and bad politics.

There is plenty to argue about regarding the scope of constitutional powers and the meaning of Article II, whether it is the bounds of the commander in chief's power, or the meaning of the vesting-of-executive- power clause, or other matters that have been debated for more than two centuries. In the twenty-first century, one can accept the realities of modern presidential governance and take that argument one step further by making a logical and even respectable normative argument that the separation-of-powers system has outgrown its usefulness—that the American public mind seeks and prefers executive power, very much in the way Clinton Rossiter described it in his forgotten 1950s classic *The American Presidency;* that it has no patience for a national legislature that has failed to adapt to the twentieth, much less to the twenty-first century; that Congress needs a strong executive hand more than ever before;[67] and that twenty-first-century America needs an executive- centered system of governance, despite the risks of such an unabashed express turn to executive power. Indeed, political scientist Harvey Mansfield very nearly makes this case when he argues that "the rule of law must yield to the need for energy."[68] But the unitarians do not rest their arguments on any such "living Constitution" view, because their ideological restraints impel them to justify their actions and theory on originalism, which leads us back to the faux "scholarship" of a few lawyers that is the fountainhead of the unitary theory. The Bush presidency was entitled to make a case for a more bold and powerful presidency. But the Bush unitary executive is an honest reading of the Constitution only if the reader is standing on her or his head at the time. Therefore, the Bush presidency was not, in any important sense, a "Constitutional presidency"—it was rather a contempt-of-Constitution presidency, and that is the legacy the Bush administration leaves to its successors. Finally, if the Constitution can be said to mean the opposite of what it says, then the document simply has no meaning.

Notes

The author wishes to thank Mary McGuire for her assistance.

1. Louis Fisher, *The Politics of Shared Power* (College Station: Texas A&M Univ. Press, 1998), xii.

2. Richard E. Neustadt, *Presidential Power and the Modern Presidency* (1960; New York: Free Press, 1990), 29 (page references are to the 1990 edition).

3. John Locke, *Of Civil Government* (Chicago: Regnery, 1955), 125. See James P. Pfiffner's superb discussion of Locke and other theorists in *Power Play: The Bush Presidency and the Constitution* (Washington, DC: Brookings Institution Press, 2008), chap. 1.

4. Garry Wills, *A Necessary Evil* (New York: Simon and Schuster, 1999), chap. 5. See also Robert J. Spitzer, *President and Congress* (New York: McGraw-Hill, 1993), 13–16.

5. Alexander Hamilton, James Madison, and John Jay, *The Federalist Papers* (New York: New American Library, 1961), 322.

6. Clinton Rossiter, *1787: The Grand Convention* (New York: New American Library, 1966), 55.

7. Roger Davidson, "'Invitation to Struggle': An Overview of Legislative-Executive Relations," *Annals of the American Academy of Political and Social Science* 499 (Sept. 1988): 11.

8. Harold Hongju Koh, *The National Security Constitution* (New Haven, CT: Yale Univ. Press, 1990), 75–76.

9. Wills, *A Necessary Evil*, 85.

10. Ibid., 86.

11. Max Farrand, ed., *The Records of the Federal Convention*, 4 vols. (New Haven, CT: Yale Univ. Press, 1966), 2:34.

12. Robert J. Spitzer, *The Presidential Veto* (Albany, NY: SUNY Press, 1988), 9–14. The council-of-revision proposal was offered up for a vote no less than four times at the convention and was narrowly defeated each time.

13. Robert Scigliano argues precisely that the judiciary and executive "were intended by the framers of the Constitution to act, for certain purposes, as an informal and limited alliance against Congress, and that they have in fact done so." This was done, he argues, "to counterbalance the power of Congress." *The Supreme Court and the Presidency* (New York: Free Press, 1971), vii.

14. Spitzer, *President and Congress*, chap. 2; Wills, *A Necessary Evil*, 87–90; Louis Fisher, *Constitutional Conflicts between Congress and the President* (Lawrence: Univ. Press of Kansas, 2007), chap. 1. Among the Constitution's founders, Alexander Hamilton stands out as one who sought to stake out an aggressive view of executive power as President George Washington's secretary of the Treasury and de facto chief of staff. Yet Hamilton's efforts stand out precisely because they were anomalous.

15. Theodore J. Lowi, *The Personal President* (Ithaca, NY: Cornell Univ. Press, 1985), 35.

16. Woodrow Wilson, *Congressional Government* (1885; New York: Meridian Books, 1956), 23, 31 (page references are to the 1956 edition).

17. A small sampling of such writing includes Edward S. Corwin, *The President: Office and Powers* (New York: New York Univ. Press, 1957); Rossiter, *The American Presidency;* Lowi, *The Personal President;* Neustadt, *Presidential Power;* Stephen Skowronek, *The Politics Presidents Make* (Cambridge, MA: Harvard Univ. Press, 1993); Spitzer, *President and Congress;* Gordon Silverstein, *Imbalance of Powers: Constitutional Interpretation and the Making of American Foreign Policy* (New York: Oxford Univ. Press, 1997); Michael A. Genovese, *The Power of the American Presidency* (New York: Oxford Univ. Press, 2001). A superb synthesis of competing arguments about presidential power is found in Raymond Tatalovich and Thomas S. Engeman, *The Presidency and Political Science* (Baltimore, MD: Johns Hopkins Univ. Press, 2003).

18. Louis Fisher, *Congressional Abdication on War and Spending* (College Station: Texas A&M Univ. Press, 2000).

19. For example, see Michael Lipsky, *Street-Level Bureaucracy* (New York: Russell Sage Foundation, 1983).

20. Wilfred E. Binkley, *President and Congress* (New York: Vintage, 1962), 13.

21. Robert J. Spitzer, "The Presidency: The Clinton Crisis and Its Consequences," in *The Clinton Scandal*, ed. Mark J. Rozell and Clyde Wilcox (Wash-

ington, DC: Georgetown Univ. Press, 2000), 1–17; David Gray Adler and Nancy Kassop, "The Impeachment of Bill Clinton," in *The Presidency and the Law,* ed. David Gray Adler and Michael A. Genovese (Lawrence: Univ. Press of Kansas, 2002), 155–74.

22. Spitzer, *The Presidential Veto,* 71–104; Richard A. Watson, *Presidential Vetoes and Public Policy* (Lawrence: Univ. Press of Kansas, 1993); Charles A. Cameron, *Veto Bargaining* (New York: Cambridge Univ. Press, 2000).

23. Spitzer, *President and Congress,* 208; Lyn Ragsdale, *Vital Statistics on the Presidency* (Washington, DC: CQ Press, 2009), 417–34.

24. Ragsdale, *Vital Statistics,* 362; Henry J. Abraham, *Justices, Presidents, and Senators* (Lanham, MD: Rowman and Littlefield, 1999), 28.

25. *Jefferson's Letters,* arranged by Willson Whitman (Eau Claire, WI: E. M. Hale, 1950), 108.

26. Matthew J. Dickinson, "The Politics of Persuasion," in *Presidential Leadership,* ed. Bert A. Rockman and Richard W. Waterman (New York: Oxford Univ. Press, 2008), 277–310.

27. Neustadt, *Presidential Power,* 32.

28. Ibid., 28.

29. Ibid., 28, xix.

30. Ibid., 150.

31. See, for example, Bert A. Rockman and Richard W. Waterman, eds., *Presidential Leadership* (New York: Oxford Univ. Press, 2008).

32. Robert Y. Shapiro, Martha Joynt Kumar, and Lawrence R. Jacobs, eds., *Presidential Power: Forging the Presidency for the Twenty-first Century* (New York: Columbia Univ. Press, 2000); William G. Howell, *Power Without Persuasion: The Politics of Direct Presidential Action* (Princeton, NJ: Princeton Univ. Press, 2003), 8.

33. Spitzer, *President and Congress,* 259.

34. See Steven M. Teles, *The Rise of the Conservative Legal Movement* (Princeton, NJ: Princeton Univ. Press, 2008), chap. 5.

35. The Federalist Society was formed in 1982. See www.fed-soc.org/AboutUs /ourbackground.htm, accessed Oct. 5, 2006.

36. Jeffrey Rosen, "Power of One: Bush's Leviathan State," *New Republic,* July 24, 2006, 8.

37. Hamilton, Madison, and Jay, *The Federalist Papers,* 423–31.

38. James Burnham, *Congress and the American Tradition* (Chicago: Regnery, 1959); Willmoore Kendall, *The Conservative Affirmation* (Chicago: Regnery, 1963); Alfred De Grazia, *Republic in Crisis* (New York: Federal Legal Publications, 1965). See also Tatalovich and Engeman, *The Presidency and Political Science,* chap. 7.

39. A typical invocation of unitary executive power in a signing statement to

void a part of a law was that issued by Bush in his signing statement of H.R. 2863 on December 30, 2005. This bill to provide emergency supplemental appropriations included an amendment, sponsored by Republican senator John McCain (AZ) to bar cruel, degrading, and inhumane treatment of prisoners being held by the United States. Bush had opposed the amendment, but he dropped his opposition when it became clear that the measure had overwhelming congressional support. Yet his signing statement included this phrase: "The executive branch shall construe Title X in Division A of the Act, relating to detainees, in a manner consistent with the constitutional authority of the President to supervise the unitary executive branch and as Commander in Chief and consistent with the constitutional limitations on the judicial power." McCain protested the implication that Bush might decline to enforce this provision of the law, but the White House refused to explain Bush's intentions. Yet the just-quoted phrase was typical of hundreds inserted in prior and subsequent pieces of legislation. The arcane, mantralike wording ("to supervise the unitary executive") raised little attention in the first several years of Bush's presidency until the intent behind it came into public view. "President's Signing Statement of H.R. 2863," Dec. 30, 2005, in www.whitehouse.gov/news/releases/2005/12/20051230-8 .html, accessed Jan. 17, 2006; Elisabeth Bumiller, "For President, Final Say on a Bill Sometimes Comes after the Signing," *New York Times,* Jan. 16, 2006, A11.

40. Jess Bravin, "Bush's Power Play Has Key Ally," *Wall Street Journal,* Jan. 5, 2006, 12; "How Bush Has Asserted Powers of the Executive," *USA Today,* June 6, 2002, 2A; R. Jeffrey Smith and Dan Eggen, "Justice Expands 'Torture' Definition," *Washington Post,* Dec. 31, 2004, A1; Stuart Taylor Jr., "The Man Who Would Be King," *Atlantic Monthly,* April 2006, 25–26.

41. *Humphrey's Executor v. U.S.,* 295 U.S. 602 (1935); *Bowsher v. Synar,* 478 U.S. 714 (1986); *Morrison v. Olson,* 487 U.S. 654 (1988).

42. The voluminous and decades-old literature on the American bureaucracy, nearly all of which is ignored by advocates of the unitary view, confirms the constitutional, legal, and political place for agencies. Good summaries are found in Robert E. Cushman, *The Independent Regulatory Commissions* (New York: Oxford Univ. Press, 1941); Theodore J. Lowi, *The End of Liberalism* (New York: Norton, 1979); Richard J. Stillman II, *The American Bureaucracy* (Chicago: Nelson-Hall, 1987). Peter Woll addressed these issues decades ago in his standard work on bureaucracy when he noted that Hamilton's reference to unity in the presidency was cited by early critics as an impediment to the development of independent agencies. Woll's analysis was: "The fact is that the system they [the Framers] constructed supported in many particulars bureaucratic organization and functions independent of the President. It was the role they assigned to *Congress* in relation to administration that assured this result, as well as the general position Congress was to occupy in the governmental

system. . . . Congress can not only set up an administrative agency on an independent basis, but it can see to it that the agency remains independent." Woll, *American Bureaucracy* (1963; New York: Norton, 1977), 62–63 (page references are to the 1977 edition).

43. Charlie Savage, *Takeover: The Return of the Imperial Presidency and the Subversion of American Democracy* (New York: Little, Brown, 2007), 230; Presidential Signing Statements, www.coherentbabble.com/listGWBall.htm, accessed July 26, 2009; Charlie Savage, "Bush Challenges Hundreds of Laws," *Boston Globe,* April 30, 2006, A1; Savage, "Bush Cites Authority to Bypass FEMA Law," *Boston Globe,* Oct. 6, 2006, A1. These data come from the work of political scientists Christopher S. Kelley and Phillip J. Cooper. For more on signing statements, see Kelley and Ryan J. Barilleaux, "The Past, Present, and Future of the Unitary Executive," a paper presented at the Annual Meeting of the American Political Science Association, Philadelphia, PA, Aug. 31–Sept. 3, 2006; Cooper, *By Order of the President* (Lawrence: Univ. Press of Kansas, 2002); Cooper, "George W. Bush, Edgar Allan Poe, and the Use and Abuse of Presidential Signing Statements," *Presidential Studies Quarterly* 35 (Sept. 2005): 515–32; Louis Fisher, "Signing Statements: What to Do?" *Forum* 4 (2006): 1–10. Bush II is not the first president to use signing statements to balk at the enforcement of provisions of bills. But all of Bush's predecessors combined used signing statements in such a manner in about six hundred instances. Moreover, no president has ever overlain these actions with a theory in the nature of the grandiose unitary theory.

44. 542 U.S. 507 (2004); 542 U.S. 466 (2004); 548 U.S. 557 (2006).

45. Bush's vice president, Dick Cheney, has been that administration's foremost proponent of the corollary notion that presidential power was gutted in the 1970s and that it had not recovered its proper powers from then up to the present. Jane Mayer, "The Hidden Power," *New Yorker,* July 3, 2006, 44–55. This notion has been challenged from all political quarters. For example, Reagan Justice Department official Bruce Fein commented about the Bush administration's and Cheney's views of presidential power, "They're in a time warp. If you look at the facts, presidential powers have never been higher." Dana Milbank, "In Cheney's Shadow, Counsel Pushes the Conservative Cause," *Washington Post,* Oct. 11, 2004, A21. See also Shirley Anne Warshaw, *The Co-Presidency of Bush and Cheney* (Palo Alto, CA: Stanford Univ. Press, 2009).

Debate concerning the rise or demise of presidential power is more thoroughly discussed on pages 61–64, and pertinent writings that discuss this very topic can be found in note 17.

46. Theodore B. Olson, "The Impetuous Vortex: Congressional Erosion of Presidential Authority," in *The Fettered Presidency: Legal Constraints on the Executive Branch,* ed. L. Gordon Crovitz and Jeremy Rabkin (Washington, DC:

Robert J. Spitzer

American Enterprise Institute, 1989), 231; Minority Report, *Report of the Congressional Committees Investigating the Iran-Contra Affair* (Washington, DC: GPO, 1987). Dick Cheney, then a representative, was a key architect of the Minority Report, which set out many of the tenets of the unitary-executive view.

47. Bravin, "Bush's Power Play Has Key Ally."

48. See Ryan J. Barilleaux and Christopher S. Kelley, eds., *The Unitary Executive and the Modern Presidency* (College Station: Texas A&M Univ. Press, 2010).

49. Charles C. Thach Jr., *The Creation of the Presidency, 1775–1789* (1923; New York: Da Capo Press, 1969), 167 (page reference is to the 1969 edition); J. W. Peltason and Sue Davis, *Corwin and Peltason's Understanding the Constitution* (New York: Harcourt College, 2000), 151, 181.

50. Frederick A. O. Schwarz Jr. and Aziz Huq, *Unchecked and Unbalanced* (New York: New Press, 2008), 156.

51. Savage, *Takeover,* 48.

52. "Yoo Presidency, The," *New York Times Magazine,* Dec. 11, 2005, 106.

53. Savage, *Takeover,* 45; Schwarz and Huq, *Unchecked and Unbalanced,* 156.

54. Robert J. Spitzer, *Saving the Constitution from Lawyers: How Legal Training and Law Reviews Distort Constitutional Meaning* (New York: Cambridge Univ. Press, 2008).

55. See Robert J. Spitzer, "Saving the Presidency from Lawyers," *Presidential Studies Quarterly* 38 (June 2008): 329–46.

56. Alfred H. Kelly, "Clio and the Court," in *The Supreme Court Review,* ed. Philip Kurland (Chicago: Univ. of Chicago Press, 1965), 122.

57. Peter L. Strauss, "The Place of Agencies in Government: Separation of Powers and the Fourth Branch," *Columbia Law Review* 84 (April 1984): 599–602; Geoffrey P. Miller, "Independent Agencies," *Supreme Court Review* (1986): 41–97; Harold J. Krent, "Fragmenting the Unitary Executive: Congressional Delegations of Administrative Authority outside the Federal Government," *Northwestern University Law Review* 85 (Fall 1990): 62–112.

58. Steven G. Calabresi and Kevin H. Rhodes, "The Structural Constitution: Unitary Executive, Plural Judiciary," *Harvard Law Review* 105 (April 1992): 1153–1216. Calabresi is a cofounder of the Federalist Society and also worked as a lawyer in the Reagan administration.

59. Articles defending the unitary view include Gary Lawson, "Changing Images of the State: The Rise and Rise of the Administrative State," *Harvard Law Review* 107 (April 1994): 1231–54; Steven G. Calabresi and Saikrishna B. Prakash, "The President's Power to Execute the Laws," *Yale Law Journal* 104 (Dec. 1994): 541–665. Critics of the unitary view include Lawrence Lessig and Cass R. Sunstein, "The President and the Administration," *Columbia Law Review* 94 (Jan. 1994): 1–120; Abner S. Greene, "Checks and Balances in an Era of

Presidential Lawmaking," *University of Chicago Law Review* 61 (Winter 1994): 123–96; Martin S. Flaherty, "The Most Dangerous Branch," *Yale Law Journal* 105 (May 1996): 1725–1839; Neil Kinkopf, "Of Devolution, Privatization, and Globalization: Separation of Powers Limits on Congressional Authority to Assign Federal Power to Non-Federal Actors," *Rutgers Law Review* 50 (Winter 1998): 331–96.

60. Steven G. Calabresi and Christopher S. Yoo, "The Removal Power: The Unitary Executive during the First Half-Century," *Case Western Reserve Law Review* 47 (Summer 1997): 1451–1561; Steven G. Calabresi and Christopher S. Yoo, "The Unitary Executive during the Second Half-Century," *Harvard Journal of Law and Public Policy* 26 (Summer 2003): 667–801; Christopher S. Yoo, Steven G. Calabresi, and Lawrence D. Nee, "The Unitary Executive during the Third Half-Century," *Notre Dame Law Review* 80 (Nov. 2004): 1–109; Christopher S. Yoo, Steven G. Calabresi, and Anthony J. Colangelo, "The Unitary Executive in the Modern Era, 1945–2004," *Iowa Law Review* 90 (Jan. 2005): 601–731. These arguments were published as Steven G. Calabresi and Christopher S. Yoo, *The Unitary Executive* (New Haven, CT: Yale Univ. Press, 2008).

61. Lawson, "Changing Images of the State," 1231.

62. Particularly effective critiques of the unitary view are found in Lessig and Sunstein, "The President and the Administration"; Kelley and Barilleaux, "The Past, Present, and Future of the Unitary Executive"; and Louis Fisher, "The 'Unitary Executive': Ideology versus the Constitution," a paper presented at the Annual Meeting of the American Political Science Association, Philadelphia, PA, Aug. 31–Sept. 3, 2006; Barilleaux and Kelley, *The Unitary Executive and the Modern Presidency*.

63. Schwarz and Huq, *Unchecked and Unbalanced*, 156–57.

64. Hamilton, Madison, and Jay, *The Federalist Papers*, 322; Fisher, "The 'Unitary Executive,'" 1. See also Louis Fisher, "The Unitary Executive and Inherent Executive Power," *University of Pennsylvania Journal of Constitutional Law* 11 (2009).

65. See Spitzer, *Saving the Constitution from Lawyers*, chap. 4.

66. George Will, "The 'Unitary Executive,'" *Washington Post*, May 4, 2008, B7; Bruce Fein, "Executive Nonsense," *Slate Magazine*, July 11, 2007, at www.slate.com/id/2170247/, accessed Oct. 14, 2008; Fein, "Carts before Horses," *Slate Magazine*, Aug. 31, 2007, at www.slate.com/id/2173106/, accessed Oct. 14, 2008; see also Fein, *Constitutional Peril: The Life and Death Struggle of Our Constitution and Democracy* (New York: Palgrave/Macmillan, 2008); David Iglesias, "Out of Bounds," *Slate Magazine*, June 13, 2008, at www.slate.com/id/2193365/, accessed June 14, 2008; Joseph Baldacchino, "Conservatism Can Be Revived: Unmasking Neocons Just a Beginning," *Epistulae* 3 (Sept. 25, 2008), 1; Claes G. Ryn, "Power Play," *American Conservative*, Oct. 6, 2008, at www

.amconmag.com/article/2008/oct/06/00025/, accessed Oct. 15, 2008; Gene Healy, *The Cult of the Presidency: America's Dangerous Devotion to Executive Power* (Washington, DC: Cato Institute, 2008), 19–33. For more on the problems with Yoo's view of the commander-in-chief power, see Spitzer, *Saving the Constitution from Lawyers,* 103–14.

67. In a mostly forgotten essay, Samuel Huntington argued in 1965 that the power over legislation should simply be taken from Congress and given to the president, reserving to Congress only administrative oversight and constituent service. See "Congressional Responses to the Twentieth Century," in *The Congress and America's Future,* ed. David Truman (1965; Englewood Cliffs, NJ: Prentice-Hall, 1973), 34 (page reference is to the 1973 edition). For more about criticisms of Barack Obama for adopting at least some of Bush's positions on secrecy and executive power, see Maura Reynolds, "A Mottle of Transparency," *CQ Weekly,* July 20, 2009, 1698–1705.

68. Harvey C. Mansfield, "The Case for the Strong Executive," *Wall Street Journal,* May 2, 2007, at www.opinionjournal.com/federation/feature/?id=110010014, accessed Oct. 15, 2008.

THE FUTURE OF THE WAR PRESIDENCY

The Case of the War Powers Consultation Act

William G. Howell

Scholars have long bemoaned the Congress's inability to check the president's war powers, the failure of Congress's own members to take up their own constitutional obligations, and the resulting imbalance of power in foreign policy that has thus been birthed. But when an extraordinarily unpopular president unapologetically trumpeted the expansion of executive war powers, when the protracted Iraq war was taking its toll on American blood and treasure, and when newly elected Democratic majorities in Congress failed to do much about it, principled critiques gave way to outrage. The years Bush was in office are debatably defined solely by the development of presidential power.

Condemnations most commonly follow especially audacious displays of executive unilateralism and congressional acquiescence, neither of which were in short supply during the presidency of George W. Bush. Recall a few of the audacious displays of executive unilateralism or congressional acquiescence during that period that prompted condemnations from critics: Bush's signing statement refusing to abide by the central tenets of the 2005 antitorture legislation;[1] Justice Department memos that gave the president power as commander in chief to excuse strict interrogation techniques, even those considered by many to be torture; the Congress's banal Abu Ghraib hearings; refusal by the administration to apply the Geneva Convention to Guantanamo Bay prisoners; and the 2007 troop surge that took place at approximately the same time the Democrats took over Congress, promising a new policy for the Iraq war. Each of these episodes, and plenty more besides, attracted its share of anger and demands for policy reform.

In many ways, Barack Obama picked up where Bush left off in 2008. To the considerable consternation of his political base, Obama during his first eighteen months in office maintained operations at the Guantanamo Bay detention facility, significantly increased U.S. troop levels in Afghanistan, ramped up the activity of drone aircraft on the Pakistan-Afghanistan border, and further resisted efforts by the courts to monitor the treatment of enemy combatants. And while his gestures toward diplomacy won him, rather extraordinarily, a Nobel Peace Prize in 2009, Obama did not back down from the threats posed by Iran's ongoing nuclear program or North Korea's sinking of a South Korean vessel in the spring of 2010.

Occasionally political observers will fix their attention on the structural arrangements that define presidential-congressional relations and allow presidents to achieve so much of what they want when waging foreign wars. Both for the celebrity of its membership and the media attention that accompanied its final report, the 2008 National War Powers Commission (hereinafter the Commission) represents perhaps the most important effort in the past quarter century to reform the domestic institutional machinery of war. Any effort to understand the future of the American presidency, especially the presidency during times of war, would do well to reflect upon what the Commission had to say.

The Commission counted within its ranks two former secretaries of state, former and current senators, national security advisers, U.S. attorneys general, university presidents, governors, deans, and high-ranking military officials. And the Commission's final report received extensive domestic and international media coverage, much of it sympathetic. Upon release of the Commission's report in July 2008, cochairs and former secretaries of state James Baker and Warren Christopher placed a lengthy op-ed in the *New York Times*. Thomas Omestad of *U.S. News and World Report* called the Commission's recommendations "one of the more practical attempts to deal with the accumulation of presidential power." And according to syndicated columnist David Broder, the Commission "devised a clever way to signal a healthy change toward bipartisanship in foreign policy."[2]

The Commission's report found receptive audiences in Washington's corridors of power. In the fall of 2008, Baker and Christopher testified before Congress about the Commission's recommendations. A number of individuals with close ties to President Barack Obama—including Abner Mikva, John Podesta, and Joe Biden—either served on the Commission, testified before it, or indicated vocal support for its recommendations. And in December 2008, Obama himself met with Baker and Christopher to discuss the report.[3]

What did the Commission recommend? Rather than lambaste an imperial president and a feckless Congress, as so many before had done, the members of the Commission sought to offer a more measured tone and a constructive voice to ongoing debates about the domestic politics of war. While expressly withholding judgment on the conduct of previous and ongoing wars, the Commission kept its gaze on the future. "Our aim was to issue a report that should be relied upon by future leaders and furnish them practical ways to proceed in the future," Baker and Christopher wrote in their opening letter. They intended to offer recommendations that would clarify the obligations of presidents and members of Congress during the lead-up to war, that would calm, if not settle, the partisan bickering that so often accompanies military deployments, and, crucially, that bipartisan majorities could accept. Baker and Christopher hoped that their report would avoid the fate of so many of its predecessors—"collecting dust rather than catalyzing changes in policy."[4]

The specific changes promoted by the Commission were packaged as a legislative proposal: the National War Powers Consultation Act (WPCA). The principal objective of the WPCA, which the Commission hoped Congress would enact into law in 2009, was to augment the quality and frequency of interbranch dialogue. Hence, the WPCA establishes a set of guidelines—some binding, others not—for how the president and Congress ought to communicate with one another during the lead-up to war. These guidelines were intended to strengthen Congress's ability to extract from the executive branch information about a prospective military venture, but also to require members of Congress to take a clear position (either in support or in opposition) on an impending war. The WPCA promises to replace secrecy with forthrightness, obscurity with transparency, happenstance with order. In the process, the public should better understand what their elected officials know and think about war, strengthening the foundations of democratic accountability and, by extension, the quality of foreign policy.

I am skeptical that the WPCA can deliver on such promises. As a citizen, I share many of the Commission's concerns about the haste with which individual presidents lead us into war and the reticence of individual members of Congress to publicly state their views about a war until after the president has committed the nation's military (and reputation) to a particular course of action. I applaud the Commission's efforts to offer a set of recommendations that might be enacted, not in some imagined, idealistic polity, but in the one that we currently have. I doubt, though, that once on the books, the WPCA will substantially alter how our nation goes to war. The reason is simple: the WPCA underestimates the politics that animate interbranch relations during times of war, politics wherein the major cleavages are defined by partisan affiliations rather than institutional loyalties and wherein the public shows little appetite for punishing elected officials who neglect their constitutional obligations. The WPCA probably satisfies the first requirement of any policy reform, that of doing no harm. But I doubt that it will do much good, either.

This essay proceeds according to the following path. The first section outlines the major provisions of the WPCA. The second critically examines the possibility that the WPCA, even if enacted, will force members of Congress or presidents to behave in systematically different ways than they currently do. The third and final section briefly reflects on how certain elements of the WPCA, in conjunction with more fundamental changes to the underlying politics of war, might create the kinds of changes that the Commission seeks.

THE WAR POWERS CONSULTATION ACT

The 1973 War Powers Resolution establishes the current legal framework for Congress and the president to initiate military action abroad. Enacted in the waning months of the highly divisive Vietnam War, the resolution requires that the president "in every possible instance" consult with Congress before introducing military forces into foreign hostilities.[5] Within ninety days, the president then must secure formal authorization for the war; and should he (someday she) fail to do so, then he must withdraw. If the president does obtain the necessary approval, he must submit regular reports to Congress about the war's progress.

Reiterating observations of numerous other scholars, the Commission claims that the War Powers Resolution has proved "impractical and ineffective." It is impractical, the Commission argues, because presidents openly flout it, Congress refuses to stand by it, and the judiciary will not even affirm its constitutionality. And it is ineffective, the Commission insists, because elements of the resolution certainly are unconstitutional, especially in light of the Supreme Court's rejection of the legislative veto in *INS v. Chadha*.[6] Most disturbing, though, the War Powers Resolution does nothing to "encourage dialogue or cooperation between the branches,"[7] leaving presidents, members of Congress, and their staff to interact with one another only when it suits their own political needs or personal fancies. As a practical matter, the War Powers Resolution has proved utterly incapable of forcing individuals within either branch of government to divulge information or express opinions that they would prefer to keep private.

And from the Commission's perspective, therein lies the single biggest problem with the contemporary state of affairs: the lack of interbranch consultation about how best to utilize the military to protect national interests abroad. The Commission also expresses concerns about the damage done to the rule of law by a disregarded War Powers Resolution and about the "divisiveness and uncertainty" that the Resolution has propagated. But the Commission worries most about the poverty of existing dialogue about how the nation addresses emergent and ongoing foreign crises. Moreover, the Commission insists, an interest in greater consultation represents the "unifying theme" of all efforts to amend the War Powers Resolution. Hence, the members of the Commission claim as their primary objective the establishment of "a constructive, workable, politically acceptable legal framework that will best promote effective, cooperative, and deliberative action by both the President and Congress in matters of war."[8]

From the Commission's telling, the benefits of greater consultation are substantial and far-reaching. Through consultation, presidents will draw from a deeper well of expertise before initiating military action. Members of Congress, at long last, will have a "seat at the table" where major U.S. foreign policy decisions are made.[9] And the public will have more information on which to hold elected officials accountable. All of these are seen by the Commission as intrinsically good. But consultation also serves an instrumental objective: the development of "better decisions" about war, which reliably garner "more lasting popular support."[10] To wit, the Commission approvingly cites Alexander Bickel's observation: "Singly, either the President or Congress can fall into bad error. So they can together too, but that is somewhat less likely, and in any event, together they are all we've got."[11] Through consultation and deliberation, presidents must defend their preferred policies against the considered judgment of experts from throughout the federal government. And so doing, they will be forced to assemble a larger coalition of active support than is currently required—all of which results in a government that wages only those wars that are absolutely necessary and a military that enjoys the domestic political support it needs to succeed on the battlefront.

To foster such consultation, the Commission recommends that we replace the War Powers Resolution with the Commission's own legislative initiative, the WPCA. The WPCA requires the president to consult with—as distinct from merely notify—a newly created Joint Congressional Consultation Committee, on which will sit high-ranking party officials as well as chairpersons and ranking minority members of those congressional committees dealing with foreign affairs. Though urged to meet with the Joint Committee before a military venture, under exigent circumstances the president may choose to wait as many as three days after the initiation of conflict before doing so. Furthermore, consultation is required only for "significant" wars, which the statute defines as military operations that are expected to last at least one week. Predeployment consultation requirements are waived for minor ventures, training exercises, or emergency defensive actions. Once troops are in the field, though, the president must meet with the Joint Committee every two months and honor a variety of reporting requirements.

Under the WPCA, members of Congress have obligations of their own. If Congress fails to authorize a war before it begins, then within thirty days of its initiation the chair and vice chair of the Joint Committee must introduce to both the House and the Senate identical concurrent resolutions calling for the war's approval. Should these resolutions fail in either chamber, any member of Congress can introduce a resolution expressing Congress's disapproval of the military venture. Such a resolution must be voted on within five days of its submission. Although a resolution of disapproval is not binding unless the president signs it or Congress overrides a presidential veto, the Commission anticipates that the mere act of forcing members to vote will "promote accountability and provide members of the Joint Congressional Consultation Committee incentive to actively engage the president."[12]

By all indications, the Commission does not expect that congressional resolutions, by themselves, will redirect U.S. foreign policy. Rather, these resolutions are viewed as means to an end: they are valuable to the extent that they foster intra- and interbranch consultations about war. Rather than blindly call for more deliberation, the Commission offers the vehicle for its actual realization, because its members fully expect that demands for further information, active debate, and introspection will precede the casting of public votes on war. The Commission's work intends to serve a single objective: to encourage greater consultation between the executive and legislative branches. The word *consultation* appears more than one hundred times in the Commission's final report and in the title of its proposed statute. If we take the Commission on its own terms, then, the success or failure of the WPCA unambiguously rides on its ability to encourage each branch of government to share its opinions and information about prospective and ongoing military ventures far more than it currently does; and, one hopes, Congress and the president will factor these opinions and this information into the decisions they make about war.

A CRITIQUE OF THE WPCA

It is important to evaluate the WPCA in the spirit in which the Commission offers it. Hence, I will not engage the longstanding debate about the dual wartime imperatives of deliberation on one side and action on the other. For the purposes of this essay, I assume, as the Commission does, that increased consultation is an unqualified good. And for the moment, let us further accept the Commission's (highly controversial) claims that neither the Constitution itself nor the history of U.S. warfare offers clear insights into the appropriate division of war powers between Congress and the president. I will assume, as the Commission does, that all sides in contemporary constitutional debates about presidential and congressional war powers have a reasonable basis for their claims. Finally, I have nothing to say about the WPCA's prospects of passage. Here again, I will not question the Commission's assertion that its members have settled on the legislative initiative with the best chances of becoming law.

I want to reflect upon whether the WPCA can be expected to alter, in any meaningful sense, the interbranch dynamics that precede military deployments. It is on this possibility that the Commission's final report prides itself. The report repeatedly states the Commission's intention to offer a "pragmatic approach" for how Congress and the president can work out their differences about war. As their guiding principle, the members of the Commission seek to develop a proposal that will "maximize the likelihood" that the president and Congress will more productively consult with each other.[13] The Commission has no interest in offering symbolic reform. Rather, its legislative proposal intends to deliver results.

But notice that to deliver results, the WPCA must be self-enforcing. Do not count on the judiciary to ensure the good behavior of either Congress or the president. Though the Commission cites the judiciary's unwillingness to affirm the constitutionality of the War Powers Resolutions as among that statute's central failings, the Commission offers no reason to expect things to be any different under the WPCA. The WPCA's success, therefore, depends upon the inclination of both Congress and the president to abide by its central provisions. But will they? I suspect not. And to see why not, one must understand the core motivations that have guided presidential and congressional behavior for at least the past seventy-five years, during which time an avalanche of public expectations and aspirations has fallen before the White House and partisan politics have regularly trumped institutional loyalties on Capitol Hill. In the following two subsections, I reflect upon how presidents and members of Congress are likely to respond to a newly enacted WPCA.

The WPCA and the Executive Branch

If members of Congress are best thought of as single-minded seekers of reelection, as David Mayhew argued more than thirty-five years ago,[14] then presidents are single-minded seekers of power. In his essay for the conference "The Future of the American Presidency," Robert Spitzer puts it well: "Power is the presidential narcotic."[15] Individual presidents may have ulterior motivations: enacting good public policy, undoing the work of their predecessors, responding to a perceived public mandate, or securing their place in history. But to accomplish any of these things, presidents need power. And so it is power they seek.

Evidence abounds of presidents seeking—not to mention guarding and nurturing—power. Past presidents have relied upon executive orders, executive agreements, proclamations, and national-security directives in lieu of legislation and treaties; building and rebuilding an administrative apparatus around the presidential office; emphasizing the importance of loyalty when appointing individuals to the more distant reaches of the federal bureaucracy; issuing signing statements, which allow them further opportunities to reinterpret the meaning of laws; directly engaging the public; and, more recently, invoking the unitary theory of the executive to justify their actions. While different presidents from different parties may advance different policy agendas, all presidents, in one way or another, seize upon opportunities to fortify their influence over the writing, interpretation, and implementation of public policy.

None of this suggests that presidents exercise all the power that they would like. Presidents are seekers of power, not paragons of power. And ample scholarship emphasizes the historical contingencies and institutional constraints that limit a president's ability to exercise his unilateral powers, centralize authority, politicize the appointments process, issue public appeals, or refashion the political universe. Some basic facts about lawmaking further limit the president's ability to have his way: executive orders and executive agreements are not perfect substitutes for laws and treaties; signing statements do not have any legal enforceability at all; and as Richard Neustadt recognized a half century ago, the formal powers that presidents retain are entirely insufficient to meet the extraordinary expectations deposited at the White House's doorstep.[16] Even in the policy domain where all observers concede that presidential power reaches its apex—in war—presidents often must confront mobilized opposition within Congress and the courts. Presidential power is now, as it likely always shall be, contested.

But a basic point remains: over the nation's history, presidents have managed to secure a measure of influence over the doings of government that cannot be found either in a strict reading of the Constitution or in the expressed authority that Congress has delegated. This discretionary influence of presidential power encompasses a major pillar of recent scholarship on the modern presidency. Article II of the Constitution is notoriously vague. As a practical matter, Congress cannot write statutes with enough clarity or detail to keep presidents from reading into them at least some discretionary authority. And for their part, the

William G. Howell

courts have established as a basic principle of jurisprudence deference to administrative (and by extension presidential) expertise.[17] It is little wonder, then, that through ambiguity presidents have managed to radically transform their office, placing it at the very epicenter of U.S. foreign policy.

By way of example, consider the mileage that President Bush derived from the 2001 Authorization for the Use of Military Force (AUMF). According to that law, the president was authorized to use all necessary and appropriate force against those nations, organizations, or persons he determined had planned, authorized, committed, or aided the terrorist attacks that occurred on September 11, 2001, or those that had harbored such organizations or persons, in order to prevent any future acts of international terrorism against the United States by such nations, organizations, or persons. President Bush cited this language to justify actions ranging from military deployments in Iraq, to the warrantless wiretapping of U.S. citizens, to the indefinite detainment of enemy combatants at Guantanamo Bay, to the adoption of "enhanced interrogation techniques," to the seizure of funds held by charities suspected of supporting terrorist activities. As the Iraq and Afghanistan wars and the war on terror proceeded, the adjoining branches of government looked upon such interpretations with increasing skepticism. But President Bush held steadfast to an expansive reading of the law and the seemingly limitless authority it conferred upon his office. As the U.S. Department of Justice put it, the AUMF "does not lend itself to a narrow reading." Quite to the contrary: "The AUMF places the President's authority at its zenith under *Youngstown*."[18]

Presidents regularly offer narrow interpretations of those laws that they oppose on policy grounds or that restrict their authority. Here again, President Bush provides a case in point. In the wake of the Abu Ghraib scandals, Congress enacted the Detainee Treatment Act of 2005, which, among other things, forbade the use of torture against any individuals held in U.S. custody. The bill enjoyed overwhelming bipartisan support, ensuring its enactment over a presidential veto. Bush, therefore, opted to issue a signing statement that neutered (or at least sought to neuter) the law's most restrictive provisions on the president's ability to wage a largely clandestine war on terror. In particular, Bush asserted his intention to interpret the law within the context of his broader constitutional authority to protect the nation from external threats. As President Bush put it, "The executive branch shall construe [the law] in a manner consistent with the constitutional authority of the President . . . as Commander in Chief"—a constitutional provision, not surprisingly, that the president interprets much more broadly than do most constitutional law scholars.[19] Of course, this law will not stop any president from engaging in inhumane conduct; it seems that it is still the prerogative of the president to weigh the issues at hand and use his authority to make any decision he deems appropriate.

The members of the Commission do recognize the self-serving ways in which presidents interpret laws. Indeed, when making their case against the War Powers Resolution, the members point out that "presidents have regularly involved the country's armed forces in what are clearly 'hostilities' under the terms of the statute, while claiming the statute is unconstitutional or not triggered in that particular case."[20] The Commission gives us no reason to believe, however, that things will be especially different under their new statutory framework. Nothing about the WPCA fundamentally alters the core incentives of presidents to seize and control the federal government's war powers.

It is of some note, then, that the War Powers Consultation Act offers plenty of ambiguities of its own, each ripe for presidential exploitation. Take, for instance, the requirement that the president consult with Congress in cases of "significant armed conflict." When is an armed conflict "significant"? And does every military deployment represent a "conflict"? Answers to these questions are hardly straightforward. Recall that Truman labeled Korea a "police action." In the 1960s, both Kennedy and Johnson, in turn, insisted that they were deploying U.S. military personnel only to "train and advise" local Vietnamese forces. According to Reagan, Lebanon was a "rescue and peacekeeping" operation, and Grenada was merely a "rescue" mission. In each of these cases, presidents redefined their actions in ways that allowed them to avoid the very kinds of consultations that the Commission now hopes to foster. Ambiguities, moreover, do not stop here.

What constitutes sufficient "consultation"? Must presidents share all that they know about a foreign crisis? And if not, what are presidents to do when members of Congress either demand too much—or, for that matter, too little—information about military plans? Is the executive branch obligated to track down new information in response to congressional queries? And if so, how much time are the officials charged with this task allowed, and what opportunities do members of Congress have for follow-up? The ambiguities continue further still.

Consider, for instance, the expansive exceptions that the Commission grants to presidents under the WPCA. Presidents, for instance, need not consult with Congress about "limited acts of reprisal against terrorists or states that sponsor terrorism." Paul Findley and Don Fraser, former legislators who voted for the War Powers Resolution, ask: "Who identifies 'terrorists'? Who defines 'terrorism'? Who determines which are 'states that sponsor terrorism'? Who defines 'limited'? The president alone."[21] And with the freedom to define the law, and powerful incentives to skirt it, it is not at all clear how the WPCA will substantially increase the quality or frequency of consultation between the various branches of government.

As the law is written, presidents can readily claim to honor the WPCA without providing genuine consultation. There is good reason to expect that they will do exactly this. Presidents, even when pressed by copartisans in Congress, have powerful incentives to resist sharing intelligence, strategy, or other information that they consider sensitive. For their part, members of Congress have incentives to occasionally skirt their own constitutional or statutory war obligations. As the lead-up to the Iraq war demonstrated, the Republican-controlled Congress did not lack the legal tools to consult a Republican president. For reasons that the next subsection describes, Congress lacked the political incentives to do so.

The WPCA and the Legislative Branch

When presidents flout elements of the WPCA, as they most certainly will, can we expect Congress to do much about it? No, at least not consistently. The WPCA does not provide Congress with anything that cannot already be found in Article I. Constitutionally, Congress has the power to express its views about a war, either in support or in opposition; to demand that the president provide information about either a prospective or an ongoing military war; and to pass other bills to authorize, end, or otherwise govern a war. The fact is, Congress regularly chooses not to exercise these powers at its disposal. A variety of contributing factors explain why. I will focus, though, on the relevance of partisan politics.

To begin, citizens need to recognize a basic fact about our nation's legislature: Congress does not act as an institution to fulfill its basic constitutional obligations. Rather, it is members of Congress who do so individually. Members of Congress mainly act as individuals or with other members in coalitions to see their policy objectives advanced, build consensus for their policy positions, and bolster their chances at reelection. And the probability that these members will challenge claims about the national interest and the use of military force—demanding presidents to share information and adjust their planning—critically depends upon the alignment of their partisan affiliations. Democrats within Congress regularly and predictably support Democratic presidents, just as Republican members of Congress back Republican presidents. Across party lines, though, political cleavages regularly erupt.

Recall that Republican members of Congress almost uniformly voted in favor of the 2002 AUMF, while Democrats were split evenly. Those Democrats who broke party ranks and supported the president, however, represented districts and states where Bush had performed especially well in the 2000 presidential elections. Persistently and unavoidably, party politics and electoral incentives inform Congress's willingness to stand by the requirements of any constitutional provisions or law, very much including those found in the WPCA.

None of this is new. The voting patterns behind the AUMF had a long historical lineage. Throughout the past half century, partisan divisions have fundamentally defined the domestic politics of war. While perhaps most apparent during the divisive Vietnam and Iraq wars, partisan politics also infused the vaunted era of "Cold War consensus," when Republicans hounded Truman over his prosecution of the Korean War and thereby drove his approval ratings down into the high twenties.

A variety of factors help explain why partisanship has so prominently shaped the contours of interbranch struggles over military deployments during the modern era. To begin with, some members of Congress face electoral incentives to increase their oversight of wars when the opposing party controls the White House. A congressional member's willingness to grant a president broad discretionary force during times of war largely depends on the member's partisan beliefs and can be swayed by two major factors: whether presidential approval ratings increase when the president exercises force abroad and whether presidential approval ratings serve as an electoral benefit to his copartisans in the Congress. It is the opposition party that has the greatest political incentives to highlight any failures, missteps, or scandals that might arise in the course of a military venture.

It also bears recognizing that the making of U.S. foreign policy hinges on how U.S. national interests are defined and the means chosen to achieve them. This process is deeply, and unavoidably, political. Only in very particular circumstances—a direct attack on U.S. soil or on Americans abroad—have political parties temporarily united for the sake of protecting the national interest. Even then, partisan politics have flared as the costs of war have mounted.

Issues of trust further fuel these partisan fires. In environments where information is sparse, individuals with shared ideological or partisan affiliations find it easier to communicate with one another. The president possesses unparalleled intelligence about threats to national interests, and—despite the dictates of the WPCA—the president is far more likely to share that information with members of his own political party than with political opponents. Whereas the commander in chief has an entire set of executive-branch agencies at his beck and call, Congress enjoys relatively few sources of reliable classified information. Consequently, when a president claims that a foreign crisis warrants military intervention, members of his own party tend to trust him more often than not, and members of the opposition party are predisposed to doubt. In this regard, congressional Democrats' interrogations of Bush administration officials represented just the latest round in an ongoing interparty struggle to control the machinery of war. And with Barack Obama in the White House, it is Republicans now who are most likely to challenge the president's foreign policy.

My own research with Jon Pevehouse shows that the president's propensity to exercise military force steadily declines as members of the opposition party pick up seats in Congress. In fact, it is not even necessary for the control of Congress to switch parties; the loss of even a handful of seats can materially affect the probability that the nation will go to war. Estimating a wide range of statistical models and datasets on military deployments, we find that the partisan composition of Congress systematically covaries with the frequency with which presidents send troops abroad, the probability that presidents will respond to particular crises happening around the globe, and the time it takes for the United States to marshal a response.[22]

The partisan composition of Congress also influences its willingness to formally initiate the kinds of deliberative activities that the Commission wants to encourage. According to Linda Fowler, the presence or absence of unified government systematically covaries with the frequency of foreign policy hearings held within Congress. Fowler demonstrates that when the same party controlled both Congress and the presidency during the post–World War II era, the number of hearings about military policy decreased; but when the opposition party controlled at least one chamber of Congress, hearings occurred with greater frequency. Likewise, Douglas Kriner has shown that both congressional authorizations of war and legislative initiatives that establish timetables for the withdrawal of troops, cut funds, or otherwise curtail military operations critically depend on the partisan balance of power on Capitol Hill.[23] These findings have clear implications for the WPCA.

Copartisans within Congress are unlikely to force the president to consult with them more regularly than they already do. Members of the opposition party, meanwhile, may well challenge the president. They will do so, however, not out of a shared sense of duty to defend laws enacted by previous regimes, but because they have powerful political incentives to criticize opposition presidents who take our nation to war. And because they recognize these political incentives, presidents tend to resist the demands for information sharing that follow.

THE FUTURE OF THE WAR PRESIDENCY

The Commission argues that the War Powers Consultation Act constitutes a "practical replacement of—and improvement on—the War Powers Resolution."[24] The basis for this claim lies in its appeal to common sense and the purported benefits of increased dialogue across the branches of government. I submit, though, that whether a proposal is "practical" critically depends upon whether it conforms to the underlying political incentives of those who would carry it out and whether there exist political actors who will reliably enforce provisions that presidents, at least, have powerful incentives to disobey.

Because it underestimates the domestic politics of war, the War Powers Consultation Act is not practical at all. Interbranch contestations over war are fundamentally political, not legal, in nature. And these contestations cannot be legislated away. As James Madison tells us in Federalist No. 48—and almost all important insights about presidential power trace back to Madison—we must not place our trust in "parchment barriers against the encroaching spirit of power."[25] Neither laws nor constitutional provisions, no matter how precisely stated, will set things right once and for all. And most certainly no statute that overlooks the deeply political incentives that guide members of Congress and presidents can be expected to restore an appropriate balance of power across the branches of government.

This caution applies to much more than war. Governance reforms that preserve existing political incentives almost always disappoint. Though they hold out promises of harmony and cooperation—features rarely found in a system of separated and federated powers—they do not, in any meaningful sense, reshape the actual operations of governance. To produce the kind of lasting change that Baker and Christopher seek, we must find ways to reorient and redefine domestic politics itself. We must reduce the partisan divisions that define relations between the legislative and executive branches. We must, as voters, hold political actors accountable at the ballot box for decisions they make about issues that do not immediately affect their political jurisdictions. And we must reinvigorate and reshape the kinds of extraconstitutional checks on executive power—parties, interest groups, the media—that at least since Jefferson have shaped the possibilities for presidents to advance their domestic and foreign policy agendas.

None of this is easy. More often than not, efforts to change politics either fall short of their intended goals or produce results that their progenitors neither intended nor wanted. I do not pretend to know how one most effectively changes politics so that the president and Congress will better conform to different notions about how we, as a nation, ought to go to war. I am confident, though, that the relevant action space is in politics and that party cleavages, more than anything else, define the possibilities for meaningful reform. This is work best left not to lawyers or constitutional law scholars, but to community organizers, media outlets, lobbyists, party activists, and scholars of political behavior.

Presciently, the Founders anticipated that the proper division of war powers would not be negotiated once and for all. Rather, it would be subject to continued contestation between the branches of government. As Edward Corwin so famously put it, the Constitution issues an "invitation to struggle" over the foreign policy machinery.[26] It's a struggle that no statute—neither the War Powers Resolution nor the proposed War

Powers Consultation Act—can hope to settle once and for all. And it's a struggle that is largely immunized from reforms that do not account for the underlying political incentives of those individuals and parties who participate in it.

NOTES

1. Charlie Savage, "Bush Could Bypass New Torture Ban," *Boston Globe*, Jan. 4, 2006, www.boston.com/news/nation/washington/articles/2006/01/04/bush_could_bypass_new_torture_ban/?page=full, accessed June 28, 2010.

2. James A. Baker and Warren Christopher, "Put War Powers Back Where They Belong," www.nytimes.com/2008/07/08/opinion/08baker.html?_r=1, accessed June 28, 2010; Thomas Omestad, "Clearing Up a President's War Making Powers," http://politics.usnews.com/news/politics/articles/2008/07/09/clearing-up-a-presidents-war-making-powers.html, accessed June 28, 2010; David S. Broder, "Fixing How We Go to War," www.washingtonpost.com/wp-dyn/content/article/2008/07/09/AR2008070901936.html, accessed June 28, 2010.

3. Huffington Post, "Obama Meeting James Baker and Warren Christopher, Chairmen of War Powers Commission," www.huffingtonpost.com/2008/12/10/obama-meeting-james-baker_n_150101.html, accessed June 28, 2010.

4. Baker and Christopher, "Put War Powers Back" (opening letter of the 2008 National War Powers Commission), 4.

5. "War Powers Resolution of 1973," http://policyalmanac.org/world/archive/war_powers_resolution.shtml.

6. *INS v. Chandra*, 462 U.S. 919 (1983).

7. Baker and Christopher, "Put War Powers Back," 7.

8. Ibid., 44, 25, 41.

9. Ibid., 31.

10. Ibid., 28.

11. Ibid., 26.

12. Ibid., 39–40.

13. Ibid., 7.

14. D. R. Mayhew, *Congress: The Electoral Connection* (New Haven, CT: Yale Univ. Press, 1974).

15. Robert Spitzer, "Is the Constitutional Presidency Obsolete?" paper presented at the conference "The Future of the American Presidency," Regent Univ., Virginia Beach, VA, Feb. 6, 2009.

16. R. E. Neustadt, *Presidential Power and the Modern Presidents* (New York: Free Press, 1990).

17. Landmark Supreme Court cases that have condoned the use of presi-

dential expertise include *Myers v. United States, Humphrey's Executor v. United States, United States v. Nixon,* and *Bowsher v. Synar.*

18. U.S. Department of Justice, "Legal Authorities Supporting the Activities of the National Security Agency Described by the President," Jan. 19, 2006.

19. Edward Lazarus, "How Much Authority Does the President Possess When He Is Acting as "Commander in Chief"? Evaluating President Bush's Claims against a Key Supreme Court Executive Power Precedent," http://writ.news.findlaw.com/lazarus/20060105.html, accessed June 28, 2010.

20. Baker and Christopher, "Put War Powers Back," 25.

21. Paul Findley and Don Fraser, "The Battle over War Powers," *Los Angeles Times,* Sept. 22, 2008, http://articles.latimes.com/2008/sep/22/opinion/oe-findley22.

22. W. G. Howell and J. C. Pevehouse, *While Dangers Gather: Congressional Checks on Presidential War Powers* (Princeton, NJ: Princeton Univ. Press, 2007).

23. L. Fowler, *Dangerous Currents: Party Conflict at the Water's Edge* (forthcoming); D. Kriner, "Hollow Rhetoric or Hidden Influence: Domestic Political Constraints on the Presidential Use of Force" (Ph.D. diss., Harvard Univ., 2006).

24. Baker and Christopher, "Put War Powers Back."

25. James Madison, Federalist No. 48.

26. E. Corwin, *The President, Office and Powers, 1787–1948: History and Analysis of Practice and Opinion* (New York: New York Univ. Press, 1957).

OPPORTUNITIES AND CHALLENGES IN PRESIDENTIAL COMMUNICATIONS

Brandice Canes-Wrone

At the beginning of Barack Obama's presidency, there was a sense that the White House had a greater capacity than ever before to use public communications to advance the president's agenda. Obama himself is clearly a gifted orator who can draw an enormous audience at a moment's notice. Moreover, his campaign was renowned for its effective use of contemporary technologies like YouTube, e-mail, and text-messaging.[1] Joe Trippi, Howard Dean's campaign manager for the 2004 Democratic primaries, surmised that Obama's communications machinery could create "the most powerful presidency that we have ever seen."[2]

Yet history suggests that pundits and politicians commonly overestimate a president's ability to utilize communications for policy-related purposes. For instance, Lawrence Jacobs and Robert Shapiro observe that "the fundamental political mistake committed by Bill Clinton and his aides [regarding Clinton's health care proposal] was in grossly overestimating the capacity of a president to 'win' public opinion and to use public support as leverage to overcome known political obstacles." George W. Bush, while not known as a rousing orator, still received praise early on for a "three-pronged" communications strategy that combined "personal charm, carefully scripted events and the artful use of surrogates."[3]

Given the history of inflated expectations for any president to utilize public communications, how should we evaluate Obama and future presidents' possibilities in this domain? Is it reasonable to think that presidents now enjoy a greater capacity than their predecessors did to utilize public communications for policy-related purposes? In this essay I assess the opportunities and challenges that the president faces in this sphere of influence, a sphere that scholars suggest has become increasingly central to presidential policymaking.[4] My assessment addresses factors that any president would face, given recent developments in communications and politics, in addition to factors that are specific to Obama's presidency and the current political context.

Section 1 reviews what the academic literature has to say about earlier presidents' ability to utilize communications for policy purposes. This literature produces a set of what Gregory Hager and Terry Sullivan have termed "presidency-centered predictions,"[5] which are independent of the specific president.[6] Section 2 identifies two major topics about which scholarship has little to say and that seem particularly timely. Section 3 discusses recent developments that afford the president potentially new ways to affect policy by reaching out to the public. Section 4, by comparison, focuses on developments that may impede the president's capacity to do so. I conclude by discussing the extent to which the original set of predictions requires updating.

1. A Brief Overview of the Literature

Numerous influential works highlight the limits of a president's ability to alter the policy preferences of the public. According to George Edwards, in his aptly titled book *On Deaf Ears,* presidents—even charismatic ones—cannot move public opinion in the ways that pundits and presidential advisers commonly expect. Edwards makes his point by, among other things, marshaling evidence about public opinion on a variety of policies for which presidents Reagan and Clinton advocated. Lawrence Jacobs and Robert Shapiro provide complementary evidence via a detailed case study of Clinton's efforts to reform health care.[7]

Some scholarship suggests that highly popular presidents have a limited ability to alter citizens' preferences about certain types of policies. For instance, Benjamin Page and Robert Shapiro demonstrate that a popular president who makes repeated appeals about a policy can increase support for that policy by five to ten percentage points, although this effect is not statistically significant at conventional levels. Samuel Kernell utilizes public-opinion data regarding President Truman's efforts to generate public support for the Truman Doctrine to argue that popular presidents can exercise opinion leadership in foreign affairs; in particular, Kernell shows that citizens who approved of Truman were swayed by his appeals for foreign aid to Turkey and Greece.[8] Other research similarly suggests that popular presidents can move public opinion on foreign policy matters.[9] More generally, scholarship finds that when the public is not well informed about an issue and the president faces limited domestic opposition to his position—such as is often the case in foreign policy—then opinion leadership of a magnitude of five to ten percentage points is feasible.[10]

In contrast to this evidence that presidents, no matter how popular they are, have only a limited ability to convince voters to support particular policies, there is a good deal of evidence that presidents can alter the public salience of issues.[11] In other words, presidents can affect the degree to which citizens know and care about a particular issue. To highlight just one recent study, Matthew Eshbaugh-Soha and Jeffrey Peake demonstrate that when a president speaks about an issue, media attention to that issue increases.[12] The effect is particularly strong when presidents make repeated statements about a policy for which media attention was initially low.

This scholarship on issue salience indicates that presidents should be able to use policy appeals to garner policy influence. In particular, given that legislators are more responsive to public opinion on issues that are salient,[13] presidents have an incentive to appeal to voters about issues on which they want Congress to become more responsive to public opinion. Thus a president can gain influence by strategically increasing the salience of issues. Presidents should not, however, try to alter voters' preferences unless these preferences are ill-formed and the president faces limited domestic opposition on the issue. This limitation is particularly relevant for domestic policy. On almost any given domestic policy initiative, presidents can anticipate opposition from interest groups. Moreover, citizens are apt to have reasonably well-formed preferences.

Research on presidential speech-making lends support to this characterization of the chief executive's incentives. For instance, in previous work I present evidence that a president gains legislative influence from publicizing initiatives that are in line with public opinion. In addition, I find that for foreign policy, presidents have a greater capacity to achieve policy goals by publicizing initiatives that are not initially popular. This evidence comes from an examination of the nationally televised, non-obligatory policy addresses of presidents Eisenhower through Clinton in addition to a more detailed study of these presidents' public appeals about budgetary proposals.[14]

Scholarship of major historical cases also confirms the predictions. For instance, in Samuel Kernell's book about presidents "going public," the major example of a successful domestic policy appeal involves Reagan's 1981 budget and tax proposals, which were popular even before Reagan went public to promote them. Likewise, Lawrence Jacobs and Robert Shapiro's analysis of Clinton's efforts to craft public opinion about health care shows the limits of the president's ability to do so.[15] Other support can be found in research on George W. Bush's efforts to secure passage of the Patriot Act,[16] Clinton's budget battles with the 104th Congress,[17] and Truman's appeals about the Truman Doctrine.[18] The major findings of the literature in the category of public opinion can be summarized as follows.

- The president will generally not be able to move U.S. public opinion from opposing to supporting policies, or from supporting to opposing policies.
- When citizens' preferences on an issue are not well-formed— for example, they "don't know" whether they support or favor a policy—and when a president does not face substantial opposition on the issue from other political actors, he can shift these preferences in favor of particular policies if he is popular.
- On most domestic policy issues, citizens will have well-formed preferences and the president will face substantial opposition to his proposals from other political actors. On some foreign policy issues, neither of these conditions will hold. Accordingly, presidents can more easily shift opinion in favor of specific proposals on foreign policy issues.
- Even when presidents cannot move public opinion for or against a particular policy, they can alter the salience of issues.

And the major findings in terms of policy influence are these:

- Presidents can gain legislative influence by going public about issues on which they want Congress to be more responsive to public opinion.

- Popular presidents can further enhance their influence by issuing repeated appeals on issues for which the American public has ill-formed preferences and on which the president does not face significant political opposition. By and large, these issues will involve foreign policy.

2. Two Gaps in the Literature

As the literature review details, a good deal of scholarship treats the question of presidents' ability to use political communications to sway U.S. public opinion and policy. However, scholarship has failed to adequately address two pressing topics that twenty-first-century presidents face concerning communication. First, researchers lack evidence about the ability of U.S. presidents—or the chief executives of other nations—to use political communications to influence public opinion outside their home country. Second, researchers know little about how a president can best use public communications to explain policy decisions the president has already made.

These topics seem particularly relevant for several reasons. With respect to the first, President Obama has indicated that his administration will make extensive efforts to communicate directly with the mass publics of other countries. For example, he promised to give a major address from the capital of a Muslim country within his first one hundred days, and he gave his first formal television interview as president to Al-Arabiya, a Dubai-based network.[19] The second topic is timely given new communications developments along with the ever-increasing importance of executive orders and other forms of unilateral presidential action.[20]

International Public Opinion

Scholarship regarding U.S. presidents and international public opinion has largely focused on the extent to which anti-American sentiment affects the "soft power" of the United States. Robert Keohane and Peter Katzenstein, in their edited volume on anti-American sentiment around the world, recognize that "the direct and immediate consequences of anti-Americanism are surprisingly hard to identify."[21] At the same time, they point out several potential long-term consequences. These include a lack of international cooperation on transnational issues such as terrorism and the possibility that anti-American opinion will gradually develop into a bias against any policy originating from the United States. The same volume suggests that radical anti-Americanism, or fundamental opposition to the United States and its values, is not widespread in the Middle East.

Obama entered his presidency with international surveys reporting worldwide optimism that he would improve relations between the United States and other nations.[22] However, if we extrapolate from what we already know about a president's ability to lead domestic opinion, international "Obamamania" will not enable the president to shift opinion on issues for which citizens have entrenched preferences based on accurate information. Thus it is worth emphasizing that on many foreign policy issues—for instance, the existence of U.S. military bases in Saudi Arabia or the level of NATO troops in Afghanistan—opinion in the relevant foreign nation(s) is already fairly well-formed.[23] What the president can do, according to research on domestic opinion, is bring certain issues to the attention of foreign publics and alter opinion where it is not already well-formed.

Moving beyond the existing literature, the president would appear to have at least two further opportunities on the international stage. First, there is the hope that he might alter misconceptions. For instance, Steven Kull finds that vast majorities of the citizens of Morocco and Egypt believe that the United States does not really support the creation of a viable Palestinian state.[24] By publicizing U.S. government support for a two-state solution, Obama can conceivably alter a frame of reference that may be based on U.S. policy from several decades ago.

Second, the president might lessen what Keohane and Katzenstein term radical anti-Americanism.[25] Of course, one does not want to be naive about radical anti-Americanism; a president cannot simply make such sentiment disappear by giving a few speeches. Still, one would like to think that communications efforts by the president can help, particularly when supported by agencies such as the U.S. Information Agency. The Bush administration had its own initiatives aimed at improving the U.S. image in the Middle East and elsewhere.[26] Unfortunately, we lack scholarship regarding the conditions under which a president's communications to foreign publics can alter public sentiment abroad or advance U.S. interests.

Explaining Policy Positions

The literature on politicians' attempts to explain policy positions is, if anything, even sparser than that on leadership of international opinion. Beginning with John Kingdon, congressional scholars have argued that a member's capacity to explain a policy decision to constituents affects the member's willingness to support a proposal.[27] Given new means for directly reaching voters, for instance through e-mail and Web sites, the possibilities for presidents to explain policy choices are arguably greater than ever before. Yet the literature has little to say about the conditions under which voters are receptive to information from a president or other politician concerning why a particular decision was made. For instance, does it make a difference whether the president tries to persuade citizens before or after the policy action has been taken? Do citizens even care whether the president makes an effort to persuade them about the wisdom of a significant policy action, especially if he does not need their support to take it?

Answers to these questions are important because presidents are increasingly enacting policy through executive orders, directives, and other forms of unilateral action.[28] If the president makes no effort to explain these decisions, and voters oppose them or do not understand why they are necessary, then over time these voters may lose trust in the president. Moreover, because these policies can be overturned by a veto-proof majority of congressional members or a subsequent president, a lack of public persuasion could have long-term effects even if not short-term ones.

In sum, while political science has a good deal to say about certain topics regarding presidential communications, significant gaps exist in the literature. Compounding these gaps are technological and societal changes that have created new opportunities, as well as new challenges, for presidential communications.

3. NEW OPPORTUNITIES

President Obama can exploit novel ways to reach large numbers of people, both here and abroad. Domestically, the public is significantly more tech-savvy now even than it was in 2001, when George W. Bush took office. Internationally as well, technologies such as the Internet have disseminated at an extraordinary rate since 2000. These developments should facilitate new ways of reaching large audiences as well as micro-targeting messages.

Domestic Communications

Within the United States, Internet usage increased 65% between 2000 and 2008 (see fig. 1). In the years between the 2000 election of George W. Bush and the 2008 election of Barack Obama, Internet usage increased from 44% to 73% of the population. Moreover, Internet usage is no longer the purview of the young; even among those age fifty-five and older, a majority of households now access the Internet at home.[29]

The president can take advantage of Internet usage in a variety of ways, some of which the Obama administration has already begun using. First, he has revamped the weekly presidential address. While George W. Bush made his radio addresses available via audio and written text on his White House Web site, Obama has updated the tradition by employing video and transmitting the speeches through YouTube, a cultural phenomenon that was not even available when Bush assumed office. The first weekly address was downloaded more than six hundred

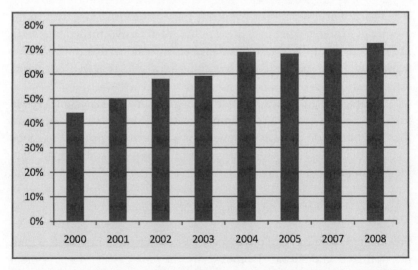

Figure 1. Internet usage in U.S. population (percentages). *Sources:* 2004–2008, Nielson/NetRatings; 2000–2003, International Telecommunication Union, Internet World Stats, www.internetworldstats.com/am/us.htm, Jan. 26, 2008.

thousand times on YouTube within the first two days of posting and more than 1 million times by February 2009.[30]

Second, and potentially more ground-breaking, are the efforts the administration is making to exploit the e-mail list developed during his campaign. Obama and his aides have created Organizing for America, a group dedicated to mobilizing a list of 13 million supporters to promote Obama's policy goals. While U.S. law prohibits the president from using e-mail lists developed during a campaign for policy purposes,[31] the Obama administration has legally sidestepped this restriction by working through the Democratic National Committee (DNC). In particular, the DNC first e-mailed the 13 million supporters to see if they would like to join Organizing for America.

The official purpose of the group is to encourage supporters to help shape mass opinion by promoting Obama's agenda to their friends. In addition, and much to the dismay of some Democratic congressional staff, the list could rally the supporters to pressure legislators to enact Obama's proposals. David Plouffe, who is helping to launch Organizing for America, has promised in response to this concern that "this is not a 'call or e-mail your member of Congress' organization."[32] At the same time, it is hard to imagine that the list would not at some point be used to advance Obama's agenda if Congress attempted to block that agenda. As Andrew Rasiej, a founder of Tech President, observes, "He [Obama] created his own special interest group . . . because the same people that made phone calls on behalf of him are now going to be calling or e-mailing their congressman."[33]

The medium of e-mail also creates other opportunities. It allows for the dissemination of information that might be difficult to transmit via television or radio, such as numbers or illustrations. Moreover, like postal mail, e-mail abets micro-targeting. Scholarship suggests that candidates focus on different sets of issues in television advertisements versus targeted mailings.[34] This research pertains to campaigns, but it seems reasonable to presume that President Obama will find televised addresses more suitable for dealing with certain issues and micro-targeted communications such as e-mail more suitable for others.

Of course, and in keeping with the notion that e-mail communications will work quite differently from traditional forms of presidential communications, the e-mail list does not blanket the general public but instead is made up of Obama supporters. Thus, while the Committee of

Concerned Journalists has expressed unease about the Obama administration's efforts to "create their own journalism," it is unlikely to be a news outlet that reaches most Americans.[35] Indeed, Obama's best use of the e-mail list might be to explain to some of his core supporters decisions that are controversial; these decisions might even be ones that are too "moderate" or "conservative" for the hard left.

YouTube and e-mail lists are but two mediums the new president is likely to add to the stable of techniques commonly employed by the White House (whether unilaterally or, in the case of e-mail, in conjunction with the DNC). The White House has already made efforts to refurbish the official Web site of the president in order to "expand and deepen . . . online engagement" with Obama's political activities.[36] Given that one-third of the 75% of Americans who own a mobile phone text-message on a daily basis, it is hard to imagine that the president's communications staff will ignore that outlet.[37] Yet as much as this presidency is likely to expand domestic communications strategies, the opportunities for new ways of reaching international audiences are arguably even larger.

International Communications

In just the years since George W. Bush took office, regular usage of the Internet and satellite television has expanded dramatically around the world.[38] Of course, the most repressive governments have made efforts to limit access to these forums. However, citizens have found ways to get around such restrictions. For instance, while Saudi Arabia forbids the creation of private radio and television stations on its own land, citizens watch the satellite station MBC, which is based in Dubai and funded by (private) Saudi investors.[39] Likewise, even in China, which has engaged in extensive censorship of the Internet, the government firewall is easily overcome. James Fallows recently observed, "As a practical matter, anyone in China who wants to get around the firewall can choose between two well known and dependable alternatives."[40] Thus, while government attempts to limit citizens' access are not completely ineffective—fear of the government will affect behavior—recent technologies have arguably made government censorship of information more difficult.

The Middle East, where President Obama has promised to make special efforts in terms of presidential communications, has participated

Table 1. Growth of Internet and satellite TV usage in select Middle Eastern nations

	Internet usage		Satellite TV
	% Population (2008)	% Growth since 2000	% Households who own dish
Bahrain	34.80	525.00	99 (2008)
Egypt	8.3 (2007)	1085.71	12 (2003)
Iran	34.90	9100.00	Banned but "widely watched"
Jordan	18.20	785.10	50 (2003), 91 (2005)
Kuwait	34.70	500.00	97 (2003), 94.2 (2007)
Lebanon	23.90	216.70	75.8 (2008)
Morocco	15.00 (2007)	4933.00	61 (2003), 75 (2006)
Qatar	37.80	1070.00	81 (2003), 94.9 (2007)
Saudi Arabia	22.00	3000.00	93.9 (2007)

Sources: Internet usage: Internet World Stats, Usage and Population Statistics, http://www.internetworldstats.com/, Jan. 26, 2009; satellite TV, 2003 statistics: Carole Chapelier and Ada Demleitner, "Satellite Television in Arab Societies," InterMedia Report 2463/04, April 2004; satellite TV, 2005–2008 statistics: Arab Advisors Group, Media Survey (for given year); satellite TV, Iran: BBC News Country Profile: Iran, http://news.bbc.co.uk/2/hi/middle_east/country_profiles/790877.stm, Jan. 26, 2009.

in this dramatic growth of Internet and satellite television usage. Table 1 documents this increase in nine Middle Eastern nations: Bahrain, Egypt, Iran, Jordan, Kuwait, Lebanon, Morocco, Qatar, and Saudi Arabia.

As table 1 shows, at least one-third of the population uses the Internet in Bahrain, Iran, Kuwait, and Qatar. More than one-fifth of the population is online in Lebanon and Saudi Arabia. In all of these countries, the rate of growth since 2000 has been stupendous. In every case it has at least doubled, and in a majority of the countries it has increased tenfold. In Iran, for instance, Internet usage has gone from less than 1% of the population in 2000 to nearly 35% in 2008.

Satellite television is also widespread in the region. In all but two of the countries, at least 75% of surveyed households own a satellite dish.[41] Even in Iran, where owning a dish is illegal, BBC News reports that "foreign satellite TV channels are widely watched" and that "this is largely tolerated by the authorities."[42] The data on satellite television, while less conducive to making intertemporal comparisons, suggest that usage is growing.[43] This increased access to mediums that are not controlled by the state improves the U.S. president's ability to engage foreign publics directly.

Although shortwave radio has long afforded the capacity for direct communication, the newer technologies offer several advantages. First, research suggests that people are more likely to overcome trust problems when visual rather than purely voice-based mediums are utilized.[44] Accordingly, televised interviews and speeches may be more effective than radio addresses in curbing radical anti-Americanism. Second, these mediums make it possible to reach audiences that might not tune in to radio programs.

Several factors specific to Obama and the 2008 presidential race should further advance the president's ability to exploit these newer technologies to improve public sentiment regarding the United States. The presidential race generated enormous interest abroad.[45] This interest should permit Obama (at least initially) to command a substantial audience when he reaches out to foreign publics. Furthermore, Obama's personal characteristics—his upbringing in Indonesia, his race, and his Muslim ancestry—afford him the opportunity to emphasize America's openness to different races, religions, and backgrounds.

4. Challenges

It is easy to be impressed by the new opportunities for communications the White House has at its disposal. However, new challenges have accompanied these opportunities. In fact, recent studies of White House communications have tended to focus on the difficulties presidents now face in getting their messages across to the public. Moreover, while these studies focus on the U.S. public, new challenges also exist with respect to international audiences.

Most significantly, the proliferation of media outlets has decreased the president's ability to command the public's attention. As Matthew Baum and Samuel Kernell document, the rise of cable has caused presidents since Carter to experience a declining audience share for prime-time addresses.[46] Coverage by the major networks used to leave television viewers with few options other than to watch the president's speech, but now viewers can switch to a multitude of other channels. Consequently, while Nixon, Ford, and Carter could count on approximately 50% of households to tune in to a prime-time presidential address, Clinton's average audience share was only 30%.

Moreover, on a day-to-day basis, the president can expect less media coverage. Since 1980, network television news coverage of the president has declined, as has "hard" news coverage of politics more generally.[47] Jeffrey Cohen surmises, "It may seem odd to suggest that the amount of presidential news has declined given the creation of dedicated news channels on cable and the 24/7 news cycle, as well as the immediate access to breaking news on the internet. . . . However, the news sources that the largest number of people use for their news, still the network evening news broadcasts and major daily newspapers, have replaced some hard news and president news with soft news and features."[48] Thus, presidents can anticipate less policy-related coverage by the traditional news sources.

As Cohen's quote attests, these traditional sources remain the most popular ones. However, fewer and fewer Americans are utilizing these sources.[49] For instance, in 1993, 60% of Americans watched the nightly news, while in 2006 only 28% did. Likewise, while in 1994, 58% read a daily newspaper, in 2006 only 40% read a print or online newspaper on a daily basis. Of course, some of this audience share has gone to cable news outlets such as CNN and Fox News. However, the overall effect has been a decline of approximately ten percentage points in the proportion of the population that obtains daily news.[50]

Further exacerbating this challenge is the fact that the remaining audience is increasingly likely to seek out sources that confirm preexisting views.[51] Liberals can watch MSNBC, conservatives Fox News. Furthermore, as Cass Sunstein has documented, news consumers can "increasingly 'filter' what they see."[52] Online papers enable readers to create tailored versions that limit what the reader encounters. Blogs provide Web links that confirm the perspective of that blogging community and avoid listing links that would challenge this perspective. Consequently, citizens are less and less likely to become exposed to alternative viewpoints through news consumption. Instead, news consumption often serves to reinforce preexisting biases about particular politicians, policies, and debates rather than to offer new perspectives, information, or ideas.

All of these changes—the increased tendency of citizens to seek out news sources that confirm particular political viewpoints, the declining audience for hard news, and the smaller audience share that presidents receive for prime-time addresses—have led scholars to declare an end to the "golden age of presidential television."[53] Of course, as I have already argued, presidents themselves can utilize the newer communications technologies. So the end of the "golden age of presidential television" will be met with new types of communications strategies. However, many of these newer mediums are ones that are readily available to other political actors, too. Accordingly, while the president still has a relative advantage in his ability to command public attention, the size of this advantage has diminished over time.

Take, for instance, Obama's group Organizing for America. While the current size of 13 million is more than three times that of major groups such as the National Rifle Association, which has 4 million members, and Moveon.org, which has 3.2 million members, it is one-third the size of the AARP, which has 40 million members.[54] Likewise, just as Obama can place a weekly address on YouTube, so can the majority or minority leader (or anyone else, for that matter). And while the president can still use prime-time addresses to exhort voters to pressure their congressional members, interest groups can now more easily and quickly contact their members for the same purpose. Using e-mail, online phone banks, and Web videos, interest groups can provide members with an immediate and unmediated response to a president's claims. Ken Kollman documents how groups have increasingly focused on these sorts of "outside lobbying" techniques.[55]

In contrast to all of these new challenges for the president in the domestic arena, in the international arena the newer technologies have largely presented opportunities. The president has never had the ability to command public attention abroad in the way he has at home. Thus the proliferation of alternative media sources has arguably been a net benefit to the president's communications capacities in other nations. At the same time, because these sources are also available to groups and personalities that are antagonistic to the United States, the White House faces new challenges in terms of combating the messages put forth by these entities. For instance, despite the fact that U.S. funding helped establish the Qatar-based satellite station Al Jazeera in 1996, the station later chose to broadcast videos by Al-Qaeda leaders Osama bin Laden and Sulaiman Abu Ghaith in which they defended the September 11 attacks on the United States.

5. Updating of Predictions

Do these changes alter the original set of predictions about the ability of U.S. presidents to sway public opinion and policy? If so, how? I would argue that the basic predictions are still relevant. Despite the end of the "golden age of presidential television," presidents can still use speeches and other communications to alter the salience of issues. The most popular media sources may not provide as much hard news as they did two decades ago, but the chief executive can still obtain coverage on major policy initiatives. If Congress blocked a major presidential proposal that was popular with voters, the president would still be able to reach out to the public and increase his prospects for legislative success.

At the same time, the president remains limited in his ability to shift voters' preferences on issues on which they already have well-formed opinions. This will be the case even for highly charismatic and popular presidents. Thus, on an issue like abortion or even union organization, Obama is unlikely to convert opposing opinion to support or vice versa. By contrast, on issues where a substantial portion of the public "don't know" their position, and particularly where Obama faces little opposition from other political elites and interest groups, he may be able to sway the "don't knows" into his favor.

Within the first two years of Obama's presidency, we have witnessed his attempt to shift public opinion on the health care debate. While an entire paper or book could be written about these efforts, it is fair to state that Obama did not succeed in significantly altering individuals' policy preferences, despite his initially high popularity.[56] If anything, Obama sacrificed his popularity by persistently trying to alter public opinion. Because health care is an issue on which people tend to have well-formed preferences, this sequence of events fits well with the basic set of predictions I have laid out.

While arguing that the basic set of predictions remains relevant, I also contend that it is in urgent need of an important type of updating. Namely, we could use additional predictions that address the opportunities and challenges of our time. For instance, when are presidents most likely to be effective at changing foreign publics' misconceptions of U.S. policy? How, if at all, can presidential communications help abate anti-American sentiment abroad? On the domestic front, can e-mail and Web sites be useful for explaining policy actions? Answers to these

Brandice Canes-Wrone

sorts of questions would not only deepen our understanding of the presidency but also potentially provide useful information for presidents.

NOTES

1. Sarah Lai Stirland, "The Tech of Obamamania: Online Phone Banks, Mass Texting, and Blogs," *Wired,* Feb. 14, 2008, www.wired.com/politics/law/news/2008/02/potomac_primaries, Jan. 26, 2009. As just one example, the campaign text-messaged supporters on the date of their state's primary, reminding them of the election and providing them with a phone number they could call to locate their polling station.

2. Chris Cillizza, "Obama Makes a Point of Speaking of the People, to the People," *Washington Post,* Dec. 14, 2008, A5.

3. Lawrence R. Jacobs and Robert Y. Shapiro, *Politicians Don't Pander: Political Manipulation and the Loss of Democratic Responsiveness* (Chicago: Univ. of Chicago Press, 2000), 115; Peter Roff, "Bush's Three-Pronged Offensive," United Press International, Feb. 21, 2001. See also "Bush's First Month Sets Stage for Future Success, Say Wellesley College Political Science Professors," AScribe Newswire, Feb. 14, 2001.

4. See Brandice Canes-Wrone, *Who Leads Whom: Presidents, Policy, and the Public* (Chicago: Univ. of Chicago Press, 2006); Samuel Kernell, *Going Public: New Strategies of Presidential Leadership,* 4th ed. (Washington, DC: Congressional Quarterly Press, 2007); and Stephen Skowronek, *The Politics Presidents Make: Leadership from John Adams to George Bush* (Cambridge, MA: Harvard Univ. Press, 1993).

5. Gregory L. Hager and Terry Sullivan, "President-Centered and Presidency-Centered Explanations of Presidential Public Activity," *American Journal of Political Science* 38 (1994): 1079–1103.

6. By contrast, "president-centered" explanations focus on the characteristics of the individual who is holding office.

7. George C. Edwards III, *On Deaf Ears: The Limits of the Bully Pulpit* (New Haven, CT: Yale Univ. Press, 2003); Jacobs and Shapiro, *Politicians Don't Pander.*

8. Benjamin I. Page and Robert Y. Shapiro, *The Rational Public: Fifty Years of Trends in Americans' Policy Preferences* (Chicago: Univ. of Chicago Press, 1992); Kernell, *Going Public.*

9. This movement tends to reflect the change of "don't knows" to support for the president's position, rather than the change of opposition to support. See Canes-Wrone, *Who Leads Whom;* and James Meernik and Michael Ault, "Public Opinion and Support for U.S. Presidents' Foreign Policies," *American Politics Research* 29 (2001): 352–73.

10. Notably, however, research suggests that unpopular presidents can repel

116

support for a policy more readily than popular presidents can convince voters to support one. Lee Sigelman and Carol K. Sigelman, "Presidential Leadership of Public Opinion: From 'Benevolent Leader' to Kiss of Death?" *Experimental Study of Politics* 7 (1981): 1–22.

11. Jeffrey E. Cohen, "Presidential Rhetoric and the Public Agenda," *American Journal of Political Science* 39 (1995): 87–107; Kim Quaile Hill, "The Policy Agendas of the President and the Mass Public: A Research Validation and Extension," *American Journal of Political Science* 42 (1998): 1328–34; and E. E. Schattschneider, *The Semisovereign People: A Realist's View of Democracy in America* (New York: Holt, 1960).

12. Matthew Eshbaugh-Soha and Jeffrey S. Peake, "Presidential Influence over the Systemic Agenda," *Congress and the Presidency* 31 (2004): 161–81.

13. See Vincent L. Hutchings, "Issue Salience and Support for Civil Rights Legislation among Southern Democrats," *Legislative Studies Quarterly* 23 (1998): 521–44; and John W. Kingdon, "Models of Legislative Voting," *Journal of Politics* 39 (1977): 563–95.

14. Canes-Wrone, *Who Leads Whom.*

15. Kernell, *Going Public;* Jacobs and Shapiro, *Politicians Don't Pander.*

16. David Domke, Erica Graham, Kevin Coe, Sue Lockett John, and Ted Coopman, "Going Public as Political Strategy: The Bush Administration, an Echoing Press, and the Passage of the Patriot Act," *Political Communication* 23 (2006): 291–312.

17. Canes-Wrone, *Who Leads Whom.*

18. Kernell, *Going Public.* See also Jeffrey K. Tulis, *The Rhetorical Presidency* (Princeton, NJ: Princeton Univ. Press, 1987), for analysis of the development of presidential rhetoric over the course of the twentieth century.

19. Michael D. Shear and Glenn Kessler, "Obama Voices Hope for Midwest Peace in Talk with al-Arabiya TV," *Washington Post,* Jan. 27, 2009, A3.

20. William Howell, *Power Without Persuasion: A Theory of Unilateral Action* (Princeton, NJ: Princeton Univ. Press, 2003).

21. See Joseph S. Nye, *Soft Power: The Means to Success in World Politics* (New York: Public Affairs, 2004), for a description of soft power, which is the ability to influence countries through attraction or co-option, as opposed to force or explicit rewards; Robert O. Keohane and Peter J. Katzenstein, "The Political Consequences of Anti-Americanism," in *Anti-Americanisms in World Politics,* ed. Robert O. Keohane and Peter J. Katzenstein (Ithaca, NY: Cornell Univ. Press, 2006), 273.

22. BBC World Service Poll, "Growing Optimism that Obama Will Improve US Relations," www.worldpublicopinion.org/pipa/pdf/jan09/BBC_Inaugural_Jan09_rpt.pdf, Jan. 27, 2009.

23. In a recent Gallup Poll, 52% of Saudi Arabian respondents stated that the

U.S. removal of military bases from the country would "very significantly improve" their opinion of the United States. By comparison, only 35% stated that U.S. aid to alleviate poverty would "very significantly improve" their opinion of the country. See Julie Ray, "Opinion Briefing: U.S. Image in Middle East / North Africa," Gallup Poll, survey conducted between May and August 2008, www .gallup.com/poll/114007/Opinion-Briefing-Image-Middle-East-North-Africa .aspx, Jan. 27, 2009. With respect to public opinion about Afghanistan, see, e.g., the Sifo poll conducted Nov. 10–13, 2008, in which only 17% of respondents supported sending more troops, 36% keeping the current level of troops, and 37% getting out of Afghanistan altogether. Angus Reid Public Opinion, www.angus-reid.com/polls/view/32295/swedes_reject_troop_increase_in_afghanistan, Jan. 26, 2009.

24. Steven Kull, "Muslim Public Opinion US Policy, Attacks on Civilians and al Qaeda," 2007, report prepared for WorldPublicOpinion.Org, www .worldpublicopinion.org/pipa/pdf/apr07/START_Apr07_rpt.pdf, Jan. 26, 2009.

25. Keohane and Katzenstein, "Political Consequences of Anti-Americanism."

26. Kennon H. Nakamura and Susan B. Epstein, "Diplomacy for the 21st Century: Transformational Diplomacy," 2007, Congressional Research Report RL34141, 17–18; USAID Press Office, "USAID Launches New Middle East Outreach Initiative with Media Summit," Press Release, May 18, 2004.

27. Kingdon, "Models of Legislative Voting."

28. Howell, *Power Without Persuasion.*

29. U.S. Census Bureau, "Household Internet Usage in and outside of the Home, by Selected Characteristics: 2007," *Statistical Abstract of the United States: 2009,* 128th ed. (Lanham, MD: Bernan Press, 2008).

30. Jim Rutenberg and Adam Nagourney, "Melding Obama's Web to a You-Tube Presidency," *New York Times,* Jan. 26, 2009, A1. By January 29, 2009, the address had more than 1 million viewings.

31. The U.S. Information and Educational Exchange Act of 1948, commonly referred to as the Smith-Mundt Act, prohibits the executive branch from dispersing "propaganda."

32. Rutenberg and Nagourney, "Melding Obama's Web," A1.

33. Sheryl Gay Stolberg, "A Rewired Bully Pulpit: Big, Bold, and Unproven," *New York Times,* Nov. 23, 2008, Week in Review Desk, 4.

34. D. Sunshine Hillygus and J. Quin Monson, "The Ground Campaign: The Strategy and Influence of Direct Communications in the 2004 Presidential Election," 2008, typescript, Harvard Univ.

35. Rutenberg and Nagourney, "Melding Obama's Web," A1.

36. "Change Has Come to WhiteHouse.gov," White House Documents and Publications, www.whitehouse.gov/blog/change_has_come_to_whitehouse_gov/, Jan. 20, 2009.

37. Pew Internet and American Life Project, "Mobile Access to Data and Information," www.pewinternet.org/Reports/2008/Mobile_Access_to_Data_ and_Information.aspx, March 2008; survey conducted in December 2007.

38. See, for instance, "Key Global Telecom Indicators for the World Tele-communication Service Sector: 1995 to 2006," from the *2009 Statistical Abstract of the United States* or the World Development Indicators database of the World Bank.

39. BBC News Country Profile: Saudi Arabia, http://news.bbc.co.uk/2/hi/ middle_east/country_profiles/791936.stm, Jan. 26, 2009.

40. James Fallows, "The Connection Has Been Reset," *Atlantic Monthly*, March 2008, 64–69.

41. I suspect these data may somewhat overstate the penetration of satellite television, given that the surveys are typically conducted in urban centers.

42. BBC News Country Profile: Iran, http://news.bbc.co.uk/2/hi/middle_ east/country_profiles/790877.stm, Jan. 26, 2009.

43. As indicated in the table, the data for 2003 versus future years are from different sources.

44. William H. Ross, Jeng-Chung Victor Chen, and Shaoyu F. Huang, "Adapting Different Media Types to Trust Development in the Supply Chain," *International Journal of Management and Enterprise Development* 4 (2007): 373–86.

45. See, e.g., Daniel Drezner, "Project Power," *Newsweek*, Jan. 15, 2009.

46. Matthew A. Baum and Samuel Kernell, "Has Cable Ended the Golden Age of Television?" *American Political Science Review* 96 (1999): 91–110.

47. Jeffrey E. Cohen, *The Presidency in the Era of 24-Hour News* (Princeton, NJ: Princeton Univ. Press, 2008); Thomas E. Patterson, "Doing Well and Do-ing Good," 2000, typescript, John F. Kennedy School of Government, Harvard Univ.

48. Cohen, *The Presidency in the Era of 24-Hour News*, 63.

49. Markus Prior, *Post-Broadcast Democracy* (New York: Cambridge Univ. Press, 2007).

50. Pew Research Center, "Biennial News Consumption Survey," released July 30, 2006.

51. Cohen, *The Presidency in the Era of 24-Hour News*; Prior, *Post-Broadcast Democracy*; Cass R. Sunstein, *Republic.com 2.0* (Princeton, NJ: Princeton Univ. Press, 2007).

52. Sunstein, *Republic.com 2.0*, 5.

53. Baum and Kernell, "Has Cable Ended the Golden Age?"; Kernell, *Going Public*.

54. For NRA membership, see "A Brief History of the NRA," www.nra .org/aboutus.aspx, Jan. 26, 2009; for Moveon.org membership, see "About the

MoveOn Family of Organizations," www.moveon.org/about.html, Jan. 26, 2009; and for AARP membership, see "AARP Celebrates 40 Millionth Member, David Squires, on AARP 50th Anniversary," www.aarp.org/states/va/articles/ AARP_Celebrates_Its_40_Millionth_Member.html, Jan. 27, 2009.

55. Ken Kollman, *Outside Lobbying: Public Opinion and Interest Group Strategies* (Princeton, NJ: Princeton Univ. Press, 1998).

56. See Frank Newport, "More in U.S. Say Health Coverage Is Not Gov't. Responsibility," www.gallup.com/poll/124253/say-health-coverage-not-gov-responsibility.aspx, May 24, 2010. See also the large set of public opinion polls at Real Clear Politics, www.realclearpolitics.com/epolls/other/obama_and_democrats_health_care_plan-1130.html, May 24, 2010.

THE FUTURE OF BIPARTISANSHIP AS A STRATEGY OF PRESIDENTIAL GOVERNING

George C. Edwards III

Every president requires a strategy for governing, for bringing about changes in public policy. One approach, which is popular with the public, is to try to create opportunities for change by reaching across the congressional aisle and attracting bipartisan support. Such support can be critical in overcoming a Senate filibuster or effectively appealing to Independents in the public, who find bipartisanship reassuring. The *Washington Post* reported that the Obama legislative agenda was built around what some termed an "advancing tide" theory: "Democrats would start with bills that targeted relatively narrow problems, such as expanding health care for low-income children, reforming Pentagon contracting practices, and curbing abuses by credit-card companies. Republicans would see the victories stack up and would want to take credit alongside a popular president. As momentum built, larger bipartisan coalitions would form to tackle more ambitious initiatives."[1]

Moreover, the president and his aides believed that a fair number of Republican lawmakers would rally behind the nation's first African American president at a time of crisis.[2] They saw his liberal programs drawing on Americans' desire for action and also counted on Obama's moderate, even conservative, temperament to hurdle the ideological obstacles that had paralyzed Washington.[3]

Democratic activists agreed. "It is quite possible to see him as liberal and having an activist agenda, but being a type of leader who does not polarize partisans and finds ways of bringing people together to work on the things where they can find common ground," said Stanley B. Greenberg, a pollster in Bill Clinton's White House. "With this type of leader, the pent-up demand for action on the economy, health care and energy allows us to reach a series of big moments where many Republicans join the process and perhaps proposals pass with overwhelming majorities."[4]

Just how realistic is the prospect that presidents will govern through obtaining bipartisan support?

OBAMA TRIES BIPARTISANSHIP

From the beginning, Barack Obama tried to strike a bipartisan pose. On the night of his election, he implored Democrats and Republicans alike to "resist the temptation to fall back on the same partisanship and pettiness and immaturity that has poisoned our politics for so long." In his press conference on November 25, 2008, the president-elect declared, "It's important . . . that we enter into the new administration with a sense of humility and a recognition that wisdom is not the monopoly of any one party. In order for us to be effective . . . Republicans and Democrats are going to have to work together."[5]

The Anti-Bush

Any move toward bipartisanship would have been a major change from the orientation of George W. Bush. Early in his first term, Bush concluded that it would not be possible to obtain Democratic support, as he had as governor of Texas, so he made few efforts at bipartisanship. He rejected the approach of obtaining the support of a broad majority of Congress through consultation, collaboration, and compromise. Instead, he centered his legislative strategy on maximizing unity among Republicans. As one of his senior political advisers declared, "This is not designed to be a 55 percent presidency. This is designed to be a presidency that moves as much as possible of what we believe into law while holding fifty plus one of the country and the Congress."[6] The White House's emphasis was to find the "right" solution and ram it through the legislature. During Bush's first term, despite narrow Republican majorities on Capitol Hill, he enacted several of his key priorities into law, such as tax cuts and prescription drug coverage under Medicare.

In the 2004 presidential election, Republican strategists concluded that there was little pliability in the electorate. As a result, they felt they could not substantially broaden their electoral coalition. Instead, they focused most of their efforts in 2004 on energizing their partisan base and encouraging turnout rather than on changing the preferences of the electorate. As Republican political strategist Matthew Dowd put it, the presidential election was "about *motivation* rather than *persuasion*."[7]

Bush's partisan strategy incited impassioned resistance, making it difficult to advance legislative proposals such as reforming Social Security and immigration policy that required bipartisan support. Moreover, his unbending approach proved self-defeating because it provoked a backlash that helped deliver the government to his Democratic critics. Obama hoped to avoid the hostility that characterized the Bush presidency.

Going the Extra Mile

As president-elect, Barack Obama did not adopt a partisan posture during the transition or the early days of his presidency. "We don't have Republican or Democratic problems. We have got American problems," Obama said after meeting with congressional leaders from both parties in an effort to obtain support for his economic stimulus package. He listened as Republicans raised concerns about waste and transparency and agreed with a suggestion by House Republican Whip Eric Cantor that the White House put the entire contents of the legislation online in a user-friendly way to see how the money was being spent. Senate Minority Leader Republican Mitch McConnell later reported, "I thought the atmosphere for bipartisan cooperation was sincere on all sides."[8]

Obama resisted inserting himself in the unresolved Senate contests in Georgia and Minnesota. Although he recorded a radio advertisement for the Democratic candidate in Georgia, he did not visit there, to avoid appearing to be too political. The president-elect also won praise from conservatives for retaining Robert Gates as defense secretary, for naming Gen. James L. Jones as his national security adviser, and for selecting the moderate Timothy F. Geithner, who had helped draw up the Bush administration's Wall Street bailout plan, as his Treasury secretary. He named three Republicans, including Gates, to his cabinet.

Shortly after being named White House chief of staff, Rahm Emanuel signaled to Republicans that the president-elect wanted to work alongside them. He met with Senate Republican leaders, gave them his cell phone number and personal e-mail address, and promised to return any communication within twenty-four hours. He told them to call at any hour if they needed to reach him, and he asked them to submit their ideas for the economic recovery plan and other issues of potential agreement.[9]

On ABC's *This Week* on January 11, 2009, Obama hinted at an inclusive and interactive approach when he spoke of a "collaborative . . . process" that would produce a great compromise in which "everybody" would "have to give" to confront gaping federal deficits. Rahm Emanuel declared that Obama was committed to "coupling" the public investment prized by liberals with "deadly serious spending reform" in areas from military procurement to entitlements that could appeal to conservatives.[10]

A few days before his inauguration, the president-elect was the guest of honor at a dinner at conservative columnist George Will's Chevy Chase home. Others attending were some of the Right's most prominent commentators, including syndicated columnist Charles Krauthammer, CNBC television host and commentator Lawrence Kudlow, *Weekly Standard* editor William Kristol, *New York Times* columnist David Brooks, *Wall Street Journal* editorial page editor Paul Gigot, *Wall Street Journal* columnist Peggy Noonan, and Fox News commentator Michael Barone. "Obama's a man who has demonstrated he is interested in hearing other views," said Krauthammer.[11]

In yet another gesture of goodwill, Obama frequently sought John McCain's advice on national security matters, including potential nominees, and kept him fully briefed on his thinking. Obama also made McCain the guest of honor at a dinner on the night before the inauguration.[12]

Rahm Emanuel and Lawrence H. Summers, Obama's economic adviser, met privately with Senate Republicans the day before the Senate voted on freeing the remaining $350 billion in Troubled Asset Relief Program (TARP) funds. Even Republicans who were not persuaded by the consultation said they were impressed by the candor of the two men. "I think they have been pretty impressive," said Senator Mitch McConnell of Kentucky, the Republican leader. "They are saying all the right things, and I think they did themselves some good in the briefing." The president-elect also telephoned some senators, including Republican Olympia J. Snowe, urging them to release the money.[13]

Once he took the oath of office, Obama dispatched a top official to brief congressional Republicans before he issued executive orders on terrorism detainees. He also met with the leaders of both parties in Congress, in keeping with his campaign promise of bipartisanship. Yet in a polite but pointed exchange with House Republican Whip Eric Cantor, the president noted the parties' fundamental differences on tax policy toward low-wage workers and insisted that his view would prevail. "We just have a difference here, and I'm president," Obama told Cantor. Obama was being lighthearted, and lawmakers of both parties laughed.[14]

The president went further on the stimulus bill. He made Republican-favored tax cuts a key component of his stimulus plan, at the cost of complaints from his fellow Democrats. At Obama's urging, Democrats also stripped from the bill provisions such as aid for family planning services and restoration for the National Mall that Republicans had ridiculed as wasteful spending and unrelated to economic stimulus. The president met with congressional leaders of both parties at the White House. Most impressively, the day before the House voted on the bill, Obama traveled to Capitol Hill and spent three hours speaking, separately, to the House and Senate Republican caucuses. GOP members emerged saying nice things about him. White House chief of staff Rahm Emanuel also met with eleven of the more moderate Republicans at the White House that evening.[15]

The day's debate contrasted with the president's conciliatory gestures, as did the lack of Republican support for the president. Nevertheless, Obama followed the House vote with a cocktail party at the White House for the House and Senate leaders of both parties.[16] The president also invited some members from both parties to the White House to watch the Super Bowl on the eve of the Senate debate.

In addition, congressional Democrats allowed Republicans to offer amendments on the floor during debate, and the House Appropriations Committee held a formal mark-up session to deal with amendments to the economic stimulus bill. Democrats even convened a conference committee on the bill. Although it was largely irrelevant to the final agreement because its members met after Senate Democrats and three Republicans had already cut a deal on the plan, Republicans had yet another venue for expressing their dissent.[17]

The president also reached out to Republicans and conservative interests outside of Congress. He obtained the support of both the National Association of Manufacturers and the U.S. Chamber of Commerce for the stimulus bill. In addition, four Republican governors, California's

Arnold Schwarzenegger, Connecticut's Jodi Rell, Florida's Charlie Crist, and Vermont's Jim Douglas, signed a letter calling for its enactment.

Frustration

Seeking bipartisan support proved to be frustrating for the new president, however. By the second week in February, he had apparently given up on winning many Republican votes. Frustrated that debate over the stimulus bill was being dominated by Republicans' criticism and that his overtures had yielded little in the way of support from across the aisle, the president switched to publicly pressuring the Republicans and rallying fellow Democrats, with a hard-line message about his unwillingness to compromise his priorities. Democrats began a radio advertising campaign in the districts of twenty-eight House Republicans, calling them "out of step."

The president held his first prime-time press conference on February 9, three weeks into his tenure. Acknowledging that his effort to change the political climate in Washington had yielded little, he made it clear that he had all but given up hope of securing a bipartisan consensus behind his economic recovery package. The sharp tone at the news conference and at a rally in Indiana earlier in the day signaled a shift by the White House in the fractious debate over his stimulus package. With no Republicans in the House voting for the economic plan and just three in the Senate, Obama began a week of barnstorming stops that took him also to Florida and Illinois to create momentum behind his program. Gone were the soothing notes of the previous three weeks. The president offered a barbed, detailed critique of the Republican argument that his plan would just create more government jobs and authorize billions of dollars of wasteful spending.[18]

White House Chief of Staff Rahm Emanuel conducted a postmortem analysis of the battle over the economic stimulus bill in which the president's senior advisers concluded that a bipartisan approach to governing was unlikely to succeed, and Obama began scaling back his appeals to congressional Republicans.[19] Of necessity, the president would have to focus on managing and maintaining the support of members of Congress already inclined to support him.

The White House stopped hosting bipartisan "cocktail parties," and the only Republican invited to the 2010 Super Bowl party was Representative Anh Cao, the sole Republican in either chamber to support the health care bill. Republican leaders and the president spent little time together; White House and congressional aides who saw interaction described the encounters as "strained" and "scripted." In March 2010, House Republican Whip Eric Cantor recalled, "When they first came into office, I could have a meeting or two with Rahm and talk with him about the stimulus bill. But the conversations have been few and far between over the last six months."[20]

A Second Wind

Nevertheless, the president wanted the legitimacy of bipartisan support—and the votes of Republicans—for his comprehensive health care reform plan. The White House focused on persuading moderate Republican senators Susan Collins and Olympia Snowe and lavished attention on them.[21]

In April 2009, the president renewed his call for bipartisan cooperation during a White House meeting with congressional leaders of both parties. However, Senate Minority Leader Mitch McConnell said the session did little to change the equation for Republicans. "We discussed bipartisanship and—of course—that will depend entirely on what the substance looks like," he said.[22] Yet the changes the Republicans demanded were not ones the president could make. His bipartisanship was more about collegiality and civility than it was about compromise on core issues.

Still, the president made efforts. Before he made his selection of Sonia Sotomayor to replace Justice David Souter, he called every member of the Senate Judiciary Committee. "He asked if I had any suggestions for nominees," said Republican senator Charles Grassley. "This is the first time I've ever been called by a president on a Supreme Court nomination, be it a Republican or a Democrat."[23] He also called all the members of the committee in preparation for his second nomination to the Court.[24]

In October, former Senate Republican leader Bill Frist, George W. Bush health and human services secretary Tommy G. Thompson, Medicare chief Mark McClellan, California Republican governor Arnold Schwarzenegger, and New York mayor Michael R. Bloomberg (a Republican turned Independent) spoke favorably of overhauling the nation's health care system (although couched with plenty of caveats regarding the details). Most of the endorsements came at the prompting of the White House, which immediately circulated and promoted the statements in e-mails and telephone calls.[25]

After Scott Brown won the special election in Massachusetts to replace Ted Kennedy in the Senate in January 2010, the Democrats lost their ability to defeat a filibuster, and the president tried once again for bipartisan support. Obama made bipartisanship a key element of his State of the Union address eight days later. In a high-profile televised question-and-answer session at a Republican policy forum, the president sparred with House Republicans, earning praise for his agility during a gathering that was meant to put the spotlight on the minority party and force its leaders to provide alternative solutions rather than simply object to the president's plans. Neither side gave much in terms of policy, even as they professed interest in moving past the bitterness of the past year and working together. Obama promised to invite Republican leaders to the White House once a month in 2010 to talk through issues with him and Democratic leaders.

Most significantly, the president hosted a bipartisan summit on health care at the Blair House. Obama felt that such an event could be an antidote to the cynicism about Washington expressed by voters and perhaps woo a few Republicans. Some White House allies said the session proved critical in putting health care back on the national agenda. The event enabled Obama to claim the high ground on bipartisanship; after Brown's victory, he needed to be seen as reaching out to the other side. He also wanted to force Republicans to put their ideas on the table, so that the public would see the debate as a choice between two ways to attack a pressing problem, not just a referendum on what Republicans derisively called "ObamaCare."[26]

On February 25, 2010, Obama and twenty-eight lawmakers squeezed around a square of tables in the Garden Room of Blair House. After more than seven hours of discussion, the president lingered behind, shaking hands, making one last pitch for his stalled initiative. "There were some good things that came out of that," he told advisers in the Oval Office afterward. He said he wanted the final legislation to incorporate a handful of ideas Republicans raised during the session. A few aides protested, asking if the White House should not extract a few votes in return. Yet Obama still held out hope for a couple of converts. "We're going to accept some of these," he replied.[27]

On March 2, 2010, Obama sent a letter to congressional leaders of both parties offering to address some of the concerns expressed by Republicans in the health care debate. The president said that he was open to four specific ideas raised by Republicans at the daylong health care forum the previous week, including encouraging the use of tax-advantaged medical savings accounts and increasing payments to doctors who treat Medicaid patients.[28]

Administration officials made overtures to several Republicans. They spoke to Peter Roskam. They conferred with John Shadegg about ways to sell insurance across state lines and with Tom Coburn about his idea to hire undercover Medicare fraud investigators. Even so, Republicans denounced the February summit as an eleventh-hour publicity stunt and declared that they would not help pass Obama's health care bill, even if it did include some of their proposals.[29]

On March 20, 2010, the day before the final House vote on health care reform, Obama told House Democrats that the bill was a compromise measure including many Republican ideas, even though congressional Republicans were all opposing it. "This bill tracks the recommendations not just of Democrat Tom Daschle, but also Republicans Bob Dole and Howard Baker," the president declared.[30]

After the passage of health care reform, the White House focused on financial regulation. Once again, he met with Republican leaders and sought their support. Once again, however, they rejected his overtures. For example, during a meeting with leaders of Congress from both parties at the White House, Republicans, and notably their leader in the Senate, Mitch McConnell, declined to support the measure offered by Senate Democrats, arguing that it would only make bailouts of gigantic, risk-laden institutions more likely.[31]

Difficulties in Managing Bipartisanship

The prospects for success diminished further in late April. For months, Republican senator Lindsey Graham worked with Democratic senator John Kerry and Independent Joseph Lieberman to craft climate-change legislation by reconciling the needs of the business and environmental communities. They sounded out key legislators, business groups, advocacy organizations, and others interested in the issue. In an effort to convince wavering senators to embrace the package, the senators focused on lining up support among business interests the bill would impact, holding dozens of closed-door meetings with groups ranging from the American Gas Association to the National Mining Association and the Portland Cement Association.

They planned to announce their bill with considerable fanfare on the morning of April 26, 2010. On April 24, however, Graham sent a sharply worded letter to his two colleagues announcing that he would no longer participate in negotiations on the energy bill. Graham's participation was essential because his support was needed to try to obtain support from other Republicans. As a result, the announcement was canceled.

Graham was troubled by reports that the Senate democratic leader Harry Reid and the White House were planning to take up an immigration measure before the energy bill. (Graham had worked with Democrats in the past on immigration matters and was expected to be an important bridge to Republicans on that issue as well.) Graham argued that any Senate debate on the highly charged subject of illegal immigration would make it impossible to deal with the difficult issues involved in national energy and global warming policy. He said in his letter that energy must come first and that Democrats appeared to be rushing to take up immigration because of rising anti-immigrant sentiment, including a harsh new measure signed into law in Arizona a few days before.

Graham had taken a substantial risk to be the lone Republican actively working on climate-change legislation. He was infuriated that it looked like the Democrats were going to leave him hanging on a limb. "I've got some political courage, but I'm not stupid," Graham declared in an interview. "The only reason I went forward is, I thought we had a shot if we got the business and environmental community behind our proposal, and everybody was focused on it. What's happened is that firm, strong commitment disappeared."[32] Graham also feared being labeled as supporting a gas tax. "I won't introduce a bill and have the majority leader . . . say, 'I can't support that gas tax.' I will not let this get blamed on me. It would be the worst thing in the world to take the one Republican working with you and make him own the one thing you don't like."[33]

A climate-change bill, but no immigration bill, had passed the House in 2009. However, Harry Reid was running for reelection in a state with a large Hispanic population. In addition, Republicans in Arizona gave Democrats a gift when they passed what many viewed as an extreme anti-immigration bill that received national attention. Some Democratic strategists saw the chance to cement relations with Hispanics.

Nevertheless, after fellow Democrats voiced skepticism, Reid backed off from his pledge to fast-track an overhaul of the nation's immigration laws on April 27. But the damage had been done, and there was little prospect of passing either an immigration reform or an energy–climate-change bill before the midterm elections.

Obama made good-faith efforts at bipartisanship, but was there any chance of success in the political climate of the era? Not really.

PUBLIC POLARIZATION

A primary reason for the difficulty of passing major changes in public policy is the challenge of obtaining support from the opposition party identifiers among the public. We know that partisan polarization reached record levels during the presidency of George W. Bush.[34] The election of Barack Obama did not diminish this polarization, which presented an obstacle to the new president when he tried to obtain support from Republicans. We can start with the election results to understand better this context.

The 2008 Election

In 2008 party-line voting was 89.1%, the second-highest level in the history of the American National Election Studies (ANES), which goes back to 1952. This level was surpassed only by the 89.9% level in 2004. Moreover, Obama's electoral coalition contained the smallest share of opposite-party identifiers of any president elected since the advent of the ANES time series, just 4.4%.[35]

Republicans and Republican-leaning Independents not only did not support Obama. By Election Day, they perceived a huge ideological gulf between themselves and the new president and viewed him as an untrustworthy radical leftist with a socialist agenda.[36] They did not just oppose him; they despised and feared him.

If we look at the states that deviated from Obama's share of the nationwide vote (about 52.9%) by 10 percentage points or more, we find

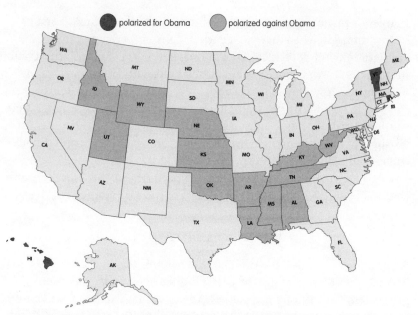

Figure 2. Polarization of states, 2008 presidential election.

that there were more "polarized" states than in any election in the previous sixty years.[37] A few states —Vermont, Rhode Island, Hawaii, and
the District of Columbia—were polarized in favor of Obama (see fig.
2). Most of the polarized states, however, voted for Republican John
McCain. The majority of these states form a belt stretching from West
Virginia, Kentucky, and Tennessee through Alabama, Mississippi, Louisiana, and Arkansas and over to Oklahoma, Kansas, and Nebraska. In
addition, Wyoming, Idaho, Utah, and Alaska were strongly in the Republican camp. Never before have many of these states voted so heavily
against a victorious Democrat.

The electoral polarization of the Bush years persisted in the 2008
presidential election, indicating that it represents more than a reaction
to George W. Bush (although he certainly exacerbated it).[38] The crucial
point, however, is that Obama has his work cut out for him to reach the
public in states that are turning increasingly red. It is possible that racial
prejudice exacerbated this polarization.[39]

Party and Ideological Divisions in the Public

The polarization evident in the 2008 election results did not end on Inauguration Day. Instead, it persisted in the underlying partisan and ideological divisions of the country.

When President Obama took office, he enjoyed a 68% approval level, the highest of any newly elected president since John F. Kennedy. For all of his hopes about bipartisanship, however, his early approval ratings were the most polarized of any president in the previous four decades. By February 15, less than a month after taking office, only 30% of Republicans approved of his performance in office, while 89% of Democrats and 63% of Independents approved.[40] The gap between Democratic and Republican approval had already reached 59 percentage points—and Obama never again reached even 30% approval among Republicans. By the one-hundred-day mark of his tenure, 92% of Democrats but only 28% of Republicans approved of his performance, a difference of 64 percentage points.[41]

The wide partisan divide in presidential approval ratings was not in itself new. From his first days in office, George W. Bush was a polarizing president, eventually the most polarizing in the history of public opinion polling. The first Gallup poll of his tenure found that he had the highest level of *disapproval* of any new president since polling began.[42] Similarly, Gary Jacobson reported that the public's initial reception of Bush reflected the widest partisan differences for any newly elected president in polling history. In the twenty-eight Gallup and CBS / New York Times polls taken before September 11, 2001, Bush's approval ratings averaged 88% among self-identified Republicans but only 31% among Democrats (Independents averaged 50%). This 57-point difference indicates an extraordinary degree of polarization.[43] Yet this gap between the assessments of Democrats and Republicans was just the beginning. In the Gallup poll of May 21–23, 2004, the difference between Bush's approval among Republicans (89%) and Democrats (12%) was an astounding 77 percentage points! That gap of 70 points or higher became common starting with Bush's fourth year in office.[44]

These were extreme and unprecedented levels of polarization.[45] No other president, dating back to Harry Truman, has had a partisan gap above 70 points in any Gallup poll in a reelection year. Moreover, Gallup had never before found such a high proportion of partisans with such strongly opposing views of a president. In the May 21–23, 2004, poll, 64% of Republicans said they strongly approved of the job Bush was doing as president, while 66% of Democrats strongly disapproved. As Gallup put it, "Bush is the only president who has had more than 6 in 10 of his party's identifiers strongly approving of him at the same time that more than 6 in 10 of the other party's identifiers strongly disapprove of him." The only other president to have more than 60% of a partisan group disapproving of him was Richard Nixon in the year of his resignation, when 61% of Democrats strongly disapproved of him. At that time, Nixon had overall job approval ratings below 30%.[46]

The fact that the public had been polarized under his predecessor was of little comfort to Obama. It merely showed the stability of the partisan divide and indicated the difficulty of reaching those identifying with the opposition party. Gallup reported that there was an average gap of 65 percentage points between Democrats' and Republicans' evaluations of the president in his first year, greatly exceeding the prior high of 52 percentage points for Bill Clinton.[47]

Moreover, ideological division reinforced partisan polarization. At the midpoint of the new president's first year in office, nearly half of Americans identified themselves as moderate or liberal white Democrats or conservative white Republicans, the poles of the political spectrum. Those in the middle were a much smaller group. Only 6% of the public said they were conservative white Democrats, and only 11% moderate/liberal white Republicans. In averaging its daily tracking polls over the July 1–August 17, 2009, period, Gallup found that the difference between white conservative Republicans and white moderate and liberal Democrats in evaluating the president's performance in office was 77 percentage points.[48]

The Democratic political organization Democracy Corps concluded from its focus groups that those in the conservative GOP base believe that Obama was "'ruthlessly advancing a secret agenda' to bankrupt the United States and dramatically expand government control to an extent nothing short of socialism."[49] These views reflect a profound sense of alienation.

Contributing to this polarization was the insulation of the opposition. Sixty-three percent of Republicans and Republican leaners reported that they received most of their news from Fox News.[50] The president's initial actions were grist for commentators on the Right, especially those on radio and cable television. They aggressively reinforced the fears of their audiences and encouraged active opposition to the White House.

PARTISAN POLARIZATION IN CONGRESS

Perhaps the most important fact about Congress in 2009 was that polarization was at a historic high.[51] According to Congressional Quarterly, George W. Bush presided over the most polarized period at the Capitol since the publisher began quantifying partisanship in the House and Senate in 1953. There had been a high percentage of party-unity votes—those that pitted a majority of Republicans against a majority of Democrats—and an increasing propensity of individual lawmakers to vote with their fellow partisans.[52] Little changed in 2009, as Congressional Quarterly found extraordinarily high levels of party-line voting even in the first weeks of the Obama administration.[53] By the end of the year, 57% of the votes in Congress were party-unity votes, just above the 56% average for the previous two decades.[54]

This polarization should not have been surprising. Republican constituencies send stalwart Republicans to Congress, whose job it is to oppose a Democratic president. Most of these senators and representatives were unlikely to be responsive to core Obama supporters. They knew their constituencies, and they knew Obama was unlikely to have much support among them. Thus, few of the Republicans' electoral constituencies showed any enthusiasm for health care reform. As Gary Jacobson put it, the partisan divisions that emerged in Congress on the health care issue were firmly rooted in district opinion and electoral politics.[55]

On the day before the House voted on the final version of the economic stimulus bill, the president took Aaron Schock, a freshman Republican member of Congress, aboard Air Force One to visit Illinois. Before an audience in Schock's district, Obama praised him as "a very talented young man" and expressed "great confidence in him to do the right thing for the people of Peoria." But when the representative stood on the House floor less than twenty-four hours later, his view of the right thing for the people of Peoria was to vote against the president. "They know that this bill is not stimulus," Schock said of his constituents. "They know that this bill will not do anything to create long-term, sustained economic growth."[56] Schock was typical of Republicans in early 2009, who viewed the stimulus debate as an opportunity to rededicate their divided, demoralized party around the ideas of big tax cuts and limited government spending.

In the 111th Congress (2009–2010), nearly half of the Republicans in both the House and the Senate were elected from the eleven states of the Confederacy, plus Kentucky and Oklahoma. In each chamber, southerners were a larger share of the Republican caucus than ever before. At the same time, Republicans held a smaller share of nonsouthern seats in the House and the Senate than at any other point in Congress's history except during the early days of the New Deal.[57] The party's increasing identification with staunch southern economic and social conservatism made it much more difficult for Obama to reach across the aisle. Southern House Republicans, for instance, overwhelmingly opposed him, even on the handful of issues where he has made inroads among GOP legislators from other regions. Nearly one-third of House Republicans from outside of the South supported expanding the State Children's Health Insurance Program, but only one-tenth of southern House Republicans did so. Likewise, just 5% of southern House Republicans supported the bill expanding the national service program, compared with 22% of Republicans from other states.

The Republican Party's losses in swing areas after 2006 accelerated its homogenization. Few Republicans represent Democratic-leaning districts. As a result, far fewer congressional Republicans than Democrats must worry most about moderate public opinion. Fully 31 of the 40 Republican senators serving in 2009 (31 of 41 in 2010), for example, were elected from the eighteen states that twice backed Bush and also opposed Obama. Five other senators represented states that voted for Bush twice and then supported Obama. Just six Republican senators were elected by states that voted Democratic in at least two of the past three presidential elections. One of these lawmakers, Arlen Specter of Pennsylvania, switched parties to become a Democrat.

Table 2 shows the impact of these constituency cross-pressures on voting of Republican senators in 2009. The Republican senators representing states that voted consistently Republican in presidential elections voted in a considerably more conservative direction than their party colleagues from states that were more likely to support Democratic presidential candidates. Moreover, most Republican senators represented reliably Republican states.

In addition, Republican members of Congress faced strong pres-

Table 2. Senate Republican conservatism by partisanship of state, 2009		
Times states voted Republican in 2000–2008 presidential elections	Number of senators	Average conservative score[a]
0	3	60
1	2	69
2	5	73
3	31	82
Source: Ronald Brownstein, "Serving behind Enemy Lines," *National Journal*, April 24, 2010. *Note:* [a] Calculated by *National Journal*, which ranks members along a liberal-to-conservative continuum.		

sure to oppose proposals of the other party. Senators Max Baucus and Charles Grassley, the leaders of the Senate Finance Committee's negotiations over health care reform, both confronted whispers that they might lose their leadership positions if they conceded too much to the other side. Iowa conservatives even threatened that Grassley could face a 2010 primary challenge if he backed Baucus. In a similar vein, the executive committee of the Charleston County, South Carolina, Republican Party censored Republican senator Lindsey Graham because "U.S. Sen. Lindsey Graham in the name of bipartisanship continues to weaken the Republican brand and tarnish the ideals of freedom, rule of law, and fiscal conservatism."[58] Two months later the Lexington County Republican Party Executive Committee censored him for his stands on a range of policies, which, it charged, "debased" Republican beliefs.[59]

In January 2010, 55% of Republicans and Republican leaners wanted Republican leaders in Congress, who were following a consistently conservative path, to move in a more conservative direction.[60] In perhaps the most extreme expression of this orientation, four months later the Utah Republican party denied longtime conservative senator Robert Bennett its nomination for reelection. The previous month, Republican governor Charlie Crist had to leave his party and run for the Senate as an Independent in Florida because he was unlikely to win the Republican nomination against conservative Marco Rubio. A year earlier, Republican senator Arlen Specter of Pennsylvania switched parties, believing there was little chance he could win a Republican primary against conservative Pat Toomey.

Similarly, House Republicans with any moderate leanings were more concerned about the pressures from their right than about potential fallout from opposing a popular president. The conservative Republican Study Committee—which included more than 100 of the 178 House Republicans—called for enforcing party unity on big issues and hinted at retribution against defectors. Conservatives also raised the prospect of primary challenges,[61] as they did in the 2009 race to fill the seat in New York State's twenty-third congressional district. Led by Sarah Palin and Dick Armey, conservatives forced the Republican candidate to withdraw from the race shortly before Election Day.

Compounding the pressure has been the development of partisan communications networks—led by liberal blogs and conservative talk radio—that relentlessly incite each party's base against the other. These constant fusillades help explain why presidents now face lopsided disapproval from the opposition party's voters more quickly than ever, a trend that discourages that party's legislators from working with the White House.

These centrifugal forces affect most the Republican Party. The Right has more leverage to discipline legislators because, as we have seen, conservative voters constitute a larger share of the GOP coalition than liberals do of the Democratic Party. The Right's partisan communications network is also more ferocious than the Left's.

Given the broad influences of ideology and constituency, it is not surprising that Frances Lee has shown that presidential leadership itself demarcates and deepens cleavages in Congress. The differences between the parties and the cohesion within them on floor votes are typically greater when the president takes a stand on issues. When the president adopts a position, members of his party have a stake in his success, while opposition party members have a stake in the president's losing. Moreover, both parties take cues from the president that help define their policy views, especially when the lines of party cleavage are not clearly at stake or are not already well established.[62] This dynamic of presidential leadership was likely to complicate further Obama's efforts to win Republican support.

THE BOTTOM LINE

Given what we know about the prospects of bipartisanship, we should expect that such a strategy for governing would fail—despite the White

House's efforts. And that is exactly what happened. The Senate approved the president-elect's request to release the TARP funds by a 52-42 margin, but only six Republicans voted for Obama's request. House Republicans were even more uniform in their opposition to the economic stimulus bill, the new president's highest priority. Minority Leader John Boehner told his caucus in a meeting before the president arrived that he was going to oppose the House package and that they should too. Similarly, the next day's debate contrasted with the president's conciliatory gestures. In the end, all but eleven Democrats voted for the plan, but not a single Republicans supported it. Even after negotiations with the Senate that pared down the cost of the bill, no Republicans voted for its final passage.

The president did little better with Republicans in the Senate than in the House. Only three GOP senators supported each version of the stimulus bill: Olympia Snowe and Susan Collins of Maine and Arlen Specter of Pennsylvania—the three most moderate Republican senators. (Soon after, Specter switched parties and became a Democrat.) Adding insult to injury, Republican senator Judd Gregg of New Hampshire withdrew as nominee for secretary of commerce, citing "irresolvable conflicts" with the president over his economic stimulus plan. "We are functioning," he added, "from a different set of views on many critical items of policy."[63]

Supported by the likes of Rush Limbaugh (who declared that he hoped Obama's presidency failed) and Sean Hannity (who denounced the stimulus bill on Fox News as the European Socialist Act of 2009), Republicans found their voice in adamant opposition, just as they did with Bill Clinton in 1993 and 1994. Even in the glow of a presidential honeymoon, in the context of Obama's outreach efforts, and in the face of a national economic crisis, they chose to employ harsh language and loaded terms such as "socialism" to describe his policies. Rediscovering the shortcomings of budget deficits and pork-barrel spending, Republicans ran radio advertisements in the districts of thirty Democrats, accusing them of "wasteful Washington spending." It is no surprise that the budget resolution for fiscal 2010 did not garner a single Republican vote in either chamber.

In June, the House passed the landmark American Clean Energy and Security Act, designed to curb U.S. greenhouse-gas emissions. It attracted only eight Republican representatives. When the House voted on the health care reform bill on November 7, 2009, it received only one Republican vote. The sole supporter was Representative Anh Cao of Louisiana, a freshman from a New Orleans–based district that went 75% for Obama. His victory resulted from two unique factors. First, his opponent, incumbent representative William J. Jefferson, was under indictment on federal corruption charges. Second, Hurricane Gustav pushed the congressional election in that district into December, when Democratic turnout was much lower than during the presidential election the previous month. When it came to voting on the final version of the bill, no Republicans in either House voted in support of the White House.

La Plus Ça Change . . .

Despite its efforts, bipartisanship was not a success for the Obama White House and is unlikely to be a successful strategy for governing in the immediate future. Critical features of the context of the Obama presidency, especially the high levels of partisan polarization in the public and Congress, made it unlikely that the president would obtain any significant Republican support for his core initiatives. Only if Obama adopted Republican policies would he receive Republican support. Yet no one should have expected him to become a hard-right conservative.

Some political commentators imply that all the president has to do to obtain the support of the public or Congress is to reach into his inventory of leadership skills and employ the appropriate means of persuasion, but such a view is naive. There is no silver bullet.

It is especially important to recognize that successful leadership is not found in the dominant chief executive of political folklore who restructures the contours of the political landscape, altering his strategic position to pave the way for change. Rather than persons who create the conditions for important shifts in public policy, such as attracting bipartisan support, effective leaders are the less heroic facilitators who work at the margins of coalition-building to recognize and exploit opportunities in their environments. President Obama will be no exception.

NOTES

1. Shailagh Murray, Michael D. Shear, and Paul Kane, "2009 Democratic Agenda Severely Weakened by Republicans' United Opposition," *Washington Post*, Jan. 24, 2010.

2. Scott Wilson, "Bruised by Stimulus Battle, Obama Changed His Approach to Washington," *Washington Post*, April 29, 2009.

3. John Harwood, "'Partisan' Seeks a Prefix: Bi- or Post-," *New York Times*, Dec. 7, 2008.

4. Quoted ibid.

5. Transcript of press conference on Nov. 25, 2008, Clips & Comment, www.clipsandcomment.com/2008/11/25/transcript-barack-obama-news-conference-the-economy-november-25-2008/.

6. Quoted in Ronald Brownstein, *The Second Civil War* (New York: Penguin Press, 2007), 240–48, 252, 287, quote on 246.

7. Ibid., 229–30, 249–52, 287–96; Dowd quoted in Robert Draper, *Dead Certain: The Presidency of George W. Bush* (New York: Free Press, 2007), 230.

8. Quotes from David D. Kirkpatrick, "Obama Reaches Out for McCain's Counsel," *New York Times*, Jan. 19, 2009; Jeff Zeleny and David M. Herszenhorn, "Obama Seeks Wide Support in Congress for Stimulus," *New York Times*, Jan. 6, 2009.

9. Jonathan Weisman and Laura Meckler, "Obama Reaches Out to Republicans," *Wall Street Journal*, Dec. 15, 2008, 10; Jeff Zeleny, "Initial Steps by Obama Suggest a Bipartisan Flair," *New York Times*, Nov. 24, 2008.

10. Ronald Brownstein, "Two Visions of Leadership," *National Journal*, Jan. 17, 2009.

11. Howard Kurtz, "Obama Charms Even a Night's Grand Ol' Party," *Washington Post*, Jan. 15, 2009, C1.

12. Kirkpatrick, "Obama Reaches Out."

13. Quotes from Carl Hulse, "Obama Team Makes Early Efforts to Show Willingness to Reach Out to Republicans," *New York Times*, Jan. 19, 2009; David M. Herszenhorn, "Obama Officials Ask Senate G.O.P. to Back Release of Bailout Money," *New York Times*, Jan. 15, 2009.

14. Jackie Calmes and David M. Herszenhorn, "Obama Presses for Quick Jolt to the Economy," *New York Times*, Jan. 24, 2009.

15. See Dana Milbank, "The Republicans Are Smiling, but They're Not Buying," *Washington Post*, Jan. 28, 2009, A3; Jackie Calmes and Carl Hulse, "Obama, Visiting G.O.P. Lawmakers, Is Open to Some Compromise on Stimulus," *New York Times*, Jan. 28, 2009; Jackie Calmes, "House Passes Stimulus Plan despite G.O.P. Opposition," *New York Times*, Jan. 29, 2009.

16. Calmes, "House Passes Stimulus Plan."

17. Carl Hulse, "Short-Circuiting Bipartisanship Is Nothing New for Congress," *New York Times*, Feb. 14, 2009.

18. Peter Baker, "Taking on Critics, Obama Puts Aside Talk of Unity," *New York Times*, Feb. 10, 2009.

19. Wilson, "Bruised by Stimulus Battle."

20. Mark Leibovich, "Missing Element in Obama's Ties with G.O.P. Leaders: Good Chemistry," *New York Times*, Feb. 24, 2010; Cantor quoted in Peter Baker, "The Limits of Rahmism," *New York Times Magazine*, March 14, 2010.

21. See, for example, John Harwood, "The President's Best Hope in the G.O.P.," *New York Times*, Sept. 20, 2009; Sheryl Gay Stolberg, "Taking Health Care Courtship Up Another Notch," *New York Times*, Sept. 27, 2009.

22. Quoted in Kathleen Hunter, "GOP Lawmakers Unmoved by Obama Overtures of Bipartisanship," *CQ Daily News*, April 23, 2009.

23. Peter Baker and Adam Nagourney, "Sotomayor Pick a Product of Lessons from Past Battles," *New York Times*, May 28, 2009.

24. Sheryl Gay Stolberg, "A Brisk First Round on Supreme Court Search," *New York Times*, April 22, 2010.

25. Michael D. Shear and Ceci Connolly, "Reform Gets Conditional GOP Support: Urged by the White House, Republicans Speak Up for Bipartisan Health Fix," *Washington Post*, Oct. 7, 2009.

26. Sheryl Gay Stolberg, Jeff Zeleny, and Carl Hulse, "The Long Road Back," *New York Times*, March 21, 2010; Ceci Connolly, "How Obama Revived His Health-Care Bill," *Washington Post*, March 23, 2010.

27. Connolly, "How Obama Revived His Health-Care Bill."

28. David M. Herszenhorn and Robert Pear, "Obama Offers to Use Some G.O.P. Health Proposals," *New York Times*, March 2, 1010.

29. Connolly, "How Obama Revived His Health-Care Bill."

30. "Remarks by the President to the House Democratic Congress," White House Transcript, March 20, 2010, www.whitehouse.gov/the-press-office/remarks-president-house-democratic-congress.

31. Sheryl Gay Stolberg and David M. Herszenhorn, "Obama Finds G.O.P. Resistance in Meeting on Financial Bill," *New York Times*, April 14, 2010.

32. Quoted in Juliet Eilperin, "On Climate Bill, Democrats Work to Overcome Graham's Immigration Objections," *Washington Post*, April 26, 2010.

33. Quoted in Ezra Klein, "Sen. Lindsey Graham: 'I Care Equally about Immigration and Climate Change,'" *Washington Post*, April 29, 2010.

34. See Gary C. Jacobson, *A Divider, Not a Uniter: George W. Bush and the American Public*, 3rd ed. (New York: Longman, 2010).

35. If independent leaners are included as partisans, the figure rises to 8.0%; only John F. Kennedy attracted fewer (7.1%). These figures are from Gary C. Jacobson, "Barack Obama and the American Public: From Candidate to Pres-

ident," paper delivered at the "Conference on the Early Obama Presidency," Centre for the Study of Democracy, Univ. of Westminster, London, May 14, 2010, 6–7.

36. Ibid., 7–11.

37. Jay Cost, "Electoral Polarization Continues under Obama," RealClear-Politics HorseRaceBlog, Nov. 20, 2008.

38. See Jacobson, *A Divider, Not a Uniter.*

39. Michael Lewis-Beck, Charles Tien, and Richard Nadeau, "Obama's Missed Landslide: A Racial Cost?" *PS: Political Science and Politics* 43 (Jan. 2010): 69–76.

40. Gallup Daily tracking averages for Feb. 9–15, 2009, Gallup, www.gallup.com/poll/116479/barack-obama-presidential-job-approval.aspx.

41. Gallup Daily tracking averages for April 20–26, 2009, ibid.

42. Gallup Poll, News Release, Jan. 5, 2001.

43. Gary C. Jacobson, "The Bush Presidency and the American Electorate," *Presidential Studies Quarterly* 33 (Dec. 2003): 701–29.

44. See, for example, Jeffrey M. Jones, "Bush Ratings Show Historical Levels of Polarization," *Gallup News Service,* June 4, 2004.

45. This point is nicely illustrated in Jacobson, *A Divider, Not a Uniter,* chap. 1.

46. Jones, "Bush Ratings Show Historical Levels."

47. Jeffrey M. Jones, "Obama's Approval Most Polarized for First-Year President," Gallup Poll, Jan. 25, 2010, www.gallup.com/poll/125345/Obama-Approval-Polarized-First-Year-President.aspx.

48. Gallup Poll Daily Tracking polls from July to mid-August 2009, including more than 47,000 interviews, www.gallup.com/poll/122672/Conservative-Democrats-Liberal-Republicans-Hard-To-Find.aspx.

49. Charlie Cook, "Intensity Matters," *National Journal,* Oct. 24, 2009.

50. Pew Research Media Attitudes Survey, July 22–26, 2009, The Pew Research Center for the People & the Press, http://people-press.org/report/543/.

51. Nolan McCarty, Keith T. Poole, and Howard Rosenthal, *Polarized America: The Dance of Ideology and Unequal Riches* (Cambridge, MA: MIT Press, 2006).

52. Shawn Zeller, "Party Unity—Parties Dig In Deep on a Fractured Hill," *CQ Weekly,* Dec. 15, 2008, 3332–41.

53. John Cranford, "This Change Isn't Very Hopeful," *CQ Weekly,* Feb. 17, 2009, 335.

54. Richard Rubin, "Party Unity: An Even Thicker Dividing Line," *CQ Weekly,* Jan. 11, 2010, 124.

55. Jacobson, "Barack Obama and the American Public," 18–19.

56. Peter Baker, "Bipartisanship Isn't So Easy, Obama Sees," *New York Times,* Feb. 13, 2009.

57. Ronald Brownstein, "For GOP, a Southern Exposure," *National Journal,* May 23, 2009.

58. Bruce Smith, "Graham Censured by Charleston County GOP," *State,* Nov. 12, 2009.

59. Lexington County Republican Party, "Lexington County Party Passes Resolution of Censure for Lindsey Graham," accessed at www.lcrp-online. com/1.html.

60. Pew Research Center for the People and the Press poll, Jan. 6–10, 2010.

61. Alan K. Ota, "GOP Moderates See Political Benefits in Opposing Obama's Economic Agenda," *CQ Today,* Feb. 6, 2009.

62. Frances E. Lee, *Beyond Ideology: Politics, Principles, and Partisanship in the U.S. Senate* (Chicago: Univ. of Chicago Press, 2009), chap. 4.

63. Jeff Zeleny, "Gregg Ends Bid for Commerce Job," *New York Times,* Feb. 13, 2009.

OUR CONTINUING CULT OF THE PRESIDENCY

Gene Healy

In addressing our continuing cult of the presidency, I shall answer five critical questions, which speak to the status of presidential power today.

1. Has the presidency become too powerful?
2. Would the Founders approve of today's presidency?
3. Does the presidency threaten our system of checks and balances?
4. To what extent has the presidency contributed to public distrust of government?
5. Do we as Americans rely too much on presidential leadership to solve our problems?

The answers, as I see them, are "yes," "no," "yes," "it's complicated," and "yes."

In the course of this essay, I'll say more about each of these questions, but my main focus will be on the last one: "Do we as Americans rely too much on presidential leadership to solve our problems?" I think that's the central question, and I think it's obvious that the answer is yes. Our national tendency to ask too much of the office is the source of most of our dissatisfaction with it. We look to the presidency to solve problems it was never designed to solve, problems that no single man or woman could solve—problems that may well be beyond the capacity of any political institution, however constituted, to solve.

Worse still, the irrational expectations we invest in the office drive the growth of presidential power. When you ask a man to perform miracles, don't be surprised when he seeks powers to match that responsibility. And, having demanded the impossible, don't be surprised when you're disappointed with the results. When it comes to the presidency, we demand what we cannot have, and as a result, we usually get what we do not like. As Theodore Lowi has noted: "There are built-in barriers to presidents' delivering on their promises, and the unlikely occasion of one doing so would only engender another round of new policies, with new responsibilities and new demands for help. . . . This is a pathology because it escalates the rhetoric at home, ratcheting expectations upward notch by notch, and fuels adventurism abroad, in a world where the cost of failure can be annihilation."[1] That dynamic has left us with a presidency that is a constitutional monstrosity: at once menacing and ineffectual.

On the campaign trail in 2008, presidential candidate Hillary Clinton declared, "We need a president who is ready on day one to be commander in chief of our economy."[2] It seemed an odd phrase at the time, given that the Constitution contemplates no such role for the federal government's chief executive officer. But two years into the Obama era, "commander in chief of the U.S. economy" seemed to fit. After all, as a result of the financial crisis, we had a president who could appoint a czar to set executive pay at major companies—a president who could fire the CEO of GM without so much as a courtesy call to major shareholders.

And yet, despite his vast powers, President Obama seemed unable to meet the public's enormous expectations for the office. By spring 2010, his approval rating was below 50 percent and dropping, as hundreds of thousands of gallons of oil spilled into the Gulf of Mexico and the punditocracy chastised him for looking weak, ineffectual, and uncaring.

This essay examines the growth of executive power and responsibility in the Bush and Obama presidencies. Both presidents amassed enormous power in a period of deep public frustration with presidential leadership. Partisans on each side of the political aisle have offered ideological explanations for Bush's and Obama's drives for increased power. Just as the Left saw neoconservative influence as the reason for the Bush power grab, the Right interprets Obama's domineering presidency as a direct result of his allegedly quasi-socialist ideology.

I'll argue that "We the People" can't get off that easily. In the twin crises that bookended the first decade of the 2000s—9/11 and the financial meltdown of 2008–2009—it was Americans' demands for bold presidential action that provided powerful incentives for concentration of power in the executive branch. As Lowi has suggested, the "Pogo

Principle" is the key factor driving the presidency's growth: "We have met the enemy, and he is us."

WITH GREAT RESPONSIBILITY COMES GREAT POWER

Surveying the pedagogical materials of the late 1960s, political scientist Thomas Cronin concluded that the president described in America's textbooks was "Superman." Americans no longer thought of the president as a constitutional officer with an important, but limited, job. Instead, they expected the president to swoop in and vanquish all manner of threats, foreign and domestic. The president had become a heroic figure who, "by attacking problems frontally and aggressively, and interpreting his power expansively, can be the engine of change to move this nation forward."[3]

Much has changed in the more than forty years since Cronin wrote those words, but the president's job description still requires a superhero. And, to reverse the credo of another comic book hero: with great responsibility comes great power. If the president is charged with righting all the country's and the world's wrongs, he's going to seek the power he needs to discharge those responsibilities. Over the course of the twentieth century, that dynamic fed the presidency's growth. And as a result, the presidency has become far more powerful than our Constitution's Framers ever expected it to be.

Would the Founders approve of today's presidency? Surely not. Even Alexander Hamilton, the Founding generation's leading advocate of a muscular presidency, might be given pause by some of the unitary executive theory's most outlandish claims—and he'd likely shrink from the notion that the buck stops with the chief executive on matters ranging from health care, to unemployment, to the progress of liberty abroad.[4]

But that in itself is not sufficient reason to regret the presidency's growth. After all, there are many aspects of modern American life from which certain Founders might recoil. We needn't regret the fact that we've become a rapidly urbanizing commercial republic just because it would have offended Jefferson's agrarian sensibilities, nor are we compelled to reject paper money simply because Madison did.[5] The Founders weren't oracles, after all; they were, like all of us, flawed persons of limited vision. *The Federalist* itself warns against a "blind veneration for antiquity."[6]

That said, we shouldn't ignore the Founders' views when we evaluate the modern presidency. If we want to be governed by law and not by men, then it matters whether the Constitution that the Founding generation drafted and ratified authorizes the powers that the modern president claims. If it doesn't, and we decide nonetheless that those powers are necessary, the Framers set up an amendment process through which we can delegate new powers.

But before we authorize or acquiesce to those powers, it's worth reflecting on the reasons they decided not to concentrate enormous unchecked power in the chief magistrate's hands. The Founders believed that there were limits to government's ability to solve social problems, that human nature was fallible, that man was easily corrupted by power, and that unchecked power was therefore exceedingly dangerous. The science of human nature has advanced dramatically since the late eighteenth century; but nothing we've learned seriously challenges their central insights.[7]

THE POGO PRINCIPLE AND PRESIDENTIAL POWER IN THE BUSH YEARS

"The accumulation of all powers, legislative, executive, and judiciary, in the same hands . . . may justly be pronounced the very definition of tyranny," Madison wrote in Federalist No. 47.[8] Seeking to maximize its freedom to respond to the 9/11 attacks, the Bush administration made a number of highly controversial constitutional claims, claims that made the modern presidency resemble Madison's nightmare. Among other things, the administration claimed that

- the president has, in the words of administration official John Yoo, "the right to start wars"—and he doesn't need any permission from Congress;[9]
- the president has virtually unlimited power to tap phones and read e-mail for national security purposes—and he doesn't need to ask a judge for a warrant; and[10]
- the president can seize American citizens on American soil and lock them up for the duration of the war on terror—perhaps forever—without ever having to answer to a judge.[11]

The conventional narrative holds that the constitutional innovations of the Bush years—warrantless wiretapping, the torture memos, the use of signing statements to nullify provisions of perfectly valid laws—were the handiwork of a cabal of ideologues, led by Dick Cheney, that had long believed America had made an enormous mistake by trying to cabin presidential power after Watergate. The conventional narrative isn't wrong—it's just incomplete. What also drove the power grab was unrealistic public expectations about the level of protection the president can and should provide against terrorism.

In his swan-song press conference on January 12, 2008, an enervated President Bush grew momentarily animated when asked about the damage to America's "moral standing" that resulted from Guantanamo Bay and "enhanced interrogation" techniques. Bush shot back:

> All these debates will matter naught if there's another attack on the homeland. The question won't be, you know, "Were you critical of this plan or not?" The question's going to be, "Why didn't you do something?"
>
> Do you remember what it was like right after September the 11th around here? In press conferences, in opinion pieces and in stories that sometimes were news stories and sometimes opinion pieces, people were saying, "How come they didn't see it? How come they didn't connect the dots?"
>
> Do you remember what the environment was like in Washington—I do—when people were hauled in front of Congress and members of Congress were asking questions about, "How come you didn't know this that or the other?"[12]

"Why didn't you do something?" Much of the Bush administration's relentless drive to expand its powers can be explained as an attempt to avoid ever having to answer that question again. Former Office of Legal Counsel head Jack Goldsmith, a dissenter from the Bush administration's absolutist theories of executive power, often clashed with Dick Cheney's deputy David Addington, perhaps the administration's most zealous advocate of those theories. But Goldsmith understood why Addington was so unrelenting: "He believed *presidential power was co-extensive with presidential responsibility.* Since the president would be blamed for the next homeland attack, he must have the power under the Constitution to do what he deemed necessary to stop it, regardless of what Congress said."[13] As Goldsmith put it, any post-9/11 president, whether Republican or Democrat, will be "acutely aware that he or she alone will be *wholly responsible* when thousands of Americans are killed in the next attack" and will act accordingly.[14]

It is, of course, perverse to hold the president "wholly responsible" for terrorist attacks on American soil. In an open society of 300 million people, no president can provide perfect protection against determined fanatics whose choice of targets is virtually limitless. But Goldsmith is probably right about the political calculus that informs executive-branch decision making. If presidents believe that their political opponents and the electorate at large will hold them accountable for providing protection that no free society can provide, they're likely to seek powers that no free society ought to let them have.

The political aftermath of Hurricane Katrina shows that those pressures can drive the growth of presidential power even in areas far removed from the threat of terrorism. In business or in government, no executive will long tolerate responsibility without authority. And in late summer 2005, when New Orleans was under water and desperate for assistance, the president found himself held accountable for failing to take actions he didn't have clear legal authority to take. As Colby Cosh of Canada's *National Post* put it at the time, "the 49 percent of Americans who have been complaining for five years about George W. Bush being a dictator are now vexed to the point of utter incoherence because for the last fortnight he has failed to do a sufficiently convincing impression of a dictator."[15]

To be sure, the administration deserved plenty of blame for bungling the disaster relief tasks it had the power to carry out. But it soon became clear that the public held the president responsible for performing feats above and beyond his legal authority. One almost had to feel sorry for Michael "Heckuva Job" Brown(ie), the disgraced former Federal Emergency Management Agency head, when he was obliged to appear on Capitol Hill a month after the hurricane to inform an irate Representative Chris Shays (R-CT) that in our federalist system, the FEMA chief has no power to order mandatory evacuations or to become "this superhero that is going to step in there and suddenly take everybody out of New Orleans." "That is just talk," Shays responded. "Were you in contact with the military?"[16]

For a president beleaguered by public demands, seizing new powers can be an adaptive response. Small wonder, then, that the Bush administration promptly sought enhanced authority for domestic use of the military. Although few in the media noticed at the time, the president received that authority. On October 17, 2006, the same day he signed the Military Commissions Act, ratifying many of the powers he'd long claimed to try enemy combatants via military tribunals, the president also signed a defense authorization bill that contained gaping new exceptions to the Posse Comitatus Act of 1878, the federal law that restricts the president's power to use the standing army to enforce order at home.

The new exceptions to the act gave the president power to use U.S. armed forces to "restore public order and enforce the laws" when confronted with "natural disasters," "public health emergencies," and "other . . . incidents"—a catchall phrase that radically expands the president's ability to use troops against his own citizens.[17] Under it, the president could, if he chose, fight a federal War on Hurricanes, declaring himself supreme military commander in any state where he thought conditions warranted it. And it came about as a direct result of the public's demands that the president protect Americans from the hazards of cyclical bad weather. Thanks largely to Senator Patrick Leahy (D-VT), that provision was repealed in January 2008, but the outsized public expectations that gave rise to it haven't abated.[18] When disaster strikes, all eyes still turn to the president, and the public demands, "Why didn't you do something?" And so long as we Americans look first to the president for the cure to whatever ails us, we can hardly complain when presidents seek to enhance their powers.

IS PRESIDENTIAL POWER THE POWER TO PERSUADE?

There's another conventional narrative that says that the backlash that resulted from the Bush administration's extravagant claims of inherent presidential power made Bush the rare president who left the office weaker than he found it. "By trying to strengthen the presidency [Cheney] weakened it," Stuart Taylor and Evan Thomas write in a January 2009 *Newsweek* cover story. Jack Goldsmith echoes their critique, declaring that we should be "less worried about an out-of-control presidency than an enfeebled one."[19]

In this case, there's a lot less to be said for the conventional wisdom. It's true that the judiciary has moved to check presidential power in recent years, challenging the Bush team's assertions of unilateral power to dispose of enemy combatants as they see fit. Congress, however, remains a "Broken Branch," as eager as ever to delegate away its constitutional responsibilities.[20] And at a time when the Treasury secretary is busily reshaping the commanding heights of finance with precious little input from Congress, it's hard to understand how anyone could think that the executive branch has lost power over the years since 2001.

In fact, one of the more interesting aspects of the Bush legacy is the challenge it offers to the argument presented in one of the seminal texts of presidential scholarship, Richard Neustadt's *Presidential Power and the Modern Presidents*. That book, first published on the cusp of the New Frontier in 1960, emphasized that "presidential power is the power of persuasion."[21] It insisted that presidential unilateralism—direct commands, based on an appeal to the president's formal, constitutional powers—did not work.

In his contribution to the conference "The Future of the American Presidency," Robert J. Spitzer documented how, armed with unitary executive theory, the Bush administration used "constitutional/command authority" to expand its powers, undermining Neustadt's argument that presidential success comes from use of "the power to bargain," rather than executive fiat.[22] As Professor Spitzer explained, President Bush expanded his powers not by cajoling Congress and the public, but through "command, not persuasion, and constitutional command at that."[23]

There's another, perhaps less direct, way in which the second Bush presidency undermines Neustadt's perspective. Neustadt maintains that political capital is key to a successful presidency—that presidents need to husband that capital, employing it strategically to achieve their aims.

But if presidential power is "the power to persuade," how do we explain the growth of presidential power in George W. Bush's second term? A year after his reelection, with his popularity plummeting as a result of Katrina and the Iraq War, George W. Bush had lost the ability to persuade virtually anyone. And yet, while he was on his way toward becoming the most reviled president in thirty years, President Bush continued to amass powers that his predecessors could hardly dream of.

As one of its last major acts, in October 2006 the 109th Congress responded to the Supreme Court's June 2005 *Hamdan* decision with legislation authorizing military commissions. Among other things, the Military Commissions Act (MCA) of 2006 declared that the Geneva

Convention did not apply to noncitizen detainees and that terrorist suspects could not challenge their detention in American courts.[24] In the administration's view, the latter provision applies even to legal residents of the United States, so long as they're not citizens. In fact, under the statute's definition of "unlawful enemy combatant" the president arguably has the power to seize American citizens.[25]

A month after the MCA's passage, the voters elected a Democratic Congress, but the new majority proved utterly unable to prevent the president from sending more troops to fight a war that most Americans by then considered a disaster. In August 2007, eager to leave town for summer recess, Congress passed the Protect America Act (PAA), which effectively legalized the National Security Agency surveillance program, removing the Foreign Intelligence Surveillance Act (FISA) court from individualized review of wiretaps of Americans' phone calls and e-mails when the government "reasonably believe[s]" that the targeted person on the other end is outside the United States.[26] In the summer of 2008, after that law expired, Congress passed the FISA Amendments Act, which left very little of the original Foreign Intelligence Surveillance Act standing. Like the PAA, the FISA Amendments Act removed the requirement for individualized warrants. Instead, FISA court judges would approve the parameters of executive surveillance programs, without access to information about the targets to be observed or the factual basis for observing them.[27]

The last months of the Bush administration repeated the pattern that had prevailed throughout Bush's two terms: the announcement of an unprecedented crisis, demands for new presidential powers to meet that crisis, and—after some perfunctory grumbling—Congress's capitulation to presidential demands. By October 2008, Bush Treasury secretary Henry Paulson looked a lot like the modern equivalent of a Roman dictator for financial affairs, using a broad delegation of authority from Congress to decide which companies would live or die, based on the $700 billion he'd been authorized to commit.

But perhaps Bush's success in manipulating a compliant Congress isn't fatal to Neustadt's argument. One could argue that the growth of presidential power during an extended period of presidential unpopularity is nonetheless consistent with the Neustadt thesis: that in an atmosphere of crisis the president nonetheless exercised "the power to bargain," persuading Congress to amplify his powers. Neustadt's main examples, after all—Truman's firing MacArthur and seizing the steel companies and Eisenhower's use of the army to enforce desegregation in Little Rock—showcase the limits of presidential unilateralism.[28] Perhaps it's a caricature of Neustadt's thesis to reduce it to a statement that presidential popularity translates to power. If Congress rolls over for an unpopular president, hasn't that president by definition exercised the power to persuade?

Fair enough. But even if aspects of the Neustadt thesis remain valid, the Bush experience suggests that presidential scholars ought at least to adjust the importance they attribute to political capital and the power to bargain.

Madison expected the branches themselves to maintain the proper separation of powers. Ambition would counteract ambition, and congressmen, judges, and presidents would each fight to maintain their institution's place in the constitutional order. But Madison's vision hasn't worked out as planned. Individual presidents have more than enough incentive to protect their power, but individual congressmen are more interested in getting reelected, and it's rare indeed than any legislator gets punished by his constituents for shirking his constitutional responsibilities or delegating too much power to the executive branch. Nor did either Madison or Neustadt envision the post-9/11 political environment, in which even an exceptionally unpopular president could invoke the threat of terrorism to garner new powers.

Another of our suggested questions is "Does the presidency threaten our system of checks and balances?" For insight into that question, consider what White House spokesman Tony Fratto had to say in December, after Congress voted down legislation that would bail out American automakers, and President Bush decided unilaterally to do what Congress refused to do. Fratto said, "Congress lost its opportunity to be a partner because they couldn't get their job done. . . . This is not the way we wanted to deal with this issue. We wanted to deal with it in partnership. What Congress said is . . . 'We can't get it done, so it's up to the White House to get it done.'"[29] As Fratto and the administration saw it, by not giving the president the power to bail out the automakers, Congress "lost its opportunity to be a partner," and the president had every right to order the bailout anyway.

Some commentators saw that decision as yet another example of Bush administration lawlessness.[30] The administration claimed that it had the power to act under the Emergency Economic Stabilization Act of 2008, passed to allow the purchase of toxic mortgage-backed securities. That law gives the secretary of the Treasury the power to buy "troubled assets" from "financial institutions." But how could that statute be used to buy shares in banks—some of which, such as Wells Fargo, weren't themselves "troubled"—or lend money to carmakers, which surely can't qualify as "financial institutions"? Having repeatedly insisted that he could not be bound by validly enacted statutes in matters related to national security, the president, it seemed, had decided he couldn't be bound by clear statutory language when it came to addressing the nation's economic woes.

The truth was actually more disturbing. A closer look at the TARP statute reveals that Congress wrote legislative language so irresponsibly broad that the administration actually had a colorable argument that it could reshape the bailout as it saw fit. Under the law, a "troubled asset" is "any . . . financial instrument" the secretary of the Treasury "determines the purchase of which is necessary to promote financial market stability," and "financial institution" is defined as *"any institution, including, but not limited to,* any bank, savings association, credit union, security broker or dealer, or insurance company, established and regulated under the laws of the United States or any State, territory, or possession of the United States."[31] Various members of Congress expressed their anger that the president had gone from buying toxic assets, to recapitalizing banks, to bailing out carmakers—shifting priorities almost daily regardless of what Congress believed it had authorized. But after signing on to legislative language that broad, their outrage was more than a day late and $700 billion short. Once again, on a core issue of governance, Congress had abdicated its legislative responsibilities, preferring to leave the hard decisions to the man with whom the buck stops.

THE CULT OF THE PRESIDENCY IN CAMPAIGN 2008

By the time both major parties had settled on their candidates for the 2008 race, it had become clear that whoever won would, as Yale Law professor Jack Balkin observed, inherit "more constitutional and legal power than any president in US history."[32] And both campaigns struggled to prove that their man was worthy of that power, making exorbitant promises and describing their respective candidates as

God-touched beings, come to deliver Americans from all that plagued them.

There's good reason that modern presidential candidates talk the way they do. Professional politicians know their business, after all, and the promises they make, the ways in which they describe the presidency, reflect their best judgment of what the public demands. Thus, their rhetoric tells us much about what the office has become.

In the revival-tent atmosphere of Barack Obama's campaign, the preferred hosanna of hope was "Yes we can!" We can, the Democratic candidate promised, not only create "a new kind of politics" but "transform this country," "change the world," and even "create a Kingdom right here on earth."[33] With the presidency, it seems, all things are possible.

One of John McCain's more effective campaign ads skewered Obama's messianic posturing. Mockingly titled "The One," the McCain ad mixed clips of Obama speeches with video of Charlton Heston as Moses, parting the waters. "And the world shall receive [Obama's] blessings," the narrator intoned.[34]

But *both* parties viewed the presidency in quasi-religious terms. The Republican party also spoke of the office as a font of miracles and the wellspring of national redemption. In his keynote address at the Republican National Convention in St. Paul, former New York City mayor Rudy Giuliani declared that we could "trust [John McCain] to deal with anything that nature throws our way, anything that terrorists do to us. . . . We will be safe in his hands, and our children will be safe in his hands" (he's got the whole world in his hands).[35]

Candidate McCain began his acceptance speech with a note of humility, which was a sharp contrast to the biographical video that introduced the speech. Among other things, the video described McCain's near-death experience in 1967, when a missile accidentally went off on the deck of the USS *Forrestal,* causing a catastrophic fire. "One hundred and thirty-four men lost their lives," the narrator said, but "John McCain's life was somehow spared. Perhaps *he had more to do.*"[36] Apparently, McCain was chosen by God as well.

But perhaps we shouldn't blame presidential aspirants for portraying themselves in such an exalted fashion: the vast responsibilities and vast powers the office entails almost seem to *demand* an anointed figure. There was a revealing moment in the first presidential debate in September 2008, when moderator Jim Lehrer asked the candidates:

"Are you willing to acknowledge, both of you, that this financial crisis is going to affect the way you *rule the country* as president of the United States?"[37] What was telling was what the candidates *didn't* say: neither McCain nor Obama objected to Lehrer's phrasing. Both, it seems, were perfectly comfortable with the idea that it's the president's job to "rule the country."

OBAMA ON PRESIDENTIAL POWER

We don't have George W. Bush to kick around anymore, and one has to look back nearly six decades to identify a president that the American public has been quite as happy to see the back of. But the conditions that encouraged and facilitated the Bush administration's staggering view of executive power—a supine Congress combined with the public's seemingly boundless demand for presidential salvation—persist.

Critics of the Bush approach who hoped Barack Obama would be "our first civil libertarian president" saw those hopes dashed in the administration's first two years.[38] But that shouldn't have been a surprise. Our experience with the modern presidency suggests that we cannot right the constitutional balance simply by electing a new president from a different party. From Truman's and Johnson's undeclared wars to the warrantless wiretapping carried out by Franklin D. Roosevelt, Kennedy, Johnson, and Nixon, the Imperial Presidency has long been a bipartisan phenomenon.

In fact, our previous Democratic president, Bill Clinton, went even further than his predecessors in his exercise of extraconstitutional war powers. Prior presidents had frequently launched military actions in the face of congressional silence. But Clinton's war over Kosovo in 1999 made him the first president to start a war in the face of several congressional votes denying him the authority to wage it. And the Clinton-era Office of Legal Counsel was only too willing to provide the thinly veiled legal rationales to justify that constitutional violation.[39]

Senator Obama's answers to a December 2007 executive-power questionnaire suggested that he understood Article II powers differently than either of his predecessors. "The President," Senator Obama wrote, "does not have power under the Constitution to unilaterally authorize a military attack in a situation that does not involve stopping an actual or imminent threat to the nation." Neither, in Obama's view, did he have the power to ignore statutes governing surveillance and treatment of enemy combatants.[40]

But as he came closer to winning the office, Obama reversed himself on national-security wiretapping. When he acquiesced to the FISA Amendments Act in the summer of 2008, Senator Obama broke an explicit campaign promise to filibuster any legislation that would grant immunity to FISA-flouting telecom companies. And by voting for the bill, Obama helped legalize large swaths of a dragnet surveillance program he'd long claimed to oppose.

Perhaps some were comforted by Obama's "firm pledge that as president, I will carefully monitor the program."[41] But our constitutional structure envisions stronger checks than the supposed benevolence of our leaders. Civil libertarians had good reason to fear that, once elected, Barack Obama would, like other presidents, "grow in office."

And yet, in the early days of his administration, Obama seemed determined to confound the cynics. In his first full day as president, he halted all military commissions trials.[42] At a swearing-in ceremony for senior executive branch officials, Obama told the attendees, "For a long time now, there's been too much secrecy in this city," and issued a directive to "the Heads of Executive Departments and Agencies" on interpreting the Freedom of Information Act: "All agencies should adopt a presumption in favor of disclosure, in order to renew their commitment to the principles embodied in FOIA, and to usher in a new era of open Government. The presumption of disclosure should be applied to all decisions involving FOIA."[43]

The next day, the new president ordered the executive branch to comply with federal laws governing torture and insisted that CIA interrogations comport with the techniques approved in the Army Field Manual.[44] He ordered the closure of the prison at Guantanamo Bay within a year and stipulated that Common Article 3 of the Geneva Conventions would apply to any interrogations conducted there in the interim.[45]

For a moment, this seemed like a genuine attempt at presidential self-restraint—a vanishingly rare thing. The perennial presidential ranking polls show that far too many scholars overvalue strong presidents—where "strong" is defined as one who expands the powers of the office. What the presidential rankers too often miss is that it takes a strong president to *resist* maximizing his power.

Laudable as it is, however, presidential self-restraint is far from a robust or lasting solution to the Imperial Presidency. Executive orders can be overturned, and personnel can be changed—by future presidents, or by *this president*, should political conditions change.

The threat of terrorism is no longer as vivid in the public mind as it was a few years ago, but all that could change quite rapidly. And if a bomb goes off in a subway or a terrorist carries out a shooting spree at a shopping mall, it will be very difficult for any president—particularly one whom political opponents are eager to portray as "soft on terror"— to resist expanding his powers.

Lasting restraint needs to come from external sources: the courts, the Congress, and the general public. As noted above, the Court has lately shown greater willingness to cabin presidential power in foreign affairs. However, there's little evidence that the public has moderated its demands for solving all manner of problems with bold presidential action. And Congress remains all too willing to cede vast powers to the president.

As it turned out, Obama's episode of presidential self-restraint was brief indeed. He has changed very few of the Bush-era war-on-terror policies. Jack Goldsmith, former head of Bush's Office of Legal Counsel, explains that despite new "packaging," in areas ranging from enemy combatants to surveillance, "the new administration has copied most of the Bush program," even "expanded some of it."[46]

Obama's Justice Department has fought to retain most of the Bush-era powers governing enemy combatants and surveillance. They've added a new power hardly dreamed of in the Bush era: the power to assassinate American citizens abroad, far from any battlefield.[47] They've embraced the Bush-Cheney position that the State Secrets Privilege bars the courthouse door to litigants who claim they've been harmed by warrantless wiretapping. In fact, as president, Obama has gone further still than Bush, arguing in court that, as the Electronic Frontier Foundation has put it, "the government can never be sued for surveillance that violates federal privacy statutes."[48]

Compared to Bush, Obama does represent something of a change in tone on war-on-terror issues. He's more reluctant than his predecessor to foster an atmosphere of crisis or wave the bloody shirt of 9/11. But though the Obama team has backed away from the war metaphor when it comes to international affairs and homeland security, they seem all too willing to employ the language of war and crisis to increase federal power over economic affairs. "We are at war," Vice-President-elect Joe Biden told congressional leaders in a meeting on January 5, 2009.[49] The president's inaugural address leaned heavily on the theme of crisis, and, as chief of staff Rahm Emanuel noted, "you never want a serious crisis to go to waste."[50] Though Obama has hesitated to claim that the president has the power to do whatever he wants in the name of national security, he seems quite comfortable with vast grants of power that allow him to remake the economy by executive fiat.

GREAT EXPECTATIONS

It was never terribly plausible to suppose that a man running as the reincarnation of John Fitzgerald Kennedy would reduce the presidency's power and prominence in American life. While he sought the presidency, Obama did more than any candidate in living memory to raise expectations for the office—expectations that were absurdly high to begin with. What is "the Audacity of Hope" after all, but the eternal promise of national redemption through presidential politics?

During the campaign, candidate Obama promised that as president, he would "end the age of oil in our time," deliver "nothing less than a complete transformation of our economy," and give "every American . . . the highest-speed broadband access—no matter where you live or how much money you have."

President Obama's inaugural address began somberly, emphasizing, "We are in the midst of crisis." But even in the midst of crisis, our possibilities were virtually limitless. United behind our president, we could "wield technology's wonders" to improve health care, "harness the sun and the winds and the soil to fuel our cars and run our factories," and "transform our schools and colleges and universities to meet the demands of a new age. All this we can do. All this we will do," said the new president.[51]

Obama's inaugural emphasized inclusiveness: "Our patchwork heritage is a strength," the president insisted. "Christians and Muslims, Jews and Hindus, and non-believers"—Americans "of every language and culture, drawn from every end of this Earth" would join together to renew America's greatness. But there was one sect, at least, whose membership in the American family was suspect: "cynics" weren't quite welcome. "There are some," Obama intoned, "who question the scale of our ambitions, who suggest that our system cannot tolerate too many big plans. Their memories are short, for they have forgotten what this country has already done. . . . What the cynics fail to understand is that the ground has shifted beneath them, that the stale political arguments that have consumed us for so long no longer apply."[52]

Yet, if the early polls were any indication, Barack Obama had little to fear from the cynics, who seemed pretty thin on the ground. He entered office with a 79 percent favorability rating, the highest in over three decades. Eight in ten Americans expected President Obama to improve conditions for minorities and the poor. Seven in ten expected him to improve education and the environment, and 60 percent expected him to usher in a robust economy and keep Americans safe from terrorism.[53] In fact, the only modern president to rival Barack Obama's popularity on the eve of inauguration was James Earl Carter—something that ought to have given our new president pause.

As the Carter experience suggests, in presidential politics, great expectations often lead to crashing disappointments. The so called "expectations gap"—the vast distance between what the public expects of the president and what he can realistically deliver—had been "a mainstay of the presidency literature for more than thirty years" already by 1999.[54] With few exceptions, the public has greeted each post–World War II president with an initial burst of enthusiasm, followed by dashed expectations and declining popularity. Thus, modern presidential-approval graphs strung together look like an EKG on a patient being repeatedly shocked to life—"clear!"—and then fading out again. Just as popularity tends to fade within each president's tenure, average approval ratings have been in decline from one president to the next for most of the era of the modern presidency.[55]

The Obama era began amid an infectious atmosphere of hope. But there's no reason to believe that Obama will escape what Barbara Hinckley called "the decay curve"—the steady decline in popularity that all modern presidents have experienced as the public recognizes that they're unable to deliver the miracles they've promised.[56] Obama, after all, has inherited a budgetary and financial disaster; he faces significant constraints, and he is likely to see some of his more ambitious plans run aground on fiscal reality.

Even when it comes to racial healing, Americans might do better to

moderate their expectations. Seven in ten Americans expected race relations to improve under Obama, according to a Gallup poll taken after
the election.[57] And it's not hard to understand why. The election of an
African American president shows genuine progress toward resolving
the "American dilemma," and whatever one's politics, it's an event that's
cause for celebration.

But even here, where high hopes seem justified, the modern presidency may once again disappoint. In fact, Obama's tenure may lead to
a politics that's more racially charged, and thus even more rancorous
than what we currently endure. That's so for reasons that have more to
do with the nature of the modern presidency than with Obama himself.
Americans expect the president to right the wrongs that plague us—
and we blame him when he fails. Because we invest impossible expectations in the presidency, the presidency has become an impossible job.
And once the honeymoon period inevitably fades, the modern president becomes a lightning rod for discontent, often catching blame for
phenomena beyond the control of any one person, however powerful.
In an Obama presidency, America's unhealthy obsession with race may
collide with our equally unhealthy obsession with the modern presidency—and the results might make us long for the relative placidity of
the Bush years.

Over and over again, we begin by looking to the president as the
solution to all our problems; and we end up believing he's the *source* of
all our problems. Thomas Cronin, who skewered Americans' irrational
desire for a "Superman" president, observed that "on both sides of the
presidential popularity equation, the president's importance is inflated
beyond reasonable bounds." The president's supporters exhibit "a nearly
blind faith that the president embodies national virtue and that any de-
tractor must be an effete snob," while his detractors consider him "the
cause of all personal maladies, the originator of poverty . . . the inventor
of the establishment, and the party responsible for a choleric national
disposition."[58]

If history is any guide, when President Obama fails to fully heal our
financial troubles, fix health care, teach our children well, provide balm
for our itchy souls, and so forth, his hope-addled rhetoric will seem all
the more grating, and the public will increasingly come to see him as
the source of all American woes. As his popularity dwindles, many of
Obama's defenders will view attacks on him through the prism of race,

forgetting or ignoring the fact that nearly every president eventually morphs from superhero to scapegoat in the public mind.

Unfortunately, when they look for reasons to cry racism, Obama's supporters will be able to find some examples of they're looking for. Conservatives will resent being lumped in with bigots and hit back harder, and on and on it will go. Race will take on undue relevance because the presidency is far more powerful and far more important than it ought to be.

Perhaps, then, we ought to rethink what we ask of the presidency. Our Constitution's Framers thought the president had an important job, but they never looked to him to heal all the nation's wounds and save the national soul. Far from serving as a national guardian angel, the president was to be a limited constitutional officer, whose main job was to execute the laws.

That vision of the presidency may be unromantic, but at least it's realistic. Until we return to the Framers' modest, businesslike view of the presidency, we shouldn't expect any president, however well-intentioned, to be "a uniter, not a divider" in American life.

THE PRESIDENCY IN THE TWENTY-FIRST CENTURY

Where does that leave us? After our century-long drift away from the Framers' vision, can we possibly return to a humbler set of expectations for the office and a less powerful chief executive? Predicting the future is always a dicey enterprise, but there are two long-term trends, at least, that could improve our chances of downsizing the presidency.

First, one major factor that led to the growth of the Imperial Presidency was America's increasing global role in the twentieth century and its unrivaled dominance after the collapse of the USSR. As neoconservative commentator Charles Krauthammer wrote in 1987, "Superpower responsibilities inevitably encourage the centralization and militarization of authority. . . . And politically, imperial responsibility demands imperial government, which naturally encourages an imperial presidency, the executive being (in principle) a more coherent and decisive instrument than its legislative rival."[59] As the twenty-first century progresses, the United States is likely to distance itself from those responsibilities—and, perhaps, from the presidential powers they enabled.

Fareed Zakaria predicts that China and India's rise, along with waning U.S. power, will in this century usher in "the Post-American World."[60] The U.S. National Intelligence Council recently released *Global Trends 2025: A Transformed World*. That report notes that "shrinking economic and military capabilities may force the US into a difficult set of tradeoffs between domestic versus foreign policy priorities."[61] Fifteen years from now, the United States will retain enormous military power, but "advances by others in science and technology, expanded adoption of irregular warfare tactics by both state and nonstate actors, proliferation of long-range precision weapons, and growing use of cyber warfare attacks increasingly will constrict US freedom of action."[62] It's possible, then, that shrinking American power and the emergence of new superpowers will result in the United States' behaving more like a normal country in the international sphere; and that that in turn will enable a shift to a "normalized" presidency.

The second long-term trend that may reduce the presidency's power and importance in American life is growing distrust of government, or what I'd prefer to call "skepticism toward power." It's true that too many Americans are presidential cultists. But what's easy to miss is that, on the whole, we're far less cultish than we used to be. The most important political trend of the past fifty years is the rise in distrust of government. In the late 1950s, when pollsters started tracking trust, nearly three-quarters of Americans said they trusted the federal government to do what is right "most of the time or just about always"—and most of all they trusted the president. Those numbers collapsed after Vietnam and Watergate.[63]

One of the leading experts on this phenomenon is Vanderbilt political scientist Marc Hetherington. Professor Hetherington leans left, so he takes no joy in reporting what the data have convinced him of: that the rise in distrust is going to make it very difficult for any future president to have an FDR- or LBJ-style one hundred days. But the same trend has also made it somewhat more difficult than it was sixty years ago for presidents to permanently evade legal and political checks on their power when it comes to civil liberties in wartime.[64]

In our public discourse—especially in Washington, D.C.—we tend to view distrust as a political pathology. But should we? Skepticism toward power lies at the heart of our constitutional culture, and if it makes it harder for presidents to do great works, it also makes it harder for them to abuse power.

Unfortunately, it's part of the American character that we periodically get drunk on the romance of the presidency. But, happily, it's also part of the American character that we eventually *sober up* and feel *disgusted* with ourselves. And then we take the long walk of shame back to the well-lit dorm room of *political sanity.*

The primal fact of the American identity is that we *became a nation* by throwing off a *king.* And call it cynicism, or call it skepticism toward power, but the quest to limit political power can never truly die, because it's written deep in the American genetic code. Because of that, despite all appearances, it's my hope that the cult of the presidency is a *dying cult.*

NOTES

1. Theodore J. Lowi, *The Personal President: Power Invested, Promise Unfulfilled* (Ithaca, NY: Cornell Univ. Press, 1986), 20.

2. Patrick Healy, "Clinton Calls for $30 Billion for Home Mortgage Crisis," *New York Times,* March 25, 2008.

3. Thomas Cronin, "Superman: Our Textbook President," *Washington Monthly,* Oct. 1970, 50.

4. See Louis Fisher, *Presidential War Power* (Lawrence: Univ. Press of Kansas, 1995), 18, 20–21.

5. James Madison, "Notes for Speech Opposing Paper Money," Nov. 1, 1786, http://press-pubs.uchicago.edu/founders/documents/a1_10_1s2.html.

6. Federalist No. 14, in George W. Carey and James McClellan, *The Federalist* (Indianapolis: Liberty Fund, 2001).

7. Steven Pinker, *The Blank Slate: The Modern Denial of Human Nature* (New York: Penguin, 2003).

8. Federalist No. 47, in Carey and McClellan, *The Federalist.*

9. John Yoo, "A President Can Pull the Trigger," *Los Angeles Times,* Dec. 20, 2005.

10. U.S. Department of Justice, "Legal Authorities Supporting the Activities of the National Security Agency Described by the President," Jan. 19, 2006, www.fas.org/irp/nsa/doj011906.pdf.

11. *Jose Padilla v. Commander C. T. Hanft,* 389 F. Supp. 2d 678, 690 (D.S.C. 2005).

12. "Raw Data: Transcript of Bush's Last White House Press Conference," Jan. 12, 2009, www.foxnews.com/politics/2009/01/12/raw-data-transcript-bushs-white-house-press-conference/.

13. Jack Goldsmith, *The Terror Presidency: Law and Judgment Inside the Bush Administration* (New York: Norton, 2007), 79.

14. Ibid., 189–90.

15. Colby Cosh, "Katrina-ism 6.0: The Triumph of Government?" www.colbycosh.com/old/september05.html.

16. "Former FEMA Director Michael Brown Testifies before Congress; Rescue from Rita," *CNN Live Event/Special,* aired Sept. 27, 2005, http://transcripts.cnn.com/TRANSCRIPTS/0509/27/se.02.html.

17. John Warner National Defense Authorization Act for Fiscal Year 2007, Public Law 109-364, *U.S. Statutes at Large* 109 (2006): sec. 1076.

18. National Defense Authorization Act for Fiscal Year 2008, Public Law 110-181, *U.S. Statutes at Large* 110 (2008): 122.

19. Stuart Taylor Jr. and Evan Thomas, "Obama's Cheney Dilemma," *Newsweek,* Jan. 10, 2009.

20. Norman J. Ornstein and Thomas E. Mann, *The Broken Branch: How Congress Is Failing America and How to Get It Back on Track* (New York: Oxford Univ. Press, 2006).

21. Richard E. Neustadt, *Presidential Power and the Modern Presidents: The Politics of Leadership from Roosevelt to Reagan* (New York: Free Press, 1990), 23.

22. Robert J. Spitzer, "Is the Constitutional Presidency Obsolete?" paper presented at the conference "The Future of the American Presidency," Regent Univ., Virginia Beach, VA, Feb. 6, 2009, 10.

23. Ibid., 22.

24. Public Law No. 109-366, sec. 948(b)(g): "No alien unlawful enemy combatant subject to trial by military commission under this chapter may invoke the Geneva Conventions as a source of rights"; sec. 7(a): "No court, justice, or judge shall have jurisdiction to hear or consider an application for a writ of habeas corpus filed by or on behalf of an alien detained by the United States who has been determined by the United States to have been properly detained as an enemy combatant or is awaiting such determination." However, in *Al-Marri v. Wright,* 487 F.3d 160 (4th Cir. 2007), a case involving a legal resident of the United States picked up on American soil and subjected to military detention, the Fourth Circuit Court of Appeals recently held that "the MCA was not intended to, and does not, apply to aliens like al-Marri, who have legally entered, and are seized while legally residing in, the United States."

25. Sec. 948a(1); see Robert A. Levy, "Does the Military Commission Act Apply to U.S. Citizens?" *Cato@Liberty.org,* Feb. 6, 2007, www.cato-at-liberty.org/2006/10/02/does-the-military-commission-act-apply-to-us-citizens/.

26. Protect America Act of 2007, Public Law 110-55, *U.S. Statutes at Large* 110 (2007).

27. FISA Amendments Act of 2008, Public Law 110-261, *U.S. Statutes at Large* 110 (2008).

28. Neustadt, *Presidential Power.*

29. David Cho and Zachary A. Goldfarb, "UAW Vows to Fight Wage Concessions," *Washington Post,* Dec. 24, 2008.

30. George F. Will, "End Run on the Treasury," *Washington Post,* Jan. 8, 2009.

31. Emergency Economic Stabilization Act of 2008, Public Law 110-343, *U.S. Statutes at Large* 110 (2008), emphasis added.

32. Jack Balkin, "Obama and the Imperial Presidency," *Guardian,* Nov. 12, 2008, www.guardian.co.uk/commentisfree/cifamerica/2008/nov/12/obama-white-house-barackobama.

33. Peter Hanby, "Obama: GOP Doesn't Own Faith Issue," *CNN.com,* Oct. 8, 2007, www.cnn.com/2007/POLITICS/10/08/obama.faith/.

34. JohnMcCain.com, "The One" (Streaming Video), YouTube, Aug. 1, 2008, www.youtube.com/watch?v=mopkn01PzM8.

35. "Rudolph W. Giuliani's Speech at the Republican National Convention," *New York Times,* Sept. 3, 2008.

36. Gopconvention2008, "John McCain Introduction at the 2008 Republican National Convention" (streaming video), YouTube, Sept. 4, 2008, www.youtube.com/watch?v=CPCMGs7dr90.

37. "First Presidential Debate," *New York Times,* Sept. 26, 2008.

38. Jeffrey Rosen, "Card-Carrying: The First Civil Libertarian President?" *New Republic,* Feb. 27, 2008.

39. See Major Geoffrey S. Corn, "Clinton, Kosovo, and the Final Destruction of the War Powers Resolution," *William and Mary Law Review* 42 (April 2001).

40. Charlie Savage, "Barack Obama's Q&A," *Boston Globe,* Dec. 20, 2007, www.boston.com/news/politics/2008/specials/CandidateQA/ObamaQA/.

41. Gail Russell Chaddock, "Congress Wrestles over Spying Bill," *Christian Science Monitor,* June 23, 2008, www.csmonitor.com/2008/0623/p03s02-uspo.html.

42. One judge refused his request; see Demetri Sevastopulo, "Judge Thwarts Obama's Plan to Shut Cuba Prison," *Financial Times* (online), Jan. 30, 2009, www.ft.com/cms/s/0/2a292918-ee70-11dd-b791-0000779fd2ac.html.

43. "President Obama Delivers Remarks at Swearing-In Ceremony," Jan. 21, 2008, www.fas.org/sgp/news/2009/01/obama012109.html.

44. Barack Obama, "Ensuring Lawful Interrogations," Executive Order 13491, Jan. 22, 2009, *Federal Register* 74 (16): 4894, http://edocket.access.gpo.gov/2009/pdf/E9-1885.pdf.

45. Barack Obama, "Review and Disposition of Individuals Detained at the Guantánamo Bay Naval Base and Closure of Detention Facilities," Executive Order 13492, Jan. 22, 2009, *Federal Register* 74 (16): 4897.

46. Jack Goldsmith, "The Cheney Fallacy," *New Republic,* May 18, 2009.

47. Scott Shane, "U.S. Approves Targeted Killing of American Cleric," *New York Times,* April 6, 2010.

48. Tim Jones, "In Warrantless Wiretapping Case, Obama DOJ's New Arguments Are Worse Than Bush's," April 7, 2009, www.eff.org/deeplinks/2009/04/obama-doj-worse-than-bush.

49. Jonathan Martin, "Biden on Economy: We Are at War," *Politico,* Jan. 5, 2009.

50. Gerald F. Seib, "In Crisis, Opportunity for Obama," *Wall Street Journal,* Nov. 21, 2008.

51. "President Barack Obama's Inaugural Address," http://whitehouse.gov/blog/inaugural-address/.

52. *Jose Padilla v. Commander C. T. Hanft,* 389 F. Supp. 2d 678, 690 (D.S.C. 2005).

53. Jill Lawrence, "Poll: Americans Have High Hopes for Obama," *USA Today,* Nov. 12, 2008; Michael D. Shear and Jon Cohen, "Nation's Hopes High for Obama, Poll Shows," *Washington Post,* Jan. 18, 2009, www.washingtonpost.com/wp-dyn/content/article/2009/01/17/AR2009011702822.html.

54. Richard W. Waterman, Robert Wright, and Gilbert St. Clair, *The Image-Is-Everything Presidency* (Boulder, CO: Westview Press, 1999), 4.

55. "Contemporary presidential approval ratings generally peak 10% to 15% below those achieved at the beginning of the survey era." Marc J. Hetherington, "The Political Relevance of Political Trust," *American Political Science Review* (Dec. 1998): 791. Michael A. Fitts, "The Paradox of Power in the Modern State: Why a Unitary, Centralized Presidency May Not Exhibit Effective or Legitimate Leadership," *University of Pennsylvania Law Review* 144 (Jan. 1996): 836.

56. Miller-McCune, www.miller-mccune.com/article/congratulations-mr-president-here-s-your-decay-curve.

57. Angus Reid Public Opinion, www.angus-reid.com/polls/view/americans_expect_better_race_relations_with_obama/; Sarah Kershaw, "Talk about Race? Relax, It's OK," *New York Times,* Jan. 14, 2009.

58. Cronin, "Superman," 53.

59. Charles Krauthammer, "The Price of Power," *New Republic,* Feb. 9, 1987.

60. Fareed Zakaria, *The Post-American World* (New York: Norton, 2008).

61. National Intelligence Council, *Global Trends 2025: A Transformed World* (Washington, DC: Government Printing Office, 2008), iv.

62. Ibid., xi.

63. "Trust the Federal Government, 1958–2004," *ANES Guide to Public Opinion and Electoral Behavior,* www.electionstudies.org/nesguide/toptable/tab5a_1.htm, table 5A.1.

64. Jack Goldsmith and Cass R. Sunstein, "Military Tribunals and Legal Culture: What a Difference Sixty Years Makes," *Constitutional Commentary* 19 (Spring 2002): 282, 289.

Plausible Futures

Jeffrey K. Tulis

January 20, 2009, marked the beginning of a new presidency. Did it also mark the beginning of a new political era in America? President Obama promised to "change Washington," to offer "a new kind of politics," and to be a "transformational" president. These commitments are unusually broad and deep. The usual concerns of journalists and political pundits are much narrower—about specific policy preferences and plans, about political scandal, about partisan tactics, or about political strategy. As Obama assumed the office, domestic and foreign circumstances inclined the polity to want the broader kind of leadership he promised. Transformational leaders have arisen in the past in circumstances like these—a severe economic crisis and a nation at war. It may be more than mere conventional wisdom that America has found her greatest leaders in times of greatest need.

Obama looks to Lincoln, FDR, and Ronald Reagan as models of transformative leadership. It is always wise to look to history for exemplary models as well as to avoid the mistakes of the past. But it may be an error to understand the promise and pitfalls of the present moment by analogizing them to these seemingly similar moments in the past. The error I wish to highlight is not that of Obama, who is wise to glean any and all lessons he can from studying the administrations of Lincoln, FDR, and Reagan. Obama may indeed be some kind of transformational leader—but if his presidency is successful on its own terms, he will transform the meaning of transformational leadership more than he transforms the polity he leads. That is, assuming and hoping for the best, Obama may turn the economy around and successfully contend with the threat of terrorism, for example, but nevertheless transform neither the partisan "regime" nor the constitutional regime. Put another way, should Obama successfully contend with the enormous challenges he faces, he could establish himself as a "great" president but not a transformative president, or at least not transformative in the ways Lincoln and FDR are often described.

A Critical Election?

Some elections are more important than others. The important elections signal or cause a durable shift in the partisan governing order. The notion of a "critical election," or "critical realignment," has been sharply criticized by political scientists in recent years, but it is hard to deny that Jefferson or FDR or Reagan altered the partisan landscape in ways that persisted for decades after their ascendance. Critics of realignment have focused too intently on nominal party identification and shifts (how many people identify as Republican or Democrat, or how many shift from one to the other, for example) rather than on the ideological direction of the realigning leader and the ideational content of policies fashioned under the auspices of a governing coalition.[1] Critical realignments may or may not be marked by durable shifts in party identification and they may or may not be marked by a landslide election. However, critical elections are always marked by a durable change in democratic discourse. One knows that a critical election has occurred when the basic terms of partisan debate are altered (for example, "government is not a solution to our problems, government is the problem") and when the losing party talks like the winner, tacitly accepting the new terms of debate. A striking example of this is the insistence of Republicans since the 1950s that it is unfair to suggest that they would undermine the Social Security program—indeed, that it is dirty politics to suggest that intention, an equivalent to calling Republicans unpatriotic. One is asked to forget that Republicans vigorously opposed Social Security when FDR proposed it; they insisted then that it was equivalent to "socialism." Similarly, following Ronald Reagan's stunning transformation of the partisan political order, Bill Clinton endorsed the idea that the era of big government was over, notwithstanding the fact that he was a Democrat (and notwithstanding the fact that the era of big government was not over).

In partisan-ideological terms, how important was the election of 2008? The easy answer is that it is too soon to say. One can't know whether an election alters the partisan governing order until it has done so. One could not easily outline the New Deal from the rhetoric of the 1932 campaign. Stunning electoral results are never sufficient, and they may not even be necessary conditions for durable shifts in partisan regimes. One has to wait to see what the leader says and does and whether or not he alters the political landscape in enduring ways.

A more complex answer begins with the observation that the presidential campaign of 2008 was unusual in ways that confound our normal expectations for transformative leadership. On the one hand, unlike "normal" elections, the Obama-McCain contest offered a much clearer ideological choice than the "Tweedledee, Tweedledum" choices that characterize most presidential elections in between critical realignments. On the other hand, the stark differences on domestic and foreign policy only seemed to rehearse New Deal Democratic positions, on the one hand, and Reagan Republican views, on the other. On the substantive policy choices, there was no true originality on either side. It was clear to most citizens that the electoral choice really mattered for the policy direction of the country, that the election would have significant consequences—but the anticipated policy trajectory of each choice was cognizable in very familiar political terms.

It has been observed that the precipitous collapse of the banking industry and the economic crisis more generally greatly enhanced Obama's electoral advantages. Less noticed is the fact that the economic crisis made it even more likely that Obama's substantive agenda would echo the New Deal. Had Obama come to office in an environment less defined by economic emergency, his intimations of new policies to contend with truly new challenges, global warming, cyber crime, global terrorism, and so forth might have, over time, led to a range of proposals described and defended with a truly new "public philosophy." The lingering recession has made Obama more inclined to defend an updated "New Deal" rather than some genuinely "new" Democratic program.

One could see this dynamic at work as President Obama confronted one of the greatest environmental catastrophes in American history. As oil gushed out of control and contaminated the Gulf region, Obama sought to contain the spill and to mitigate its effects on the economy, but he did not use the crisis to advance major new environmental legislation or to construct a genuinely new and transformative public philosophy.

The constraint of economic concerns and national security threats on the administration's substantive agenda underscores another aspect of the campaign of 2008 that was unusual. At the same time that Obama and McCain provided the citizenry a clear choice between conventional partisan alternatives, they agreed with each other on one truly original campaign issue. Both Obama and McCain offered themselves as reformers who would change the way politics was conducted in Washington. To be sure, rhetoric of reform by candidates running as outsiders against the Washington establishment is hardly new in American politics. What was new in 2008 was the centrality of governmental reform to the substantive agenda of both candidates. Both candidates pledged to alter the processes by which legislation was made and to diminish the role and effect of lobbyists in Congress and the bureaucracy. They both pledged to change the institutional culture of Congress and the manner of its interaction with the executive. They both pledged to reform the budget process in ways that would reduce wasteful earmarks. They both pledged to professionalize politics by toning down partisan rhetoric and by fostering bipartisan initiatives. Not since the development of the Civil Service toward the end of the nineteenth century has governmental reform been so central to a campaign agenda. This is really quite extraordinary. It is as if FDR had campaigned in 1932, in the midst of a depression, or in 1936, on the eve of war, for the Brownlow Commission (which he established in 1937 to reform the executive branch). It is as if when one asked, "What was the New Deal?" the answer was a committee to reorganize the executive branch and bring scientific management principles into public administration.

Had John McCain prevailed in the election, the reformist agenda would have been deployed on behalf of conservative policies and, more importantly, to conserve the partisan regime established by Ronald Reagan. McCain never depicted himself as a "transformational" leader. For Obama, the *mode* in which he sought to restore and extend the New Deal agenda was the core of his promise to be a transformational leader. What might he have meant? The key, I think, lies in his notion of a "postpartisan" politics. Both McCain and Obama promised more bipartisanship, but only Obama advanced the postpartisan notion. Bipartisanship refers to attempts to compromise partisan positions, to bring on board competing factions in the Congress by melding proposals from different ideological viewpoints. Obama's stimulus package was a bipartisan effort in this sense. Government spending projects proposed by the Democrats were joined to Republican tax-cut proposals. Bipartisanship is familiar enough as a political concept that Republicans have used it as a point of criticism ("The bill is not bipartisan enough"). As Republicans mounted their critique in late January 2009, Democrats became displeased with Obama's bipartisan strategy because the bill contained substantial concessions to Republicans at the very outset, leaving the Democrats disadvantaged for negotiations. Having won the election, Democrats chafed at premature concessions to the losers. But for Obama, this form of bipartisanship (where the bill proposed from the outset melds ideas from multiple viewpoints) is the first step to "postpartisanship."

In Obama's ideal "postpartisan" world, ideological posturing and ideological thinking would be replaced by problem-solving. To be sure, the diagnosis of problems, the priority of problems to be addressed, and the merits of solutions to the problems would all be informed by competing opinions. Where there are competing opinions, there will be competing factions, *The Federalist* reminds us. At the core of all political parties are competing ideas. Nevertheless, Obama's postpartisan vision rests on the hope that ideas can supplant ideologies. Ideas are subject to revision in their confrontation with the "problem." In the partisan world Obama seeks to reform, problems are subject to revision when shoehorned into standing ideologies.[2]

"What the cynics fail to understand is that the ground has shifted beneath them, that the stale political arguments that have consumed us for so long no longer apply," Obama said in his inaugural address. He went on to illustrate the pragmatic idea that is at the core of "postpartisanship." "The question we ask today is not whether our government is too big or too small, but whether it works—whether it helps families find jobs at a decent wage, care they can afford, a retirement that is dignified." The ideologue attacks or defends government. The postpartisan pragmatist attacks or defends particular programs, not government per se. Obama's position is not neutral between the New Deal ideology and the Reagan Revolution. His claim is tilted toward the New Deal because big government is here to stay. It got bigger under Reagan, in fact. But as committed as he is to government, he signals that it is open season on any particular governmental program if that program doesn't work. He makes a similar move with respect to the issue of markets. Markets are fundamental and here to stay. "But this crisis has reminded us that without a watchful eye, the market can spin out of control; that a nation cannot prosper long when it only favors the prosperous." Pragmatic regulation is required for markets to work well. Finally, with respect to defense, Obama rejects the false choice between our safety and our ideals. The false choice corresponds to familiar ideological alternatives. Facing the challenges of security as problems allows ideas to be melded rather than, as ideology does, to crowd out promising solutions.[3]

But the strongest sign that Obama means postpartisan to be post-ideological was his deployment of "truth." Truth does not reside in the familiar agendas of the Democratic and Republican parties. For Obama, time-honored virtues like honesty and hard work, courage and fair play, tolerance and curiosity, loyalty and patriotism, are true. "What is demanded, then, is a return to these truths." Truth does not inhere in ideological positions but in virtues, on the one hand, and reasoned solutions to problems on the other. "We will restore science to its rightful place," he says.[4]

Two very plausible lines of resistance have developed against Obama's postpartisanship. From the academy, conservative political theorist Harvey Mansfield argues that Obama's faith in pragmatic problem-solving does not so much transcend partisanship as camouflage a progressive partisan position in scientific rhetoric. Mansfield thinks that such faith in science is naive and undemocratic because science cannot resolve disputes over political principle.[5] From the political world, Obama's supporters worry that he has failed to lead his party and to aggressively attack Republicans. Where Mansfield sees a progressive takeover absent true democratic debate, Obama's Democratic supporters see a missed opportunity for progressive ascendance. Thoughtful conservatives and liberals describe Obama's politics and his policies in diametrically opposed ways, but they agree that he should be more avowedly partisan.

However, Obama's postpartisanship is more subtle than his critics seem to realize. Obama seeks to change the tone of Washington politics by showing how, in a large administrative republic in late modernity, many political disputes are actually practical arguments about fitting means to ends—not disputes about purposes or visions. Those practical disputes can't be magically solved by "science," but they can best be attenuated in a spirit of reasoned problem-solving. Partisan and principled differences will persist, but they need not define or dominate every governmental challenge. Under the auspices of this practical orientation, the remaining narrower range of partisan disputes, though vigorous, might be contested more civilly.

If one is skeptical that such a vision is achievable, that politics could actually be conducted under the auspices of a vision like this, one has an immediate sense of just how transformative Obama would have to be to succeed. My point here is not about the likely success of this vision, but rather the simple claim that Obama's kind of transformative leadership does not track the usual understanding of reconstructive leadership and critical eras in American history. Both critics and supporters view the Obama presidency through the lens of prior transformative moments in American political history. Critics insist that Obama's policies are more radical than they actually are, while his most partisan supporters feel his policies are not progressive enough. Ironically, Obama's promised transformation has been read through a very familiar ideological prism. Obama is trying to transform the meaning of transformational leadership, but older meanings of this form of leadership hinder his effort at pragmatic reform. In a sense, postpartisanship is partisanship less tied to organized political parties. As one of Obama's campaign staffers put it: "It gets back to being a transformational leader. A party leader isn't about transformation."[6]

Transforming the Constitutional Regime

Brilliant students of partisan regime change, such as Walter Dean Burnham, Theodore Lowi, and Bruce Ackerman, argue that partisan change in critical eras such as the Civil War and its aftermath or the New Deal transform the Constitution as well as the electoral landscape.[7] Ackerman sees partisan regime change inducing constitutional change because partisans in critical eras summon the people in their collective capacity to amend the Constitution outside the formal amending procedures. Lowi calls these partisan regime changes successive American "republics" (much like the first through fifth republics in France). They are wrong. It is true, of course, that partisan regime change has been the proximate cause of substantial change in constitutional practices on the ground. However, the changes partisans induce can be constitutionally transformative only if they alter the fundamental design. No partisan regime change in American history has done this. We have had one Republic, improved over time perhaps, but improved according to the original aspirations for which it was designed.

For Burnham, Lowi, and Ackerman, the Constitution is understood as a set of offices and practices defined by those that were operative at the time of the Constitution's adoption. The Constitution's meaning is tethered to the concrete states of mind of the founding generation (or the views in place at successive partisan refoundings) and to the extant political practices at each founding or refounding stage. For them, the reason constitutions change is that extant practices no longer serve the needs of a changed economy and society. In the understanding of these political scientists, constitutions periodically need to be transformed to contend with transformations in economy, society, and culture. What is striking about this picture is its unsophisticated understanding of constitutions.[8] In this picture, constitutions are, in their essence, settlements or bargains, not acts of political planning and design.

The American founders had a very different understanding of constitution making. Federalists and Anti-Federalists agreed that constitutions were not just about present political arrangements but also about plans to alter and configure the future. Indeed, plausible futures were the deepest source of dispute. In the late 1780s, America was an agrarian nation. Both Federalists and Anti-Federalists understood that if the Constitution was adopted, the nation would become largely urban and industrialized. Both sides agreed about this; the Federalists liked this plausible future and the Anti-Federalists disliked the prospect, but the power of constitutional decision to configure the future and the shape of the future was widely agreed among the founding generation. Prior to the adoption of the Constitution, the "national" government had a very weak, nearly nonexistent executive. Federalists and Anti-Federalists agreed that the American president would be a very strong executive. Some Federalists thought the executive would not be strong enough, while Anti-Federalists thought the president's strength was monarchical, but both sides agreed that presidents would be very strong. Both Federalists and Anti-Federalists anticipated that the national government would take over functions previously governed by states and localities. Despite a rhetorical effort to reassure nervous citizens that change would not be so dramatic, *The Federalist* explicitly anticipates the New Deal in essay number 10, where regulation "forms the principal task of modern legislation" and where property rights are deemed vital and important but not *fundamental*. Property rights derive from something more fundamental, "the diversity in the faculties of men." From the diversity and unequal talent in acquiring property the possession of different degrees and kinds of property result. *The Federalist* makes clear that property rights should generally be protected in the service of that diversity of talent and therefore might occasionally be abrogated when property acquisition itself compromised its own fundamental rationale.[9]

The conventional wisdom about regime change in political science simply misses the idea that constitutional design can be about economy, society, and culture as well as about government. Constitutions, in the classic view embraced by the founders, are designs to bring into being a future state of affairs. Thus, Federalists and Anti-Federalists alike understood that the decision to form a regime of continental scope had social, economic, and cultural consequences. They understood that the establishment of a direct and unmediated coercive relationship between the central government and ordinary citizens meant that states would become less important political entities over time. Founders could take decisions that set a nation on a course of political development without knowing precisely when the changes set in motion by the founding act would take effect. The key point is that the growth of commerce, a complex industrial economy, social needs, and a culture that put a premium on work, wealth, and material things and a government adequate to the new needs of a commercial republic were all anticipated and indeed planned.[10]

One can make the same point about race relations. The Constitution perpetuated slavery through several of its provisions. Yet, as Frederick Douglass and Abraham Lincoln both understood, the Constitution was oriented to freedom even as it temporarily held some in bondage. The just protest against bondage was induced largely by the Constitution itself. The Constitution may have been perfected by the Reconstruction amendments, for example. But they were not truly "amendments" (changes) but rather elaborations of the core commitments of the original design.[11]

Thus, partisan regime change does not induce constitutional regime change. At its best, partisan regime change has induced elaboration and perfection, not transformative constitutional change. At its worst, partisan change layers ideas on top of a still working Constitution, complicating its operation without altering its basic design. Will Obama's new kind of transformational leadership perfect the constitutional regime as previous so-called transformational leaders have? Or will he complicate and extend the problems introduced by previous partisan challenges? The election of the first African American president obviously leads one to think that this president will further advance aspirations expressed in the Preamble and the Declaration of Independence—the founding documents referred to at the top of Obama's inaugural address. Obama may well issue orders and advance legislation to provide benefits to disadvantaged minorities or to extend civil rights to gay couples, for example. However, if political reform and postpartisanship do indeed form the centerpiece of Obama's attempted realignment, it is more likely that his constitutional legacy will be restorative rather than perfectionist.

Transformation as Restoration

Obama invoked Lincoln, FDR, and Reagan at various points during the campaign, transition, and early days of his administration. Commentators have also compared his leadership project to those figures. Ironically, it may be Teddy Roosevelt, McCain's hero, who comes closer to modeling the kind of restorative leadership Obama articulates. It was T.R. who said he didn't care who got the credit as long as his adversary was going the same way; it was T.R. who laid out an economic and regulatory reform agenda to the public but left Congress discretion to craft the bill unpressured by a relentless, continuing public-speaking campaign; it was T.R. who offered moderation as the watchword of his policies and political/constitutional tactics. The principled search for the mean characterizes both the statesmanship of T.R. and the campaign and early days of the Obama administration.[12]

After the first six months of the Obama presidency, the outlines of a new kind of political transformation were becoming clearer. On the one hand, there is no new overarching public philosophy that would distinguish the array of Obama policies from those of his Democratic predecessors FDR, Kennedy, and Johnson. The understandings of justice and of the common good implicit in Obama's policies are those made explicit by New Deal and Great Society ideas. On the other hand, the sheer scope and ambition of his economic and social policies are unprecedented. The massive spending required to support an economic stimulus package, financial-sector reform and bailouts, and bailouts and restructuring of the auto industry, as well as nearly universal health care coverage, is likely to transform (for good or bad) American lives and political practices.

Obama has also begun to alter the relation of president and Congress. Unlike all recent presidents, Obama has not prepared legislation in the executive branch to be tweaked (at best) or rubber stamped (at worst) in the legislature. Instead, he has (1) established a priority or focus, (2) articulated and defended principles to guide legislation on the priority problem, (3) left the drafting of legislation to the Congress, and (4) used the advantages of his office to pressure Congress to do its job— to craft and pass legislation, rather than to campaign for a specific executive-designed bill. This political strategy alters a century of presidential practice and, if successful, may transform the way presidents lead on domestic policy and the way Congress legislates.

It is common to attribute the errors and excesses of the Bush administration to executive misjudgment and overreaching. Obama seems to understand that the pathology of modern governance lies more in the legislature than in the executive, notwithstanding his disagreements with Bush policies and practices. The failures of the Bush administration are the failure of government because aggressive executive decision was never tested by thoughtful deliberation in the legislature. Legislative deference is the root pathology of the modern constitutional order.[13] The tendency of the Congress to defer to the executive over matters that were previously subject to political contestation is deeply rooted in twentieth-century constitutional culture. In the nineteenth century, nominations to the Supreme Court were routinely contested by the Senate on the full range of considerations that influence presidential choices; for more than two hundred years, Congress more actively intervened and assessed presidential foreign policy decisions; until the mid-twentieth century, Congress took principal responsibility for budget-making; until relatively recently, "political questions" such as the status of executive agreements or executive privilege were resolved by Congress and the president, not by the courts. The exceptions to these tendencies, in our time, sometimes arise in divided government as partisan contestation becomes a surrogate for competing institutional perspectives.

Obama's postpartisanship ideal can be viewed as an effort to reform the Congress as well as to solve particular problems. It remains to be seen, however, whether the need for emergency action trumps the need for governmental reform. Will the success of a health care package

Jeffrey K. Tulis

that drew ideas from Republicans as well as Democrats set in motion a new way of doing business, or will its political legacy be polarization because it was passed along straight party lines? Can Obama's extraordinary grassroots organization, bolstered by technological savvy, usher in a new era of civic education? Or will it be remembered as just another high-tech means to attempt to pressure the Congress? These are all plausible futures, and at the midterm election of 2010, the failure of postpartisanship seems more likely.

It is ironic that the best solution to the decay of a vigorous national legislature may be presidential leadership itself. A president who seeks to recover the traditional functions and virtues of Congress in the separation-of-powers system may be a new kind of transformative leader—one who restores the constitutional order rather than perfects it. The motivation for such leadership could be the realization that George W. Bush's political interests were hindered, not helped, by the abdication of Congress. Had Congress challenged, or even seriously debated, Bush administration foreign policy, for example, the effectiveness and legitimacy of those policies might have been enhanced.

Approaching the election of 2010, Obama's political successes and setbacks confirmed the general shape of these plausible futures that were visible in the campaign and early days in office, now bringing them into sharper focus. As mentioned above, Obama secured a large economic stimulus package, a large financial bailout of the banking industry, a bailout of the auto industry followed by the forced bankruptcy of General Motors, and passage of a comprehensive health care package. His foreign and military policies have been marked by a distinct change in tone and rhetoric from those of the Bush administration, but the actual policies regarding Iraq and Afghanistan extend and do not substantially change the policies of his predecessor. The Obama administration has extended and defended in court many Bush administration policies regarding detention and trial of terror suspects, even while modifying detention and interrogation practices to be more in line with national and international values and standards of conduct. All of these efforts evidence an approach to politics more pragmatic than ideological.

The debate on health care offers an excellent case in point. No new principle marked this effort. It was offered explicitly as a version of the past, likened to other policies in place such as Medicare, and open to a variety of institutional mechanisms to advance its purposes. To be sure, fevered rhetoric from partisan critics painted the health care proposal in ideological terms—as socialism or, in the minds of some gun-toting protesters, as Nazism—but these heated criticisms only served to underscore how nonideological, how pragmatic Obama's policy actually is. If there is any merit, for example, to the "socialism" worry, it could only be a kind of slippery-slope argument that the new policy will lead to socialism. The policy itself cannot fairly be described as socialism. It was presented as a way to save and improve the American capitalist order, and indeed, the main capitalists relevant to the issue, the large insurance companies, were brought into the policymaking process.

No one can deny that the cumulative effects of these policies might dramatically transform life in America or America's place in the world. The array of new domestic spending on top of a continuing war in the Middle East offers the prospect of enormous deficits whose costs may be incalculable at this moment and whose future effects are presently unfathomable. The point I want to stress, however, is that whether Obama becomes a failed president because of the problems his policies create or a successful one because of the problems he solves, his presidency will not have transformed any core principles, any core ideas, the way previous "transformational" presidents have done. The potentially massive changes on the ground induced by Obama's pragmatism may be lasting and profound but still not regime-changing, even if life in the regime is much better or much worse than before he took office. What many are struck by, causing them to erroneously label Obama as potentially transformative, is the sheer size, the sheer mass and cost, of Obama's domestic agenda. But Obama's ambition is better understood as restorative in the sense that Obama extends and elaborates the New Deal of the 1930s and the Great Society of the 1960s, which itself was an elaboration of the New Deal. As Obama himself points out, the problem of deficits and national debt really stem from structural aspects of governance set in place long before he took office, as well as massive war spending by the Bush administration. In all these respects, Obama's debt-enhancing policies are extensions, not transformations, of past practices and policies.

The second way Obama may be changing the meaning of transformative leadership, his emphasis on the form of leadership—providing principles rather than detailed legislative proposals and deferring to the legislative work of the House and Senate—was also more evident after the first two years of this administration. During the primary campaign, Obama distinguished himself from his opponent Hillary Clinton by suggesting their differences to be more style of governance than substance of policy. One should not underestimate the importance of this point. Near the beginning of the primary season, I described Obama's view this way:

> Just beneath the surface of Obama's call for a new kind of leadership that transcends previous partisan divisions and old habits of political contestation is a new constitutional theory—or, perhaps more accurately, a better understanding of our Constitution whose meaning has been lost over time and whose principal political institutions have begun to decay. In Obama's vision, presidential success is not measured by how many detailed policy proposals he can ram through Congress. Rather, his vision sets a new standard, that presidential success will be measured by an improved functioning of the government as a whole. In this vision, the details of policy are not as important as the principles that guide policy. In this vision, it is less important to secure one's preferred version of a bill than it is to mobilize Congress to solve the problem for which the legislation was designed.
>
> In contrast, all recent presidents, and especially Senator Clinton, understand the President as the chief legislator, as the person and the place where legislation is made. She seems incensed that anyone not as technically skilled as she in legislative craftsmanship would think they are as qualified for election to the presidency. Obama understands that although the president needs to be very knowledgeable about public policy, to demonstrate that knowledge, and even, as president, to offer legislative proposals to the Congress—he has an instinctive sense that his job is to lead, not to legislate.
>
> Obama knows instinctively that Senator Clinton did not learn the major lesson from the failure of her health care plan at the beginning of her husband's term. For Obama, the lesson is that one does not take over the role of Congress, in secret meetings of unelected friends and colleagues and then insist that the presidential product be given a mere seal of approval

by the Congress of the United States. He knows that presidential leadership is much more than a matter of bargaining from a strong position but includes, as well, facilitating the work of others. Obama knows that his job will be to initiate and nurture a legislative process. He will offer a plan, to be sure. He will use his plan to illustrate the principles he wishes to guide legislative craftsmanship: that all Americans have access to health insurance and that it be affordable. He will make speeches and he will call, meet, and cajole members of Congress. But he will not substitute "administration" for "deliberation." If as Congress deliberates it becomes clear that Senator Clinton's plan accomplishes his principled objectives better than his own plan, he will embrace it, praise it, and praise her. Obama seems to understand that this sort of scenario would represent success not only because the nation's health care system would be improved, but also because it would signify that the government, not just the presidency but the government as a whole, was not broken anymore. He would show the world that some meaningful vision of democracy was still workable.[14]

This intimation of Obama's intention turned out to be an accurate description of his approach to health care once in office. Again and again, Obama insisted that his principles were more important than specific policies, and he challenged Congress to do the actual work of legislation. Many of his supporters were frustrated by this posture, and his partisan critics painted him as weak and ineffectual—but Obama sensed that his transformative potential derived as much from his new mode of leadership as it did from the policy project he proposed. Yet, like the domestic policies themselves, this "new" mode of leadership is not really new. Rather, Obama's principled deference to Congress is a restoration of a leadership mode common to the nineteenth century and early twentieth century. While Obama needed to be more aggressive than Teddy Roosevelt as the health care legislation moved to the floor of each chamber and as Senate and House bills were reconciled, his general strategy was to define principles and leave particulars to the legislature. As I mentioned previously, this style closely mirrored the leadership of Roosevelt.

Because most transformations in American politics perfect some element of the past, one may wonder whether there is a real distinction between perfection and restoration.[15] The distinction is this: transformations like the Reconstruction Amendments or the New Deal elaborate an aspiration buried in the Constitution's genetic structure. They bring to fruition something latent in the past but not previously realized. Restorations, such as Obama's, recover past ideas and practices that have been buried or covered over, making present once again something that was previously manifest and real.

One can not conclude the subject of transformational change without reflecting upon the fact that Barack Obama is the first African American president of the United States. The fact of his elevation has brought many Americans an extraordinary sense of pride, has attracted the admiration and attention of millions of people across the globe, and clearly marks a watershed in American political history. Yet, even this extraordinary change was cast in, and perhaps depended upon, a restorative orientation. Obama did not campaign as an African American but rather as a postracial politician. To be sure, race was a central topic in his campaign, but he was pushed to address it by his critics. He spoke eloquently about race, but he did not define his campaign or his presidency in racial terms. Instead, his conjunction of postpartisan pragmatism and inspirational eloquence harked back to the politics of America's greatest statesmen: Abraham Lincoln, Frederick Douglass, and most importantly, George Washington.

David Brooks recently wrote that our culture today suffers from an almost total absence of the understanding and practice of dignity. In the first year of the Obama presidency, we endured a corrupt governor of Illinois whose fall from office was marked by a complete lack of dignity or grace, a governor of South Carolina who publicly humiliated his family and himself, and a governor of Alaska who, according to Brooks, "aspires to a high public role but is unfamiliar with the traits of equipoise and constancy, which are the sources of authority and trust."[16]

But then there is Obama. "Whatever policy differences people may have with him, we can all agree that he exemplifies reticence, dispassion and the other traits associated with dignity. The cultural effects of his presidency are not yet clear, but they may surpass his policy impact. He may revitalize the concept of dignity for a new generation and embody a new set of rules for self-mastery."[17]

In the context of our time, to dignify our regime would surely be to transform it. Yet, from the wider-angle lens of our entire political history, it would be the most deeply *restorative* transformation of them all, pointing beyond the Great Society and New Deal origins of health policy, beyond the capitalism-enhancing regulatory politics of Teddy Roosevelt's Square Deal, to the very origins of the presidency itself, to the person and statecraft of George Washington, America's *prepartisan* president. Forrest McDonald's description of Washington's most important and most subtle legacy might well describe President Barack Obama: "He endowed the presidency with the capacity—and the awesome responsibility—to serve as the symbol of the nation, of what it is and what it can aspire to be."[18]

Notes

1. David Mayhew, *Electoral Realignments* (New Haven, CT: Yale Univ. Press, 2004); Byron E. Shafer, *End of Realignment? Interpreting American Electoral Eras* (Madison: Univ. of Wisconsin Press, 1991). For an excellent account of Mayhew's failure to comprehend the systemic significance of realignments, see Curt Nichols, "Reconsidering Realignment from a Systemic Perspective," *Clio* 19 (Spring–Summer 2009): 2.

2. To understand why Obama's stated objective is "postpartisan," see J. Russell Muirhead, "A Defense of Party Spirit," *Perspectives on Politics* (Dec. 2006): 713–27.

3. President Barack Obama, inaugural address, Jan. 20, 2009, www.whitehouse.gov/blog/inaugural-address/.

4. Ibid.

5. Harvey Mansfield, "What Obama Isn't Saying: The Apolitical Politics of Progressivism," *Weekly Standard*, Feb. 8, 2010. For a contrary view, see William Galston, "Freedom Agenda: Obama's Politics Aren't Anti-democratic. They're Liberal," *New Republic*, Feb. 4, 2010.

6. Cornell Belcher, quoted in Matt Bai, "Democrat in Chief," *New York Times Magazine*, June 13, 2010, 38.

7. Walter Dean Burnham, *Critical Elections: The Mainsprings of American Politics* (New York: Norton, 1971); Theodore Lowi, *The Personal Presidency: Power Invested, Promise Unfulfilled* (Ithaca, NY: Cornell Univ. Press, 1986); Bruce Ackerman, *We the People: Foundations* (Cambridge, MA: Harvard Univ. Press, 1993). In his important book, Stephen Skowronek ties his influential notion of reconstructive leadership to critical elections, but he does not argue that each of those eras signals a change in the constitutional, as opposed to partisan,

regime. Skowronek, *The Politics Presidents Make: Leadership from John Adams to Bill Clinton* (Cambridge, MA: Harvard Univ. Press, 1997).

8. This legalistic misunderstanding of constitution as tethered to the concrete intentions or extant practices at the origin or making of the document is a central premise or claim of the essays by Stephen Skowronek and Robert Spitzer in this volume, although they draw very different conclusions from this assumption. For Skowronek, the irrelevance of the Constitution to subsequently devised governing arrangements means we should think less about the Constitution. Spitzer, in contrast, is upset that contemporary presidents and scholars have abandoned the Constitution as originally understood, despite the fact that by his own account it is irrelevant to contemporary problems and circumstances.

9. See especially Herbert J. Storing, *Toward a More Perfect Union* (Washington, DC: AEI Press, 1995), chap. 14.

10. Jeffrey K. Tulis, "The Constitutional Presidency and American Political Development," in *The Constitution and the American Presidency,* ed. Martin Fausold and Alan Shank (Albany, NY: SUNY Press, 1991). See also Sotirios A. Barber, *Welfare and the Constitution* (Princeton, NJ: Princeton Univ. Press, 2005).

11. Storing, *Toward a More Perfect Union,* chaps. 6, 7.

12. See Jeffrey K. Tulis, *The Rhetorical Presidency* (Princeton, NJ: Princeton Univ. Press, 1987), chap. 4, "The Middle Way: Statesmanship as Moderation."

13. This is the subject of my forthcoming book *Democratic Decay and the Politics of Deference.* For a preview, see Jeffrey K. Tulis, "On Congress and Constitutional Responsibility," *Boston University Law Review* (April 2009): 515–24.

14. Jeffrey K. Tulis, "Obama's Beef," *Balkinization,* Jan. 30, 2008, http://balkin.blogspot.com/2008/01/obamas-beef.html.

15. I am grateful to Hugh Heclo, who raised this question at the Regents University symposium where the first draft of this essay was presented.

16. David Brooks, "In Search of Dignity," *New York Times,* July 7, 2009, A23.

17. Ibid.

18. Forrest McDonald, "Today's Indispensable Man," in *Patriot Sage: George Washington and the American Political Tradition,* ed. Gary L. Gregg II and Matthew Spalding (Wilmington, DE: ISI Books, 1999), 37.

CONTRIBUTORS

Brandice Canes-Wrone, Princeton University Professor of Politics and Public Affairs, wrote *Who Leads Whom? Presidents, Policy and the Public* (2005), which won the 2006 Richard E. Neustadt Award for the best book published on the presidency.

George C. Edwards III, Distinguished Professor of Political Science at Texas A&M University, has taught at Oxford and the University of London. His twenty-four books include *The Strategic President: Persuasion and Opportunity in Presidential Leadership* (2009).

Gene Healy, Vice President of the Cato Institute and Contributing Editor to *Liberty Magazine*, wrote *The Cult of the Presidency: America's Dangerous Devotion to Executive Power* (2008) and edited *Go Directly to Jail: The Criminalization of Almost Everything* (2004).

Hugh Heclo, Clarence J. Robinson Professor of Public Affairs at George Mason University and previously a senior professor of government at Harvard University, most recently wrote *On Thinking Institutionally* (2008) and *Christianity and American Democracy* (2007).

William G. Howell, Sydney Stein Professor in American Politics at the University of Chicago, has written *While Dangers Gather: Congressional Checks on Presidential War Powers* (2007) and *Power Without Persuasion: The Politics of Direct Presidential Action* (2003).

Stephen Skowronek, Pelatiah Perit Professor of Political and Social Sciences at Yale University, includes among his books *Presidential Leadership in Political Time* (2008), *The Politics Presidents Make* (1997), and *Building a New American State* (1982).

Robert J. Spitzer, Distinguished Professor of Political Science at SUNY–Cortland, has written *Saving the Constitution from Lawyers* (2008), *The*

Presidency and the Constitution (2005), *Politics and Constitutionalism* (2000), and *The Presidency and Public Policy* (1983).

Jeffrey K. Tulis teaches in the Department of Government at the University of Texas at Austin. His books include *The Rhetorical Presidency* (1987), *The Constitutional Presidency* (2009), and *The Limits of Constitutional Democracy* (2010).

Index

Index

Index